Happy Tails

across

New Jersey

Happy Tails *across* New Jersey

things to see and do with your dog

DIANE GOODSPEED

Rivergate Books

AN IMPRINT OF RUTGERS UNIVERSITY PRESS
NEW BRUNSWICK, NEW JERSEY, AND LONDON

Library of Congress Cataloging-in-Publication Data

Goodspeed, Diane, 1962–
Happy tails across New Jersey : things to see and do with your dog / Diane Goodspeed.
p. cm.
ISBN-13: 978-0-8135-3848-8 (pbk. : alk. paper)
1. Travel with dogs—New Jersey—Guidebooks. 2. New Jersey—Guidebooks. I. Title.
SF427.4574.N5G66 2006
917′.49044—dc22
2005028098

A British Cataloging-in-Publication record for this book is available from the British Library

Manufactured in the United States of America

To

all the dogs out there working hard to de-stress the world,

one human at a time

Contents

Happy Tails

across

New Jersey

Introduction

He is your friend, your partner, your defender, your dog. You are his life, his love, his leader. He will be yours, faithful and true, to the last beat of his heart. You owe it to him to be worthy of such devotion.

—UNKNOWN

No Dogs. No Dogs Allowed. As a dog owner and enthusiast, I hate these signs and they are everywhere. Or are they? Can you take your canine family member with you when you hike, visit the beach, or go to a park? Yes, you can. The towns and parks of New Jersey are surprisingly dog-friendly. It is simply a matter of knowing where to go and when. Rather than spending another day snoozing at home waiting for you to return, your dog can go with you. There are parks with rivers and creeks where your dog can wade or swim. There are plenty of places to hike whether you want a leisurely stroll or a strenuous day hike. Many of the beaches allow dogs once the summer swim season is over. And there are fabulous training facilities, dog parks, canine sports events, country farms, dog bakeries, and woof-wonderful pet stores all waiting to be explored.

All of our family outings include the dogs. Their enthusiasm and pure joy at being out and about adds an indefinable element of fun to our day. My dogs are always eyeing the car, looking for that open door. It does not matter to them where we go or when we go. They do not care about the weather. They do not worry if we get lost and spend an extra hour getting to a park. They do not watch the clock so a thirty-minute walk is just as good as a four-hour hike. My dogs love investigating new shops and are pretty sure it is their mission in life to taste a treat from every dog bakery in the state! My dogs (and yours) just want to go with! And any outing with a companion who is easy to please and loves every minute of your company can only add pleasure and fun.

As a dog enthusiast, I live in a dog subculture. My friends are dog trainers, breeders, and multi-dog owners. This world is filled with people who love dogs and take them everywhere, from the school bus stop to Costa Rica. You may not be ready to get your dog a frequent flyer number, but why not take your dog out to enjoy the wonderful towns, parks, and natural areas in New Jersey? Whether you have a pampered pooch, a rambunctious hound, or a family couch potato, this book will help you get going and enjoy a day out with your dog! Nope, it does not matter what kind of dog you have. Our current dog pack consists of a Border collie, a Shetland sheepdog (sheltie), and a Lhasa apso. They all take turns exploring with the family. The pack instinct runs strong and your dog, like mine, will thrive on the extra attention and both your lives will be enriched by time spent together.

Precious Cargo

When referring to car travel, I firmly believe that "dogs are people too!" If you wear a seatbelt, why not have a safety system for your dog? I believe your dog should receive the same consideration as every other passenger in your car. In a collision your dog is exposed to the same risks as those of an unsecured child. A sudden stop or sharp swerve leaves your dog unbalanced and vulnerable to injury. Recent surveys show that 78 percent of dog owners transport their pets without any sort of protection system. While this may work for the dog that only travels in the car once a year for its annual vet appointment, it is not a good idea for dogs that collect frequent travel miles.

While only a few states have started passing laws (New Jersey not being one of them) regarding the transportation of pets, there are plenty of options for traveling safely with your dog, no matter where you want your dog to ride or what kind of vehicle you have.

Car Transportation

My dogs are constantly in the car since they compete in multiple sports, which translates to lots of travel. Furthermore, they go on almost all of our family vacations. My minivan is one-half dog van and one-half people van. It is equipped with wipes, sunscreen, bug spray, napkins, Game Boys, and kids' books in the front, while in the back I carry travel collars, leashes, kennels, toys, water bottles, bowls, towels, and poop bags. While this is now *normal* for my family, I realize it is not exactly standard for most people. Even if you do not convert your minivan into a rolling dog mobile, a little advance preparation can keep the day fun and entertaining versus painful and exhausting for your dog. Your first consideration is a safety system.

A yip from Dave Barry, "Dogs feel very strongly that they should always go with you in the car, in case the need should arise for them to bark violently at nothing right in your ear."

Car Safety Systems

Options for transporting dogs are many and varied. The wide variety of methods allows you to select the one that works for your dog and your vehicle type.

Pet Carriers. The standard pet carrier is a wire crate or plastic kennel. There are many advantages to this system. Crates and kennels are easy to purchase from your local pet store, come in a wide range of sizes, and are extremely durable. A crate provides your dog with its own "seat" in the car, allowing your dog to relax for the duration of the trip. It is also easy to leave the car without worry about what mischief your furry friend will get into while you are gone. Crates also keep dog hair, dirt, and dander in one place. This can be a huge advantage after a muddy hike or a romp along the beach. Kennels and plastic crates can also be stacked, allowing you to travel with multiple dogs in a relatively small area.

Seatbelt Harness. A dog seatbelt keeps your dog in one spot while allowing freedom of movement, including that important window sniffing. The harness should attach to a buckled seatbelt or directly to the seatbelt receptacle itself. Never attach your dog's collar to the seatbelt and always use a car harness in the back seat. Air bags are as dangerous to a dog as to a child. The seatbelt that you purchase should be a two-point or three-point harness that wraps around your dog's chest and look for an attachment system that has a free-floating clip that absorbs turns and spins. A quick word of caution: your dog should never ride with her head outside the car window. Insects, dirt, gravel, and other flying debris can cause serious eye injuries.

Booster Seats. These little seats allow even small dogs to look out the window and snuffle fresh air. Most booster seats attach to the seatbelt and contain a safety harness. Do not use a booster seat that does not attach to the car or attaches the dog to the seat by its collar. Both can cause serious injuries in an accident. Safety before fun!

Loading and Unloading

Many more accidents happen while people are loading and unloading their dogs than at any other travel time. It is when the owner is distracted, the dog is excited, and the situation is not ideal. A few simple safety rules go a long way toward reducing stress and the potential for an accident.

First and foremost, never let your dog leap from the car. This is a very bad habit. You must teach your dog to wait in the car even with the car door open. (This is one of the advantages of a kennel or seatbelt harness.) Get a firm grip on your dog's collar, attach the leash, and then release him from the car. This routine should be followed strictly—even when you get home. Second, when you arrive, do not immediately get your dog out. Check out the area. Look for loose dogs, moving cars, and other hazards. More than one dog owner has been yanked off his feet by ignoring a habitat filled with chattering squirrels. And one last word of caution, know where your dog is when you close the car door. It is not uncommon for a travel-savvy dog to mistake your motions to close the car door as a signal to jump back inside. Few dogs can survive an encounter with a car door. And you should reverse these cautions when loading your pet into the car. First, always load your dog on leash. Put the dog in the car, settle him down, and then detach the leash. Second, put the dog in the car first. Your hiking gear or shopping bags will not run away if you get distracted.

Stop, Think, and Plan

It seems obvious but the basic rule of dog travel must be repeated, "Never leave your dog in the car on a hot day." This is not generally an issue for dogs that travel once or twice a year but as you become more addicted to traveling with your canine friend and the miles add up, so too will the stops. While most pet owners are very aware of this problem and diligently protect their pets in the hot summer months, it is easy to underestimate the heat in the spring and fall. Your best defense is simple. Never leave your dog in the car when the outside temperature is over 50°F and never leave your car parked in the sun. There are other ways to reduce the risk of heat stroke.

Water. Your dog should always have a full water bowl. This is one of the reasons I prefer kennels. A water bowl attached to the side of the kennel means the dogs always have clean, fresh water in the car. With a seatbelt harness, you must provide water at timely intervals during your travels. A no-spill water bowl can help. Keep several large jugs of water in your car and fill them with fresh water before each trip. On hot days, fill them with ice water for extra cool refreshment.

Fans. There are several types of portable, battery-operated fans available. Some have a base that allows you to position them wherever needed. There are also fans made to hang on dog crates and kennels. These quiet, high-powered fans direct air into the kennel, are very efficient, and are now available in large pet supply stores. Please remember that a fan only reduces heat. It will not protect a dog left parked in the sun or in an enclosed car.

Cool Pads. There are several different varieties of these on the market. Some have a water-absorbent material (same stuff as in diapers) that can be "filled" with water the day before your trip. As the water slowly evaporates off the pad, the temperature of the pad is kept cool. These do work but the pad feels slightly damp, which some dogs do not like. There are also foam pads that wick high temperatures into the pad. These high-tech pads are usually soft and make good dog beds. Either of these products can now be purchased at large pet supply stores.

Windshield Sunscreens. Used by car enthusiasts who like to protect the interior of their car from sun damage, sunscreen panels attach to the rearview mirror and sun flaps, preventing heat buildup through the front windshield. I keep one under the seat all year. When using a windshield sunscreen, remember to park facing the sun.

Emergencies

What will happen to your dog if she gets lost? What will happen to her if you get injured? While these are both (hopefully) remote possibilities, accidents tend to be very inconvenient. Your own wallet has emergency information in it and your cell phone probably contains all your own emergency contacts. What about your dog? Being prepared takes minutes and can make life a whole lot easier on your pet.

Veterinarian

Put your veterinarian's phone number in your cell phone. Question your vet with regards to emergencies. With so many emergency animal clinics now open, many vets do not offer twenty-four-hour service. Make sure you know who to use or where to go for off-hour service. My dogs always seem to prefer holiday weekends for any incident that involves blood!

Emergency Contact

I also recommend putting an emergency contact list together for your dog. This list should be in your wallet or in the glove compartment of your car next to the car registration. This is where emergency service people will find it, should you be unable to communicate. Your contact person must be capable of collecting your dog from an accident site or from the local animal shelter and should be someone who can handle and transport your dog.

Lost Dog

Accidents happen. Dogs run off and dogs get lost. Sometimes it is a fear reaction and sometimes they just disappear while chasing a squirrel or rabbit. It does not have to end in tragedy. There are several lines of defense for your dog should he find himself alone.

Socialization. This sounds strange but your dog cannot be rescued if she cannot be caught. New, unfamiliar places can make dogs nervous. A dog that is not used to people will not come when called. This is where the disaster begins to take shape. Being borderline dog crazy, I have rescued more than one dog playing on the road, sniffing around my yard, or running loose in the woods. It is always heartbreaking when the dog runs away rather than coming near to visit and get a treat if I have one handy. Some dogs will bound up to anyone, anytime, anywhere. If this is your dog, then you do not have to worry. Others are naturally shy or wary of strangers. If you have one of these, take time to socialize the dog before you travel. This is easy to do in local parks, at the kids' soccer game, or in a structured dog-training environment.

Identification Tag. The simplest and easiest protection is an identification (ID) tag. This tag can provide all the information your dog's rescuer needs. There is typically space for your dog's name, your name and town, plus one or two phone numbers. This is a must. Go to your local pet store and invest in a tag for every dog. There are plastic reflector tags that can now be customized and ready for wear in less than five minutes. Check the tags frequently for wear and tear. A dog tag that cannot be read is of no use. Your dog's rabies tag should also be attached. If you do not want to listen to the jingle of dog tags while your dog is at home, buy a second flat-buckle collar for trips, and leave it in the car for use when outdoors.

Personalized Collar. Many online pet stores offer personalized pet collars. These collars have the dog's name and your phone number stitched onto the collar. I highly recommend this investment for anyone who travels with a dog. Having your dog's name on the collar allows the person who finds him to reassure your pet that he is with friends. Having your phone number, particularly if it is your cell phone, provides your dog a direct link back to you.

Animal Recovery Program. This is another small investment that makes traveling with your dog safer. Your veterinarian can insert a tiny microchip under your dog's skin that is programmed with a unique identification number. You can then register your pet with a recovery program for a small one-time fee. Shelters, animal control officers, and rescue organizations routinely scan dogs with microchip readers. Your dog's ID number is then passed on to the recovery program, which immediately contacts you and/or your veterinarian. The two largest pet recovery programs are the American Kennel Club Companion Animal Recovery and American Veterinary Identification Device (AVID).

Equipment

One of the nicest things about a day out with your dog is that you do not need much equipment. A collar and a leash can get you started. However, there are alternates and choices for everything in life and dog equipment is no exception.

Collars

The basic is an adjustable nylon collar with a quick-snap buckle. These come in every size and color imaginable. They are cheap, easy to purchase, and come in a variety of widths and lengths, making it easy to get the right size for any dog. Alternately, a well-made leather collar will last your dog's lifetime. It will not shrink, stretch, or break. They are typically either flat or round (rolled). If you own a long-haired dog, you will have far fewer mats around the neck with a leather collar. Neither a choke collar nor a shock collar is useful for a day out with your dog. Both are training tools and require that your dog be trained to understand the corrections. No small feat and best left to professional trainers. Another choice is a harness. These are now available in leather and nylon, in all sizes, shapes, and colors. A word of caution: if your dog has a tendency to pull, do not use a harness. Since it is the same basic style used by dog sledders worldwide, it allows the dog to pull and pull hard! For dogs that pull, consider a prong collar.

- A prong collar is not a torture device created by dog haters. It is a training tool and is used by professional dog trainers every day. The prong collar lets the dog self-correct. If your dog habitually races to the end of the leash and expects you to become her pack mate, running along at full speed with her, you should consider a few walks with a prong collar. When a dog wearing a prong collar reaches the end of the leash, she gets a simple but very effective correction. I only use the prong collar on winter hikes and then only on my Border collie. She weighs enough to pull me off my feet on an icy trail so for both our protection she wears the prong as a reminder to be extra careful of tension on the leash.

Leashes

The basic is a six-foot nylon leash that comes in a variety of colors and styles to match your budget. The nylon, or leather if you prefer, leash works very well on walks about town and on short hikes. It gives your dog room to explore without getting the leash tangled on every leg, lamppost, or bush. If you are walking multiple dogs, six-foot leashes are perfect for keeping control without constantly untangling lines. The best choice for longer hikes is the retractable leash. Be careful to size the retractable to your dog's weight. A sixty-pound Labrador can snap the line on a small retractable with one good pull. On the other hand, losing your grip on a large retractable and watching it fly toward a seven-pound Maltese is not amusing. A retractable leash gives your dog twenty-plus feet of running room while keeping you in control. The braking system allows you to stop the dog at any distance and can change the retractable into a standard six-foot leash whenever necessary. I drag the brake lightly on the wheel whenever my dog is in a full run and seems to have blanked on the fact that we are attached! The noise is usually enough to get her to pull up and eliminate a dead-end spin for her and a dislocated shoulder for me! Do not use a nylon-leash (versus a thin-line) retractable on a hike. These are very heavy and your arm will fatigue long before your feet. Unfortunately, thin-line retractables pose a considerable danger to your human hiking companions. If the line wraps or rubs along bare skin, it inflicts a truly nasty rope burn.

Water Bowls and Containers

The first rule of dog travel, particularly in hot weather, is to bring enough water. Your dog needs water, just like you do, and relying on ponds, puddles, or streams for your dog's liquids is not a solution. Offer your dog water at regular intervals. Dogs that like playing with the hose or like playing with water can easily be taught to drink from a squirt bottle. Other, high-tech options are available at sports and large pet stores.

Dogs do not need nor derive any benefit from sports drinks, such as Gatorade. These drinks contain a balanced mix of water, sugar (carbohydrates), and salts (electrolytes) and are effective for rehydrating human athletes. Dogs do not need sugar and salt to rehydrate or rejuvenate tired muscles. Offer lots of water and drink the Gatorade yourself.

Pooper Scooper Bags

Yes. These are a requirement. You must carry poop bags and, even more important, you must use them. Commercial poop bags are small (4″ × 6″) plastic bags. Some have tie handles while others are colored and/or scented. You can buy them individually rolled in plastic capsules, by the hundreds in easy-pull sheets, or just use plastic bags. The trick is to carry whatever is easiest for you to use since there is nothing more unpleasant than dog poop on a walking path or hiking trail, unless it is carrying dog poop 3 or 4 miles on a trail. A little advanced planning goes a really, really long way here. First, potty your dog before you start hiking. This may take a few minutes but the time is well spent. Second, carry a plastic, disposable container in your backpack and car. Use the poop bag and then put that in the sealed container. This keeps the smell, well, contained.

Accessories

You can spend a lot of money on travel and hiking gear for yourself and almost as much on your dog if you really want to. Dog accessories range from fancy bandanas to dog-body rain suits to high-tech backpacks. Most of this is personal choice. There are a few investments that merit a mention.

Retractable Leash Pack. This is a small saddlebag pack that Velcros onto your retractable leash. The two side pouches have enough space for poop bags, keys, small cell phones, dog treats, and a bit more. The only limiting factor is the weight. These inexpensive packs fit most medium and large leashes.

Raincoat. These come in a variety of sizes and styles. Some have hoods. Others have a quilted or fleece lining for extra warmth. Some fit like horse blankets while others are true body suits. Most are machine-washable and fairly durable. When hiking in cold, rainy conditions, these can be very useful, particularly with long-haired dogs or dogs with a very thin coat. The best raincoats have overlapping buckles around the chest or straps that slip under the back legs, which keep the blanket in place when the dog runs or the wind blows the fabric around. Not all dogs need extra protection from the elements. My dogs shuddered with horror and hid behind the cat when I brought home dog coats but their favorite hiking companion, a German short-haired pointer, who has led them on several canine-thrilling jaunts, wears one from late fall to early spring.

Footwear. Paw protection is not necessary for every dog nor is it necessary under normal circumstances. However, if you are walking your dog on extremely rough, rocky terrain, across ice, or on streets covered in ice melt, paw protection is not a bad idea. These are basically dog shoes or boots. Most are waterproof and attach to the dog's foot with adjustable Velcro straps. They can be purchased at many large pet stores for a reasonable price. If you do get pooch boots, get the video camera ready. Watching your dog figure out how to walk while wearing boots for the first time is classic video fun.

Pet Sling. Dog hiking is not just for big dogs! Smaller dogs can and do enjoy a day out just like their larger cousins. If you have a small dog or puppy that has not yet worked up to a full-day hike, consider a pet sling or front backpack. Dogs weighing four to twelve pounds fit comfortably into these packs, making it easy to carry them over rough or wet terrain or for a short break.

Dog Pack. Why not let your dog share the load? A healthy dog should be able to carry from a quarter to a third of his weight in a properly fitted dog pack. There are several companies who make dog packs for almost any size dog. With a healthy, well-conditioned hiking partner, a dog pack is a very good idea for long hikes. Look for saddlebags that do not obstruct the dog's movement, allow plenty of ground clearance, and let the dog lie down, even with a fully loaded pack. Straps should be soft, wide, and fit snuggly. The pack should also have a leash hook on top. Start with short hikes and light loads, and build up gradually. The pack dog must also obey the "no swimming" rule since a wet pack is heavier and the straps are more likely to rub.

Healthy, Wealthy, and Wise

Dogs are no different than people. They live healthier, happier lives with good nutrition, daily exercise, and a few common sense precautions, such as vaccines and preventive medical care. You need to consider your dog's health and physical conditioning very carefully before adding new activities to your pet's life. There are a lot of "couch potatoes" out there in the canine world. The quality of your dog's experience and the level of fun for you both are directly proportional to the care and preparation provided before you start. Being ready for a variety of situations and using a little common sense before you set out can go a long way toward ensuring a safe and healthy journey for your dog.

Neuter or Spay

If your dog is not part of a breeding program, spay (female) or neuter (male) your pet. It is healthier for them and eliminates potential behavior problems. Intact males tend to roam more than neutered males and often find everything (trees, grasshoppers, a cloud in the sky, a blade of grass) more interesting than you. This can make training difficult and time-consuming. Intact males are often more aggressive toward other male dogs. If your male is not neutered, make sure you can control him, even in difficult situations. Female dogs often have more health problems when not spayed and will also wander more when in season. A female dog in season should never be taken out, anywhere.

Age Limits

What ages are appropriate for outdoor adventures and travel? There are guidelines but no real rules. Older dogs should be evaluated for their fitness level and the type of outing rather than their age. Puppies six months of age or less should be kept away from public places simply because they have not yet had all their vaccinations and are not protected from disease. Run them around the yard or a quiet park and get them used to collars, leashes, and walking with you. After six months, the issue becomes joint development, bone growth, and control. A dog is not full-grown until twelve to eighteen months and during that time bones are still growing and joints are still forming. Excess wear and tear during this growth time can lead to serious problems in an adult dog. Furthermore, puppies and young dogs are not always well balanced and tend to be accident-prone. However, these youngsters have a blast playing in the park, scampering through the woods, or visiting town. All of these are fantastic ways for them to learn about the world, develop great coordination, become well socialized, and bond with you. Just keep their outings to puppy duration, distances, and difficulties. And give them a lift when their little paws get pooped!

Vaccinations

Dogs are prone to a variety of viral and bacterial diseases, some of which can be quite debilitating, or even fatal, and many are difficult to treat. Prevention is essential. Your veterinarian will have implemented a vaccine program for your dog's risk of exposure to diseases. Keep in mind that as your dog travels to towns, events, and parks across the state, she is exposed to different bacteria and viruses than she was while sitting in your house. Take time to revisit her vaccination record with your veterinarian. Your dog should be covered for the following:

Rabies. This is a fatal disease of the central nervous system that can affect any warm-blooded animal. It is transmitted from animal to animal through contact with bodily fluids—typically from a bite. A rabies vaccine is required by law in New Jersey. Most counties require that a three-year vaccine be given every two years, which ensures gap-free coverage. Keep your dog's rabies vaccinations current. If your dog does tangle with a stray dog, feral cat, or wild animal, wash the wound out immediately with water and apply pressure to stop bleeding. Though it is unlikely that saliva (the body fluid responsible for transmission of rabies) remaining in the dog's wound is infectious, you should wear latex gloves while cleaning the wound. Wrap the injury to keep it clean and contact your veterinarian as soon as possible.

Booster Shots. Every year you receive a reminder to get your dog's annual shots. There are many different types of boosters made by different manufacturers. Most boosters are a combination vaccination, meaning they protect against more than one disease in one injection, including one or more of the following: distemper, hepatitis, parainfluenza, and parvovirus. Distemper is a highly contagious disease spread by contact with infected secretions. It causes fever, lethargy, discharge from the eyes and nose, vomiting, diarrhea, and eventually seizures and death. Hepatitis affects mostly young dogs less than one year of age and causes damage to the liver, kidneys, eyes, and other major organs, and can be fatal. The disease is spread through contact with infected urine. Parainfluenza is one of the viruses responsible for kennel cough. Parvovirus is an intestinal virus that causes rapid dehydration, vomiting, severe bloody diarrhea, and possibly death. The important point here is that the vaccination is prevention and protection. If your dog is vaccinated and/or tested regularly, you can forget about all of this and go about happily with your dog for years to come.

Kennel Cough. *Bordetella bronchiseptica* is the bacterium behind kennel cough. This airborne disease is highly contagious in indoor environments. It is a viral infection, which cannot be treated with antibiotics. The usual symptom is a dry, nonproductive cough. Similar to a human cold, it is generally more irritating than dangerous but you should contact your vet if you suspect kennel cough or if you want your dog vaccinated. Outdoor adventures do not typically expose your dog to kennel cough but indoor activities do. If you take a training class, show, or board your dog, this is a very wise yearly investment.

Lyme Disease. There are now vaccines to protect your pet from Lyme disease. However, if you work on protecting your pet from getting ticks, you may not need the vaccine. There are multiple tick/flea prevention products on the market today—all of which are very good at tick protection. Talk to your vet about what is best for your dog and keep in mind that many high-end pet supply stores sell tick and flea prevention at lower prices.

Fleas have changed history. More human deaths have been attributed to fleas than to all the wars ever fought. As carriers of the bubonic plague, fleas were responsible for killing one-third of the population of Europe in the fourteenth century.

Insects

Ticks, fleas, mosquitoes, deer flies, and bees can ruin your dog's day. For the most part, your dog can go outside much better protected than you can. A topical, monthly flea and tick preventive is an absolute must. These products, like Frontline, Bio Spot, and Advantix, are safe and effective at keeping fleas and ticks off your dog and are now available everywhere. Never use products intended for humans, as these often have high concentrations of DEET, which may be toxic to animals.

Parasites

Dogs are vulnerable to several internal parasites, also known as worms. These little buggers can inhabit your dog's intestines, heart, or lungs. The critical point is prevention. Protecting your pet against worms is easy and cheap when compared to the treatment costs.

Intestinal Parasites. These come in a gross variety: roundworms, tapeworms, hookworms, and whipworms. Dogs generally pickup worms from contaminated soil or from eating woodland creatures contaminated with fleas or worms. No fun but completely controllable. For most dog owners, stool tests and wormers are a regular part of your annual vet visit. These normal treatments are enough to handle most intestinal parasites. Many dogs, mine included, seem to think rabbit and deer feces are better than cat food and an occasional bite of dirt is just added roughage. These are not good habits and will cost you a fortune in stool and blood tests. With your dog on leash, you can easily discourage and prevent him from gobbling up gross stuff.

Heartworm. This disease is a serious and potentially fatal condition caused by parasitic worms living in the lungs and heart. The disease is transmitted from animal to animal by mosquitoes. The bad news is that mosquitoes in New Jersey do carry the disease. The good news is that, like rabies, heartworm is completely preventable. There are a variety of options for the prevention of heartworm infection, including monthly chewables or topicals. With your dog spending more time outdoors, heartworm protection is a must.

Weight

Today, one in every three dogs is overweight. Like their owners, American dogs are carrying around a few extra pounds. Dogs may not watch TV but they spend just as much time on the couch and, perhaps, have a few too many snacks. The risks of being overweight are the same, whether you have two legs or four, and include diabetes, heart disease, joint problems, cancer, and a shortened life span. So how exactly do you determine if your dog is overweight? There are three simple tests that will get you started on an answer. For long-haired or double-coated dogs, check the following when the dog is wet.

Ribs. With your dog standing, press gently on the skin over the ribs. You should be able to feel the ribs without effort. If you have to press hard to feel rib bones, then your dog is probably overweight.

Waist. Standing over or just slightly behind your dog while he is standing, look for a waistline. A slight indentation or tuck-in should be visible just behind the ribs and before the hips. This is your dog's waist. If the waist is not clearly visible, your dog is probably overweight.

Abdomen. Viewed from the side while your dog is standing, you should see a distinct tuck or upward curve between the rib cage and the hind legs. If the abdomen is not visible, your dog is probably overweight.

The second step is a visit to your veterinarian. Just like with humans, dogs should not be started on a diet and exercise program without being sure that the extra weight is truly from overeating and/or a lack of exercise. If your dog does need a diet, try to remove the weight gradually. Dogs do not do well on starvation diets! A few diet changes and a regular exercise program will start your pet on a healthier lifestyle and get your dog out and about with you in no time.

Fitness and Conditioning

Walking can prevent or reduce any number of physical and behavioral disorders in dogs (and their owners). It can also provide a healthy alternative to destructive habits (human or canine) but your dog must be in shape. Taking your dog to an agility class or out on a strenuous hike without some type of fitness conditioning is wrong, if not downright dangerous. Most dogs cannot spend weekdays on the couch and weekends on the go—even if they are trim and slim. Just like people, dogs need to work into an exercise program that builds muscle tone and endurance.

If you are not sure about your dog's fitness level or know for sure your dog needs to get started on an exercise program, the same rule applies. Walk, walk, walk, and then walk some more. Start with "around the block" and increase the distance gradually. Include hills slowly and add different terrains, like rocks, mud, sand, and/or logs, only after you have done some solid conditioning. You must also acclimate your dog to different temperatures. When you start your dog's fitness program, avoid the hotter parts of the day. Remember, dogs have a tough time ridding themselves of heat.

Heatstroke

With no sweat glands and only panting available to disperse body heat, dogs are much more susceptible to heat stroke than we are. Even mild heat can cause discomfort in dark-coated or long-haired dogs. A dog cannot remove her "coat" and cannot always sense when to rest. Unusually rapid panting, a bright red tongue, and/or staggering are signs of heat exhaustion. You need to cool your dog down immediately. Put cool water or cool cloths under legs, on feet, and on the tummy. Do not put cool water on the dog's back. Keep the dog quiet and in a cool spot. Offer plenty of water. If ice cubes or ice pops are available, let your dog chew the ice in small amounts. Resume activity slowly. Common sense, good conditioning, and plenty of water can minimize the risk of heatstroke.

Pads, Paws, and Claws

Dogs are sure-footed, four-footed critters with specialized paws that get them off the couch, around the block, and across the field in almost any weather. Paws provide traction, shock absorption, and come in handy for digging and scratching. Thick pads absorb more shock and increase endurance. Rough pads allow for better traction and agility. Different breeds, bred for centuries, actually have different paw shapes. The occasional dog walk or slow meander around the yard or park does not stress your dog's feet. Outdoor adventures can bring on more wear and tear. Make sure your dog's pads are in good condition. Keep their nails well trimmed and keep the fur between their pads clipped short (shear off the fur that sticks out between pads) to eliminate dirt and ice collection.

Dog First Aid Kit

Standard travel equipment should include a well-stocked first aid kit. When exploring with your dog, you should enhance your kit to cover your dog. Since many treatments require basic information about the patient to be effective, you should also keep track of how much your pet weighs and have a mental picture of the dog's healthy gums and tongue. A healthy dog's temperature should be around 101°F when taken rectally. The basic essentials in a dog first aid kit are very like those in a human's. Covering your dog may just mean switching medications and adding one or two items. You should also discuss with your veterinarian what dose to use for your dog when administering over-the-counter drugs. Do not give your dog acetominophen (Tylenol), ibuprofen (Advil), or Pepto-Bismol.

Instruments: scissors, tweezers, toenail clippers, thermometer

Cleansers and disinfectants: hydrogen peroxide, betadine, eyewash, baking soda

Topical antibiotics and ointments: calamine lotion, antibiotic ointment, styptic powder (stops toenail bleeding), petroleum jelly, 1 percent cortisone cream

Medications: Bufferin (regular aspirin causes ulcers), Imodium, Kaopectate, Benadryl

Dressings and bandages: gauze pads, nonstick pads, adhesive tape, Vet Wrap

Miscellaneous: muzzle (long piece of cloth), dog boots, Gold Bond powder

Canine Etiquette

Before bringing your dog out and about, please consider that you and your dog will not be alone. New Jersey parks, events, and trail systems are often crowded. As dog enthusiasts, we must do our part to maintain relations with the non-dog world. This means religiously cleaning up after our dogs and keeping them under control. Non–dog lovers are more receptive to a friendly, well-behaved dog. Excessive barking, frantic hunting, and arguing with other canines are no fun for others. If your dog is a bit unruly or rambunctious at home, do not expect that he will suddenly learn right from wrong and become the perfect partner when out and about!

Those readers who travel with their dogs and/or have already invested time and energy in their pup's training are probably ready for the next chapter, Trip Tips for selecting a park or event. So I am going to focus here on the family dog that has little or no experience dealing with the *outside* world. However, this is not a dog-training manual so I will stick to the basics needed to successfully enjoy a day out with your dog.

Breed Behavior

All dogs are not created equal. Although dogs are considered a species, their body size, coat length, color, and temperament varies enormously from dog to dog. Specific traits were bred into the current dogs of any given breed. Many of these selected traits drive behavior and they are *part of* the dog. For instance, it is very difficult to remove the herding instinct from a Border collie or the hunting instinct from a Welsh springer spaniel. In any breed, or even within the same litter, some dogs display more inherent instincts than others but the critical factor is to recognize what your dog's natural instincts tell him to do. If your dog's core (or soul) has a hunting dog lurking there, he is going to hunt. If your dog's core breeding tells him to herd, he will herd whatever is around—be that you, the neighborhood kids, your cat, or a passing deer. If your dog has basically been bred to be a house pet, you may actually have to encourage him to get wet and muddy.

None of this should unduly impact your desire to take your dog out. It just means every dog needs to be handled a little differently. My Border collie loves being outdoors in any weather and will hike any trail for any distance. Unfortunately, she sees a loose sheep instead of a brown deer and thinks it is her job to return the fleeing animal to me. This is why my daughter refuses to hold her leash! On the other hand our Lhasa has never seen a reason to chase anything except a fuzzy tennis ball and has never wandered more than a few feet from the family pack on a hike. He will, however, guard my backpack (which contains his lunch and/or training treats) from anyone or anything in any location. Two dogs, same environment, but two different reactions and behaviors.

In China, the "Fu Dog" is said to bring happiness and good fortune.
A great deal of the dog's early domestication took place in ancient China.
In fact, the emperor Fo-Hi actually encouraged their breeding in 3400 B.C.
It was probably in China that both dwarfing and miniaturization occurred.

Basic Training

Dogs are pack animals and teaching them to travel in a group is relatively easy. They inherently understand that rules exist and must be followed. The only problem is getting them to understand that it is *your* rules that must be followed. The place to start this adjustment, if it is needed, is at home.

With a puppy or a dog that is convinced you live by her rules (and those of you who do this know who you are), your simplest, shortest path to a well-behaved dog is through a course at the nearest dog training school that has classes tailored to family dog training. These classes will serve you and your pet well and are relatively inexpensive. An instructor watching your dog in training situations can provide feedback particular to your dog and can answer your specific questions. Be sure to let the instructor know what you want from the class. Furthermore, going to dog school gives you multiple chances to debug your traveling process and provides your dog an opportunity to mingle with her own kind, all while you are adjusting her attitude about whose rules to obey when she is away from home.

An eight-week session of classes should provide almost all your basic training. You just need a foundation to build on and time to master some canine communication skills. *Dogs cannot do what they do not understand.* Obedience training gives you a "language" to communicate with your dog and, hopefully, teaches your dog that you mean what you say. In today's world of positive reinforcement training, the use of treats and toys also makes the process fun.

Your dog should graduate from training—whether done at home or in class—with all the basic skills needed for a lifetime of happy, healthy adventures. Of course, if you and your dog enjoy class, there is no reason not to continue. However you handle this training, you need the following:

Walk on Leash

Your dog should be able to walk on a six-foot leash without pulling, circling, lagging behind, or trying to play tug. This means a loose leash—no tension. Even slight tension can wear down your hand and arm over the course of a three-mile hike. This does not mean your dog cannot be enthusiastic and pull you along to the park entrance. What it does mean is you can say, "Enough" and get him to walk calmly without straining. Walking on leash also means that your dog understands order and will stay beside or in front of you—even when that leaf pile has the best smell ever. This is important, particularly if you are walking in a group. If your dog lags behind in a sniff fest every ten feet, you will quickly get dizzy untangling yourself and/or your companions. (I have also heard that these walking single-file rules can be applied to kids but my training skills have not improved to that level yet.)

Recall

Your dog should come when called. This is critical for dogs that travel with the family. Get your dog conditioned to come immediately when you call. And make sure his recall is all the way to you and that he allows you to get a hold of his collar. A dog that returns to your vicinity is not doing a safe recall. Train it and proof it—before you need it. A reliable recall requires training in multiple situations over a long period. It is, however, something that you can continually train. Take half a dozen treats on all your outings and call your dog back to you at random times and in random situations. This will keep his recall sharp and you will be eternally grateful on the day you turn the corner and find him nose to nose with a skunk or his tennis ball bounces into the street.

Sit and Stay

This is your control zone. Your dog should sit on command (or a reasonable number of commands) and should stay put until you release her. With your dog in a reliable sit-stay, you can focus on your backpack, a conversation, the trail map, or another dog approaching. Your dog should sit quietly while you are doing something else and while you are holding her collar. Both are critical skills and should be taught immediately, even to young puppies. At the absolute minimum, your dog should sit while you get out a bag and collect the poop. This is unpleasant enough without struggling with a wandering dog. Holding a leash that has been dragged through the poop pile is enough motivation for most owners to effectively enforce the sit command. Like the recall, with a few treats and a few practices on every trip, you can keep these skills sharp. I always put my dogs in a sit when bikers or horses are passing on the trail. Tangling a leash with a speeding mountain biker or skittish horse does not bear thinking about.

Around

While not absolutely necessary, this one makes life a lot easier. The "around" command gets your dog to reverse his path around a tree or obstacle. Most dogs sniff multiple sides of trees and large obstacles, which are the equivalent of canine "chat rooms." About half the time, your dog will continue forward from the opposite side of the tree. You call him back and he returns to you—neatly encircling the tree or mailbox or log in the leash. For years, I tramped through the brush, collecting scratches and poison ivy, to unloop the leash. Then my Border collie, who inherently understood that leash walking was a three-dimensional exercise, came along. With very little help on my part (okay, none, since I did not realize what she was doing until after she figured it out), she learned to track backward around the tree before continuing forward. I am pretty sure she just got tired of delaying her walk while I fumbled around with the leash! Anyway, I now teach all my dogs—from a very early age—to correct their path. Unfortunately, this is one of those behaviors that some dogs

1. Sit and stay also works when taking photos.

understand better than others. Like I said, my Border collie did this on instinct. My Lhasa is not quite sure what he is doing or why and manages to give me the "I am humoring you only because I am nice" look through the entire exercise.

Leave It

This command is helpful when you have a natural hunter on the end of your line. It gets your dog to stop chasing down a fleeing creature, be that dog, child, bear, or squirrel, and can also tell your dog to move on from whatever has captured his attention. This command is easy to teach and reinforce with a dog on leash. Our two herding dogs need this most, especially the Border collie, who needs reminders to leave the darn sticks alone—particularly when the "stick" weighs more than she does and anyone she takes it to will require knee surgery. There is a hidden lesson here: never, never, never play fetch with sticks while walking or hiking!

Drop It

This one can come in handy in a number of places. The most obvious is when your lovable pooch picks up his first dead animal or bag of garbage. Of course, this is also when he follows the "every pack member for himself" rule, making him more likely to ignore your request to share. Ever play tug with a dead duck carcass? To avoid these delightful encounters with someone's moldy lunch bag or creature internals, have a command that gets whatever your dog just put in her mouth out again without your having to pry, tug, and pull. If you can get your dog to drop a meat bone at home, chances are she will give up the trail goody too.

Pick Up and Carry

While this is not necessarily a command, it is well worth teaching your dog to let you pick him up and carry him when necessary. It is not possible to predict every situation on every outing. I hiked three miles soaking wet in December the day I found out my Border collie would not let me pick her up. We were hiking along a river and needed to climb the side of a waterfall. There was a section of vertical rock that was easy enough to climb, even for the kids, but it was beyond what my Border collie could safely leap. Unfortunately, when I picked her up, she wiggled and twisted in complete desperation (thought I was going to get even for that duck carcass probably) and we ended up in the waterfall spray. Talk about a wake-up call! Needless to say, we now practice the pick up and carry all over the yard. This is the one that finally convinced the neighbors that I was certifiably nuts! All kidding aside, this is also a safety issue. If your dog is injured, you should be able to carry him (assuming you do not own a Newfoundland) without a fight or struggle, which could do more damage.

THE OTHER DOG

Okay, you now have a quiet, well-behaved furry companion and are ready to go anywhere, anytime. Most people immediately discover that not everyone's dog is as well-behaved and, in some cases, not even under control. Now what?

THE BASIC RULE

Dogs are literal creatures. In other words, they do not understand different rules for different situations and, for the most part, they assume the world works the same way everywhere. Dogs also have different personalities. Some dogs are very social and want to meet everyone. Other dogs are shy and would just as soon not deal with other dogs. If yours is a social animal, you need to establish meet and greet rules immediately. What you do not want is for your dog to drag you along to meet every dog she sees. This gets old. It is also dangerous. Many dogs fit in the unsocial category and some will take exception to being accosted. The simplest method is to teach your dog to walk quietly past—always. This gives you control. If the other dog is aggressive or enthused with social fever, you can just keep moving. After a year of traveling with me researching this book, my Border collie, who is sociable but shy, has perfected her own greeting. She very quickly bumps noses with the oncoming dog and then slips past while the other pooch is still "thinking" about her unusual greeting!

BODY LANGUAGE

Dog language is mostly physical. They express emotions with body language. Once you are outside with your dog, you will discover dogs everywhere. You and your dog must deal with them effectively. Sometimes the dog has an owner. Sometimes the dog is inside an invisible fence. Sometimes the dog is loose. Being able to "read" a dog's body language can be a huge advantage. When in doubt, use the head and tail as a guide since dogs express many of their emotions with tail and ear positions.

AGGRESSION. This is the most difficult to deal with but the easiest to identify. The signs include ears laid back along the head; snarling or growling with teeth exposed; tense body; fur around neck and back standing up; challenging, direct stare; rigid tail. This is a dog that is considering an attack or is serious about defending the territory.

FEAR. This is also easy to identify. The dog has ears back, flat to the head; low, tense body; tail tucked between legs; averted eyes; teeth exposed with low whines or growls. You may also see the dog slink back and forth. This dog is afraid and very worried. Generally, the tail position indicates the level of fear or anxiety. A tummy-tucked tail indicates a strong fear. A lowered tail, sometimes with a slight wag, indicates worry or anxiety.

Curious. Curiosity and excitement are easy to confuse with anger. However, the ear and body positions of an excited dog are quite different from those of an aggressive dog. The curious dog has ears perked; head up and pointed in direction of interest; steady stare but not challenging; tail position will be stiff but not rigid; whines or quick barks. You may see the dog bounce forward, prance, or wiggle.

Playful. Dogs have a whole set of body signals for play. The dog has ears up and perked forward; eyes wide and happy; tail or whole body wagging; quick barks or mock growling; relaxed body with lots of contained energy. The dog may bounce, spin, or run back and forth. The classic play invitation is issued by putting front legs on the ground and leaving the rear end high. This is the universal canine message for "Come and get me!"

Meet and Greet Etiquette

In a decade of training classes, park use, and hiking, I have only encountered an aggressive dog once and that dog was actually after the kids, not my dog. I have had much worse encounters with happy, slightly out-of-control, eager-to-meet-you dogs. Dog etiquette is simple. Ask the dog's owner before you let your dog greet his dog. Never assume a dog is friendly or that the other people want to stop for a hello sniff. I planted a very heavy foot on a young golden retriever's nose one day (Oh, yeah! His human companions were less than thrilled with me), but their pooch was about to lose that cute little black nose. Our sheltie was going through a fear stage and was horrified by the oncoming rush of canine enthusiasm! Furthermore, the couple did not *listen* when I warned them that our dog was getting aggravated. They had a friendly dog and made the mistake of assuming all other dogs were too.

Assuming that every dog on the trail or in the park or at class is glad to see your best friend is the fastest path to a bad experience. Think of it this way . . . do you expect every person you meet to stop for a chat? Even with dogs that are sociable, it is difficult to untangle legs and leashes when dogs greet on a narrow trail, crowded sidewalk, or in a class waiting area as they instinctively circle each other. It is much better to let your dog socialize during class free time or in a dog park.

Trip Tips

So you are ready for your first outing with your well-behaved, well-conditioned pooch; where should you go? The majority of this book describes hundreds of wonderful parks, towns, and events for you to share with your four-footed friend. Everyone has their own interests, however. So use the following general descriptions and cautions to decide which are best suited to you and your pooch.

Parks, Preserves, Reservations, and Reservoirs

From rugged, steep trails to paved paths meandering along placid creeks, New Jersey has it all. National, state, county, and township parks all offer wonderful doggie adventures. Unfortunately, these adventures are sometimes more than we really want. Knowing what to avoid can make your journey a lot more fun.

Park Rules

It is easy to follow the "rules" since there are only two. First, your dog must be on leash. Some park rules specifically say a six-foot leash but flexible leads are okay so long as you shorten the leash to six feet when around other park visitors. And the second rule is that you must clean up after your dog. No poop excuses! Pick it up and dispose of it correctly. In the carry in/carry out state and national parks this means taking it out of the park with you. For more information on the state parks, go to www.state.nj.us/dep/parksandforests.

Wildlife Encounters

Most woodland inhabitants take off long before your dog becomes a threat but there are a few exceptions. If you surprise an opossum, remember that their defense mechanism is to "play dead." Give the animal lots of room (they have nasty, sharp teeth) and go around. The Canada goose is another creature that does not always clear the area, particularly for smaller dogs. An odd goose or two will actually hiss and run at a dog but they are not really dangerous. On the other hand, a skunk encounter can just plain ruin the day. With your dog on a leash, you should have plenty of time to remove your dog before the skunk gets irritated. Skunks are a bit arrogant and assume you are leaving the area to them anyway.

- If you surprise a skunk or your dog manages to provoke one despite your efforts, there is a remedy. No, tomato juice as a treatment for skunk stink is a bit of a myth. An expensive skunk shampoo is also not necessary. Try the following homemade recipe.

  1 quart of 3 percent hydrogen peroxide
  2 ounces of baking soda
  1 teaspoon of liquid soap or shampoo

  Mix all ingredients and apply the whole mixture to the spray area, usually around the head (do not get in dog's eyes or nose) and let it stand for about 15–20 minutes. The mixture should bubble a bit and can be rinsed off with another regular shampoo if needed.

As for snakes, there are only two venomous reptiles found in the Garden State: northern copperheads and timber rattlesnakes. Unless cornered or teased, both types of snakes will slip away rather than attack. Avoid rocky areas, crevasses, caves, and areas where the ground cover (weed, grass or dried leaves) prevents you from seeing the ground. Snakes are solitary creatures and are seldom found in parks or along well-used hiking trails. Even when searching for them, biologists have trouble finding them. Your chances of seeing a black bear, let alone getting near one, are also remote and you can minimize the chances even more by making noise. Talk to your hiking companions (people or canines) or tie a set of bells to your pack or dog's collar. A bear's acute senses of smell and hearing alert them to your presence long before you are aware of them. If you do surprise a bear, make lots of noise, back away slowly (dragging your pooch with you), and avoid eye contact.

Poison Ivy

Although dogs are not susceptible to the skin irritations caused by poison ivy or oak, your pet can be a carrier. If your dog runs through a poison ivy patch or rubs against the vine, the oil can be on her fur. Learn to recognize poison ivy—three leaves and shiny—and avoid it! If you are walking in an area infested with poison ivy, avoid touching and petting your dog until you have a chance to wash her down.

Stop, Drop, and Roll

Nope. This is not a fire prevention drill. I am describing the ancient dog custom of rolling in the foulest-smelling stuff imaginable! Why dogs roll in *stinky stuff* is open for debate. It does not really matter why. Just be aware that your dog will roll and watch for that infamous shoulder dip. Prevention is critical. Driving home with the "smell" in your car can seriously dampen your enthusiasm for having your dog along as a travel partner.

Off-Leash Exercise

Parks are great but where do you go if you want to play or hike with your dog off leash? There are excellent options in almost all the counties for off-leash exercise as well.

Wildlife Management Areas (WMAs)

The New Jersey Division of Fish and Wildlife supports the training and conditioning of game dogs for hunting by providing eleven designated dog-training areas that are open May 1 to August 31. Within these areas, dogs are not required to be on leash. And no, you do not have to have a hunting dog. These parks may not have designated hiking trails but there are paths, many of which are easy to find and follow. Furthermore, you may take your dog off leash in *any* of the WMAs from September 1 to April 30. There is a catch, of course. WMAs are open to hunting for much of this time. For more information, go to www.nj.gov/dep/fgw/.

Dog Parks

For off-leash fun in a more controlled environment, try a *dog park.* These are typically township funded or private fenced dog runs that allow dogs to play and socialize in a natural setting. Dog parks offer dogs freedom to be, well, dogs. There are specific rules to many dog parks but most use the following guidelines as a basis.

- Use at your own and your dog's risk.
- Owners are responsible and liable for the behavior of their dogs at all times.
- Dogs must be vaccinated and have valid license/tags.
- Limit of three dogs/person. Some have lower limits so read the signs.
- Dogs must be accompanied by an adult at all times.
- Children must be eight years of age and accompanied by an adult.
- No puppies younger than four months old. Some have a six-month age limit.
- No bitches in heat.

- No food. Some also say no toys.
- Owners must clean up and remove dog feces.
- Aggressive dogs must be leashed and removed immediately.

Some of the township dog parks restrict use to residents or require that you purchase an annual pass before using the dog park. Check before you go and always read the posted rules for each individual dog park.

Beaches, Rivers, and Ponds

A place to swim, chase frogs, or soak your owner with river water—what more could a dog ask for? Water sports are "the thing" for many dogs. There are also plenty of dogs with no interest in water. If your dog does not make like a fish and dive right in, do not force the issue. Given enough exposure, most dogs will at least learn to enjoy wading. Even our water-phobic sheltie will go wading if our son goes in first. Actually, water is the only problem we encounter with our Lhasa. He loves the water and wades in to neck depth in the blink of an eye. Since I keep him in full coat, every one of his water excursions requires about four hours of fix-it grooming! Needless to say, I have been known to leap tall bushes and speed across boulder fields to stop him from wading in. Grooming issues aside, water has a plethora of other problems and issues for the owner of a water-loving dog.

Lakes, Ponds, and Rivers

Before your dog goes for a swim, check out the water for algae, pollutants, and contaminants. Look for running or moving water since it is generally cleaner. If you cannot see the bottom, which may contain sharp rocks, rusted cans, or broken glass, do not let your dog wade or swim. Avoid rapids and swiftly moving water unless your dog is a very strong swimmer. Search out the areas above rapids for good swim holes. Also, be very careful of ponds used by local fishermen who do not think about barefooted paws when they cut the line on a stuck fishhook. Use areas along streams and ponds that are obvious "swim" spots. Where others have gone and returned, your dog is safer.

Beaches

My dogs love running on the beach and there are parks that allow them to enjoy the beach with us. However, there are no dog lifeguards so safety is always the owner's responsibility. Do not allow your dog to swim very far into the surf. Swimming is natural for dogs but waves can come as a surprise. You also do not want your dog to get caught in a riptide. Another surprise for many dogs is that sea water is salty. Dogs can gulp down a lot of ocean water, especially the first time or two, so offer lots of extra water and then extra potty time.

It is also a good idea to plan on a bath when your dog gets home. Salt water dries out a dog's coat and can cause skin irritation.

Water Woes

While many dogs love water, water sports do not always treat dogs kindly. There are several common problems that you may encounter.

Hot Spots. These are skin infections caused when normal skin bacteria grow and overwhelm normal resistance. They are generally circular patches that lose hair, swell, secrete pus, and can be painfully itchy, causing the dog to scratch and lick. Moisture is a key element in the development of hot spots, and they form easily on active, outdoor dogs. Hot spot treatment is relatively simple. Isolate the spot by shaving the hair, clean it thoroughly, and apply treatment, which should include an antibiotic and a drying agent, such as Gold Bond Powder. For severe or frequent hot spots, check with your vet for the best treatment.

Dead Tail. If your dog makes like an otter at every opportunity, put the dip or swim into the first half of the walk. This gives your dog time to dry before the trip home. (Your car will thank you.) This is especially important for Labradors and other retrievers. These breeds are susceptible to a condition called cold water tail or dead tail, which is sometimes described as a sprain or a "cold in the tail." The affected tail is painful and cannot be raised. While not fatal, this uncomfortable condition is easy to avoid with a bit of planning.

Slips and Slides. Water also makes surfaces slippery. This is not knowledge that is bred into your dog. Be cautious with your dog on rocks, piers, and steep trails if the surface is wet or his paws are wet. He will figure it out but the "figuring" is through trial and error and your goal is to make sure the errors are not noteworthy.

Canine Sporting Events

Another excellent outdoor activity is to attend one of the hundreds of canine sporting events held each year in New Jersey. These events are sponsored by local dog clubs and are held under the guidance of a national dog organization, such as the United Kennel Club (UKC), National Association of Dog Agility Club (NADAC), or American Kennel Club (AKC). For more information on AKC events, go to the Events page at www.akc.org. Many of these events are in public parks, so your dog can go with you.

When your dog is a spectator, keep a respectful distance from the show area, keep her under control at all times, and pay attention to the signs and rules of the host club or organization. Young dogs, under six months, should not attend. And keep in mind that some of these events are very exciting and loud.

Rather than spend your time trying to calm your dog down, you may enjoy the event more with your dog at home.

- Please remember that the dogs entered at the show or trial are working and it is not fair for them to be distracted by a barking or out-of-control dog. If you do bring your dog, she must stay under control. And keep in mind that the human team member is also competing and may not have time to talk. If you have questions, be patient. Once the class or test is over, most dog handlers will be more than happy to talk your ear off!

All-Breed Conformation Show

Breed shows or conformation events concentrate on the unique features of each breed. Dogs are judged against their individual breed standards, which describe the ideal size, color, and temperament of the breed, as well as correct proportion, structure, and movement. All-breed shows draw thousands of entries each day and are a wonderful place to check out your favorite breed, talk to local breeders and owners, or investigate a new breed. There are also breed-specific shows, or specialties, which focus on one particular breed or a group of breeds. Due to the size of these shows, only dogs competing are allowed on the show grounds. Admission is also charged.

Obedience Trials

These trials test a dog's ability to perform a prescribed set of exercises with her handler. Each dog is scored individually and the tasks at each level increase in difficulty, for both the dog and handler. It is a thrill to watch the total concentration and close bond between the dog and handler as they complete each task. Both the AKC and UKC sponsor obedience trials in New Jersey and you will find a wide range of breeds competing. Outdoor obedience trials in public parks may allow unentered dogs to attend but indoor trials only allow competing dogs to attend and frequently charge admission. Obedience trials are frequently held in conjunction with conformation shows.

Rally Trials

In this sport, the dog and handler complete a course of ten to twenty stations, depending on the competition level, with the tasks increasing in difficulty at each level. The dog and handler proceed at their own pace through the designated stations and each station has a sign providing instructions for the skill, such as heeling backward, jumping, or circling, that is to be performed. These events are generally held in conjunction with obedience trials and the same rules apply for bringing unentered dogs.

Lure Coursing

Lure coursing is an event for sighthounds, such as the Afghan hound, greyhound, Rhodesian Ridgeback, Saluki, or whippet. A lure course tests the dog's basic ability to hunt by sight. Dogs chase an artificial lure across an open field or around an oval and are judged on their speed, endurance, agility, and ability to follow the lure. (Please note that lure coursing is not greyhound racing, although greyhounds do compete.) Sighthounds love this event and many other breeds think it looks like fun too! All of these events are open to the public, but your dog can only attend if the event is held in a public park.

The "dog" mentioned in the Bible (King James version) Proverbs 30:29–31, is an ancient Hebrew translation error.

Agility Shows

Agility is the ultimate game for dog and handler. It is also one of the most exciting canine sports for spectators. In agility, the handler directs the dog as he races the clock around the course, which has jumps, tunnels, weave poles, seesaws, dog walks, and other obstacles. All the dogs run the same course with adjustments in the allowed time and jump height, depending on the dog's size and age. While strengthening the bond between dog and handler, agility provides extreme fun and vigorous exercise for both team members. Almost all agility events are held in large parks but they are busy, noisy events. If you bring your dog, keep her under control and away from the ring fence. For specific dates on many of the agility trials in the area, go to www.fasttimesagility.com.

Herding Tests and Trials

Noncompetitive herding tests offer herding breed owners a chance to measure their dogs' basic instinct and trainability. In competitive herding trials, the trained dog shows his ability to work livestock (cattle, sheep, or ducks) through a serious of tasks, with the degree of difficulty increasing at each level. Although herding trials are simulations of farm situations, they are designed to measure and develop the characteristics of the herding breeds. Many of the herding breed clubs sponsor their own trials. Dogs not entered should not attend herding trials.

Terrier Earthdog Trials

For generations small terriers and dachshunds were bred as hunting dogs to track game above and below ground. The different levels of earthdog tests showcase these abilities. In the initial test, the dog must maneuver through a ten-foot tunnel with one right-angle turn and find the cage of rats at the end. (Please note that the rats are kept quite safe.) In subsequent tests, the distance from the tunnel, length of the tunnel, and number of turns are increased while the allowed time is decreased. Earthdog tests, many sponsored by the AKC, provide terriers an outlet for their strong instincts and excess energy. Dogs not entered should not attend earthdog trials.

Tracking Trials

The tracking test challenges the dog's ability to recognize and follow a human scent, or track, through a variety of conditions. The distance of the track and the length of time the track scent cools also increase as the dog and handler progress through the various levels. Although this is considered a "hunting" dog skill, a wide range of dog breeds compete in tracking trials. Trials are usually held in public parks, so well-mannered dogs may attend.

Hunt Tests

These tests are offered for retrievers and pointers. Hunt tests build the skills needed by a good hunting dog and are fun for dog and handler. The dog is not competing against the other dogs, but against a "standard." All three levels simulate true hunting situations with natural hazards, obstacles, and decoys. Breed groups often host their own tests and the AKC sponsors several pointer and retriever tests in New Jersey each year. Dogs not entered should not attend hunt tests.

Field Trials

The dogs that compete at these events are some of the best-trained, most highly skilled, and well-conditioned competitors in the world of sporting dogs. These complex tests require great stamina and a keen memory on the part of both the dog and handler. There are several field trials in New Jersey. Dogs not entered should not attend field trials.

Flyball

This is a relay race with four dogs on a team. The course consists of a starting line, four hurdles spaced ten feet apart, and a ball box, from which the dog retrieves a tennis ball. The dog runs back over the four hurdles with the tennis ball so the next team member can begin. The first team to have all four dogs run without errors wins. These exciting races are very popular in the South and Midwest. The closest tournaments are held in York, Pennsylvania, but there are plenty of teams practicing in Jersey. Tournaments will be held soon.

Frisbee Contests

If you can throw a Frisbee and your dog can catch, this is the sport for you! With distance-accuracy and freestyle competitions, the disc dog competitions are fabulous fun to do or just watch. Skyhoundz, the largest organizer of disc dog events, sponsor several competitions in New Jersey. These highly competitive events are also open to beginners. Canine spectators are always welcome. Check the event schedule at www.skyhoundz.com.

Dock Dogs

It's a bird. It's a plane. No, it's a dock dog! These amazing dogs leap over twenty feet before crash landing into the water. The events are sponsored by Big Air Dogs and are open to any dog, of any size, of any breed or mix. Events are always for fun and are for dogs of all abilities. Canine spectators are always welcome. Dock dogs events are not that common in New Jersey but should not be missed! Check the event schedule at www.dockdogs.com.

Township and Shelter Events

There are plenty of noncompetitive events for canines almost any weekend in New Jersey. Special events for dogs, and their people, are often held by local shelters and there are county fairs, town festivals, or local fairs that are dog-friendly. All can be great fun.

Dog Walks

A dog walk or dog walkathon is typically a local dog community fun day or shelter fundraiser event. They occur across the state on a regular basis and are usually less than 2 miles. Almost all are open to any dog with valid vaccinations. Get your dog used to walking in groups before you go and use a short leash. These noncompetitive events are a great way to make new friends.

Fairs and Festivals

You can enjoy the day with your favorite four-footed friend at many town or local organization events. Many of the fairs enjoy dog visitors. I have found (as a general rule) that if the fair or festival charges admission or uses a shuttle bus to the parking area, they do not allow dogs. At the dog-friendly fairs, organizers always recommend that you bring your dog early to avoid the "foot crush" and keep your dog on a short leash. Remember to enforce the "no visiting" rules to keep them from greeting every person in the crowd and please potty your dog well away from the events. Some festivals have dog water stations but most do not so do not forget to bring along water.

County Fairs

Almost every New Jersey county has a 4-H fair and most have a pet show. These events showcase cats, dogs, and other pets, like hamsters, hedgehogs, and frogs. The dog shows are open to the public, are free, and have a variety of categories, from best groomed to longest hair to most obedient, so everyone is a winner. Dogs must be able to handle a crowd, ignore the other pets (particularly cats and rabbits), and be able to greet the judge nicely. These events are great fun but dogs are only allowed at the fair for the pet show. For details on 4-H fairs across the state, go to www.nj4h.rutgers.edu.

Where Not to Go

This book is filled with fun places to take your dog and lists hundreds of great outings for you to share. However, there are lots of places and events that should not include your four-footed friend. Always remember that your dog is "a dog" and is sometimes safer and happier at home.

Parades

The annual Memorial Day, July 4th, and Labor Day parades are not meant for the average dog. The noises from the marching bands, car horns, and fire engines that are prominent features of these parades frighten most dogs.

Bird Sanctuaries

These are for birds and bird lovers. Even if dogs are allowed, the other visitors will not appreciate their presence.

Arboretums

Dogs and lush, hand-tended flora do not mix well. Your dog might enjoy the walk but the other visitors are sure to frown.

Pick-Your-Own Farms

As a general rule, the pick-your-own farms, particularly the strawberry, raspberry, and blueberry farms, do not allow dogs. Apple and peach orchards seem more dog-friendly but you should always call ahead for current policy.

Wildlife Refuges

These sanctuaries are for wildlife, not domestic dogs. Most have restrictions against dogs anyway.

Fireworks

Definitely not. The explosions terrify dogs and your dog will not appreciate the colorful displays anyway.

What to Bring

Before you head out, take a moment to be sure you have what your dog needs for the day.

Water

Having enough clean water for your pooch cannot be stressed enough. Extra water also comes in handy for quick cleanups. Carry a gallon of water per dog on a normal day and more on hot, humid days. A popular choice for sport dog enthusiasts is to fill a small cooler with ice water. Lift off the lid and you have a multi-dog waterer. I use old Gatorade bottles since the opening is large enough for ice cubes.

Food

For hiking trips or long days out, you pack nutritious snacks or a healthy, high-protein lunch. Your dog is burning the same amount of calories as you (perhaps more) and needs her energy resupplied as well. Packing dog food or biscuits is okay but there are better choices. Pick up a power bar specially formulated for dogs. They provide increased energy and stamina for your dog although they are a bit pricey. These bars pack a punch so feed them to your dog in quarters or thirds over the course of the day rather than as a meal. A cheaper, perhaps easier alternative is to make a treat. Putting together a healthy, portable dog treat is not hard and takes about the same amount of time as a batch of cookies.

- One of my dogs' favorite snacks is Pooch Trail Mix. It is easy to make and lasts a long time. Use low-salt ingredients whenever possible. Dogs do not need salt like humans.

Pooch Trail Mix

INGREDIENTS

2 cups	Cheerios
2 cups	Rice Chex
2 tsp	dry gravy mix (low-salt)
6 slices	bacon (low- or no-salt)
2 cups	Shredded Wheat (spoon-size)
½ cup	melted butter or margarine
½ cup	Parmesan cheese
1 cup	Lean Pupperoni dog treats (cut small)

DIRECTIONS

Preheat oven to 250 degrees. Cook bacon in microwave and tear into tiny morsels. Mix Cheerios, Chex, Shredded Wheat, bacon, and dog treats. Melt butter and blend in dry gravy and cheese powder. Turn dry mix into butter mixture and stir gently until all pieces are coated. Spread in thin layer on ungreased cookie sheet and heat until crisp, approximately 45 minutes. Let cool and store in tightly sealed container. Makes about twenty servings.

Overnights

Should your day out get extended or you want to take your dog on a vacation in the Garden State, check with the following hotel chains. All of these have a reputation for being pet-friendly. Each hotel sets their own rules and they can change so check the dog policy before you book.

Best Western
Clarion
Days Inn
Holiday Inn Express
Howard Johnson's
Mainstay Suites
Marriott Residence Inn
Radisson
Red Roof
Sheraton
Staybridge Suites
Towne Place
Westin

More Information

For more information on dogs in New Jersey, including links for many of the referenced websites and events, go to the book website at www.happytailsacrossnj.com.

You know you are a dog person when you share ice cream cones with your dog—lick for lick.

Sussex County

Organized in 1753, from a portion of Morris County, Sussex County remained a bit of a battleground with the local Indian tribes for several decades before becoming a major source of iron ore during the American Revolution. New towns and small developments were built up around the mines and by 1820, Sussex was actually one of the most populated counties in the state. Today, the population density in Sussex is among the lowest in the state. With a large part of the county's 521 square miles publicly owned, recreation is a major industry and farming is close behind. The land is green, the hills are high, the wildlife is abundant, and best of all folks are Fido-friendly. What more could an adventure-loving canine want?

Dog Day Out

One of the last northern New Jersey counties to retain its rural characteristics, Sussex promises four-footed visitors a growling good time for the day or the weekend. Huge state parks and forests offer thousands of wilderness acres, making it ideal for long hikes, water sports, and overnight camping. With so much land under national and state control, the county does not have its own park system. However, there is no bark about it—this county offers endless delights for dogs and their tag-along owners.

Delaware Water Gap National Recreation Area

This national park preserves the Delaware River and almost 70,000 acres of land along its shores. At the south end of the park, the river cuts through the Appalachian Mountains at the scenic Delaware Water Gap, and almost 40 miles to the north, the park ends at Milford, Pennsylvania. Roughly half the park is in New Jersey and half in Pennsylvania. In Jersey, the southern third of the park is actually in Warren County. Both states have a few dog-restricted areas, mostly the beaches, picnic areas, and waterfalls, but the vast majority of the park is open to four-footed visitors and it is a terrific place to spend the day with your furry friend. For directions, detailed trail maps, and park updates, go to www.nps.gov/dewa/. Maps are also available at any visitor center once you are in the park.

Blue Mountain Lakes. For hardy hiking hounds that crave wilderness experiences, go into the Blue Mountain Lake area. There are 10 miles of marked hiking trails around Blue Mountain Lake and Hemlock Pond. This is a beautiful, rugged area with few visitors. Parking is on Blue Mountain Lake Road.

McDade Trail. My dogs adore a walk along the McDade Trail. It is wide enough for multiple dog walking and we all get considerable exercise on the hills. The trail starts at the north end of the Hialeah Picnic Area and runs 5 miles north to Turn Farm. Please note that dogs are not allowed on the trail where it passes through Smithfield Beach from June 1 through September 8. This is a popular dog walk so you are sure to have company on nice weekends.

Millbrook Village. Located near the middle of the park, this restored 1800s village is a very nice place to wander with your dog. It is also much flatter than other areas of the park. One of the nicest walks is along the original road, the Columbia-Walpack Turnpike. Go south from Millbrook to the falls, which is 2 miles round trip. Another excellent canine loop is along the Rattlesnake Swamp trail, for which parking is available on CR 602. Please note that Millbrook Village is actually in Warren County.

Restricted Areas. In Pennsylvania, dogs are not allowed at Hidden Lake, Milford Beach, or on any trails at Raymondskill Falls, Dingmans Falls, Hackers Falls, and Childs Park. In New Jersey, dogs are not allowed in the Hialeah Picnic Area, Smithfield Beach, the Kittatinny Point visitor center and picnic area, Depew Recreation Site, or Watergate Recreation Site.

Delaware River Canoe Trips

Spoil your water-loving pup with a raft trip down the Delaware. Many of the river outfitters have an open-boat policy with regards to dogs, although they do recommend a canoe or raft versus a kayak. Every outfitter has specific dog guidelines so please call ahead to confirm.

Adventure Sports. In Pennsylvania in Marshalls Creek on Route 209, 570-223-0505, www.adventuresport.com.

Kittatinny Canoes. In New York in Pond Eddy or Barryville, 800-FLOAT-KC, www.kittatinny.com.

Hainesville Wildlife Management Area

This dog-training and exercise area is in Montague. With a 30-acre pond, this is a very popular spot for field trainers to work their dogs. The pond and stream offer plenty of swim spots for any water-loving canine and there are unmarked trails through the woods. From Route 206, go east on Shaytown Road. The large gravel parking area is well marked at the intersection with New Road. Remember—hunting is allowed in all WMAs and seasons extend from September to March.

High Point State Park

Located in the extreme northwest corner of the county along the Kittatinny Mountain Ridge, this park has 15,000 acres of swamp, streams, lakes, and mature hardwood forests in which your four-footed friend can nose about. There are a dozen marked trails, including a stretch of the Appalachian Trail. Ranging from a half mile to over 4 miles, with longer, tougher loops possible by combining routes, the trails vary from easy walking to difficult rock scrambling. For pooches that would rather poke around and perhaps collect ear scratches, the sculpted parklands around Lake Marcia provide the fur-pect environment. For cold weather enthusiasts, dog sledding and snowmobiling are permitted on the trails in the park south of Route 23. Trail maps are available at the park office, located on Route 23 about 7 miles north of Sussex.

One of the most famous races in the world is the Iditarod, which is a dog sled race across some of the toughest terrain in Alaska. The distance of the Iditarod is given as 1,049 miles. The distance is always over 1,000 miles, but the 49 is symbolic (Alaska was the 49th state). The actual total miles are 1,151 on the Northern Route, which is used in even-numbered years, and 1,161 on the Southern Route, which is used in odd-numbered years. The first Iditarod race started on March 3, 1973. Teams average sixteen dogs. The largest number of mushers to finish a single race was sixty-three in 1992. The closest finish was in 1978, with the first- and second-place finisher separated by one second. And a red lantern is always awarded to the last musher to finish.

Kittatinny Valley State Park

This 3,165-acre state park contains the Andover-Aeroflex Airport and Lake Aeroflex. If you and your dog are feeling lazy, there is a small picnic area at the south end of Lake Aeroflex. There are also three other ponds scattered about and multiple trails that vary in difficulty and terrain from the gravel roads to the technical terrain enjoyed by hard-core mountain bikers, who are frequent park users. This park also administers the Paulinskill Valley and the Sussex Branch Trails. These rail-trails have a wide cinder surface ideal for dog walking, particularly if you have multiple dogs. Maps for the state park and the rail-trails, which cross both Warren and Sussex Counties, are available at the park office. From Route 206 in Andover, go east on Limecrest Road.

SUSSEX BRANCH TRAIL. A rail-trail built on the old Sussex Railroad, this trail stretches 21 miles from Stanhope to Branchville. It skirts swamps, lakes, fields, and several small communities. There are several sections that make good dog hikes.

Byram. The 2-mile section in Byram is very popular with the dog-walking set. The flat trail travels north through the Allamuchy Mountain Natural Area to the southern end of Cranberry Lake, where dogs can enjoy a dip in the lake near the boat ramp. The wide trail makes it easy to walk multiple dogs. Parking is available on Waterloo Road in Byram and on South Shore Road at Cranberry Lake.

Andover. This 2-mile section is one of my dogs' favorite walks. It is flat, scenic, and relatively quiet. When snow is abundant, several local dog sled teams train on the trail here. There is a well-marked, easy access point on Route 206, just north of Andover.

Lafayette. The longest and least used part of the Sussex Trail is the 5-mile section from Lafayette north to Branchville. Local dog walkers use the trail from both towns but the middle areas are typically very quiet. Just south of Branchville, there are several shallow dog-wading spots along the Paulinskill River. Parking is available at the southern end at Olde Lafayette Village and in the middle on Augusta Hill Road, just south of Route 206. Please note that there is no parking in Branchville.

PAULINSKILL VALLEY TRAIL. For most of its 27 miles from Columbia (in Warren County) north to Warbasse Junction, this rail-trail passes through rural landscapes, northern deciduous forests, wetlands, and several small towns. Its wide, firm cinder base makes it popular with bikers, hikers, and horseback riders. For multiple dog walkers, this is an excellent choice. Although the Sussex County section of this trail is away from Paulinskill Brook, it provides four-footed hikers with lots of woods to explore and animal trails to track. There are multiple, easy access points in Sussex County. For more Paulinskill Valley Trail hikes, see Warren County.

Stillwater. Just north of the Warren/Sussex County border and just east of Stillwater, there is a parking area at Dixon Road, which is reached by driving west one mile on Fairview Hill Road from Route 94. There are very nice dog walks in both directions from the gravel parking lot, across from the Water Wheel Farm Stable.

Newton. Further north near Newton, there is a well-marked parking area at the corner of Halsey Road and CR 519, just a mile west of Route 206. Follow the trail south into the Paulinskill WMA. The area is heavily forested and quite lovely in the fall.

Chatterbox Diner is an old-fashioned fifties-style diner complete with outside car service (during summer) with waitresses on roller skates, who are sure to surprise your dog when they roll up with burgers and hot dogs for the whole family. The menu is authentic fifties and the atmosphere is pure fun. It is located where Routes 206 and 15 intersect, about 3 miles north of Newton.

Olde Lafayette Village

For a unique day trip featuring cozy shops and eateries, visit this small village. Stroll the pathways, window shop, feed the ducks, enjoy a treat with your pup from the bakery or sweet shop, or just rest together on a bench or picnic table. For wagging tails and doggie kisses, stop at The Barkery. This is also a wonderful place to socialize puppies and young dogs. It is located at the intersection of Routes 94 and 15 in Lafayette. For more information on the shops or special events, go to www.lafayettevillageshops.com.

Every Sunday from 11 to 4, the village hosts a farmer's market, which is open mid-June through early November. Items available at the market include fresh produce, fruits, dairy products, plants, flowers, breads, baked goods, cider, eggs, and other locally processed items. Special "Taste the Market" days are planned throughout the season and dogs get to nibble too!

Stokes State Forest

Located on the Kittatinny Ridge, this 15,734-acre forest has some of the finest mountain country in New Jersey. Stokes is famous for its impressive beauty and for its long section of the Appalachian Trail. If your dog could drive (and read this book and a road map), this is one of the first places he would go. All of my dogs adore the steep, often treacherous climb to the top of Sunrise Mountain and they seem to enjoy snuffling the breeze (aka a stiff wind) from the top. At the opposite end of the park is Tillman Ravine, another dog favorite. In between are a dozen different hikes of various lengths to please any type of hiker and her human chauffeur. Maps are available at the park office on Coursen Road, just off Route 206 in Branchville, and are highly recommended for the human half.

Swartswood State Park

Established in 1914 as New Jersey's first state park, Swartswood contains two lakes, Little Swartswood and Swartswood Lake. This state park has 5 miles of hiking trails, which start in the Duck Pond Multi-Use Area. The half-mile Duck Pond Trail is paved and level, while the 2.8-mile Spring Lake Trail traverses a hilly terrain along a narrow path. Trail maps are available at the park office on CR 619. From Route 94, south of Newton, go west on CR 614 for 2.5 miles. Turn right onto CR 619 and continue north to the park.

U-Cut Christmas Tree Farms

When the temperature chills and the leaves are gone, slip into a warm coat and load the dog for the traditional tree cutting. Many tree farms are dog-friendly and will even allow well-mannered dogs on the hayride to the field, although it is always wise to ask first. For directions and more information on tree farms, go to www.njchristmastrees.org.

Beaverbrook Tree Farm. In Augusta at 125 Route 206, 973-895-3526.
Holiday Tree Farm. In Augusta at 44 Augusta Hill Road, 973-948-7488.
Saint Paul's Abbey. In Newton on Route 206, 973-383-2470.
Shale Hills Farm. In Sussex at 98 Pond School Road, 973-875-4231, www.shalehillsfarm.com.
Stone Row Tree Farm. In Branchville at 242 Wykertown Road, 973-875-7968.
Wintergreen Farm. In Lafayette along Statesville Quarry Road, 973-875-8387.

Wawayanda State Park

Located in the northeast corner of Sussex, crossing into Passaic County, this 20,000-acre mountain woodland tract contains Wawayanda Lake, 20 miles of the Appalachian Trail, and over 40 miles of hiking trails. Forested hills surround Lake Wawayanda, creating a restful backdrop for canoeists, boaters, and fishermen, while steep mountains challenge casual as well as serious hikers, whether they have two feet or four. A good place to start exploring this park, which your dog would definitely drive to if she could, is the Lake Wawayanda Day Use Area. For rugged, thrill-seeking canines, try the Bearfoot Mountain Natural Area or hike up to Wawayanda Mountain from Route 94. Maps are available at the park office on Wawayanda Road in Hewitt. From Route 23, go north on Union Valley Road for 6 miles to Upper Greenwood Lake. Follow the park signs onto Warwick Turnpike. The park entrance is about 4 miles north and is on the left.

From March 8 to November 21, 1990, Bill Irwin and his Seeing Eye dog, Orient, trekked the Appalachian Trail (AT) from Georgia to Maine. The pair traveled through fourteen states, covering 2,168 miles across some of the most treacherous terrain in America. Irwin chronicled their AT experience in the book Blind Courage, *which is a must read for dog lovers.*

Whittingham Wildlife Management Area

This dog-training and exercise area is a mile west of Route 206 near Newton. It is the north end of the WMA, in which there are no lakes or streams, just woods and fields. Tractor roads meander away from the parking lot, looping around the fields. A well-marked parking lot is on Fredon-Springdale Road. Remember—hunting is allowed in all WMAs and seasons extend from September to March.

2. Kayla packing lunch on a day hike in northern New Jersey.

Paw-tacular Shopping

The Barkery

Paws, tails, and noses up! This dog bakery is top-dog fun. Bring your pooch inside and let her select from a lip-licking, delicious selection of homemade treats. You can also spoil your four-footed friend with a new toy. Located in Olde Lafayette Village at the corner of Routes 15 and 94 in Lafayette, 973-300-0035. For more information on the shops, go to www.lafayettevillageshops.com.

Farmside Supplies

Whether you have a wolfhound or a toy poodle, you should not miss this store if you get into Wantage. With everything from toys to bedding to doggie boots, this store has your hound covered from nose to tail. The store also carries a wide range of small animal, bird, cat, and horse products. It is located at 15 Loomis Road in Sussex, 973-875-3777.

J&G Discount Pet Foods

Tucked into a side street on the north side of Newton, this shop is worth sniffing out. They have every high-end dog food, including the hard-to-find brands for special and holistic diets, at a fur-fabulous price. It is located at 4 East Clinton Street, 973-579-3411.

Nature's Cove Pet Center

From fish to hounds, this shop has all creatures covered from nose to tail. The entire center of the store is two tiers of gorgeous fish tanks that canines seem to find just as fascinating as humans do. Around the edges and along the wall, you will find specialty treats, toys, and a woof-worthy selection of chewy bones. They also carry fancy dog bowls, feeders, and a nice selection of additional pamper-your-pet products. The store is in the mini-mall on Route 206 on the north side of Newton, 973-579-4886.

While traveling about in Sussex County, you can also get pet supplies at:

Pet Valu. In Stanhope in Byram Plaza on Route 206, 973-347-7088.

Tail-Wagging Training Facilities

CCI New Jersey Chapter

Canine Companions for Independence (CCI) is a nonprofit organization that enhances the lives of people with disabilities by providing highly trained assistance dogs. The New Jersey Chapter includes Canine Companion graduate teams, puppy raisers, puppy sitters, and various other multi-talented volunteers. These special folks have a variety of fundraiser events throughout the year and every year is different. The New Jersey Chapter is at 33 Sleepy Hollow Road in Andover. For more information on puppy raising or events, go to www.ccinjchapter.org.

DogDome

This facility, located off Route 284 in Wantage, specializes in agility training. Owned and operated by Diane Bauman, whose experience includes obedience, tracking, agility, and herding, this training school offers agility competitors an opportunity to train year-round with the top trainers in New Jersey, Pennsylvania, and New York. Private instruction only.

Golden Rule School for Dogs

Located in Andover, this small dog-training school offers classes for everyone. From basic household obedience to competition-level courses in obedience, rally, and agility, classes are taught by a select group of professional trainers. The school, owned and operated by Sandi Versprill, is at 23 Morris-Sussex Turnpike, just off Route 206. For more information, call 973-786-5229 or go to www.geocities.com/goldenruledogs/.

Northwest New Jersey Dog Training Club

This small dog-training club offers classes in rally, breed handling, and several types of obedience training, from puppies to competition. A friendly staff of dog lovers can get you started on a behavior fix or on a path to the show ring. The facility is located in Hamburg at 3640 Route 94, just north of the Route 23 intersection. For more information, call 973-827-1950.

Best-in-County Events

BARKS Garage Sale

Byram Animal Rescue Kindness Squad (BARKS) is a nonprofit, all-volunteer, animal rescue organization. Founded in 1973, BARKS works in association with the Byram Pound, located on Mansfield Drive in Byram Township. Fundraising events are many and varied, with the largest being the bi-annual garage sales. Held in *April* and *September* at Wild West City, these sales include household goods, sporting equipment, books, furniture, and jewelry. For more information on events, go to www.barksinc.com or call 973-300-3185.

Applewood Winery Dog Day (NY)

Slip across the state line and enjoy a day with your dog at this winery in nearby Warwick, New York. In late *June*, Applewood Winery hosts a day of fun for dogs and their people. Dog contests, including best kisser, best tail wagger, and best bark, and doggie games run all afternoon. Wine tasting, light fare, music, and raffles round out the day. All proceeds go to the Warwick Animal Shelter. All dogs must have current vaccinations. Applewood Winery is at 82 Four Corners Road in Warwick, New York. For more information, call 845-988-9292 or go to www.applewoodorchardsandwinery.com.

Abbey Glen Memorial Day

The second Sunday of *September* is the official National Pet Memorial Day. It is a Sunday set aside to remember our precious pets. Abbey Glen Pet Memorial Park offers a day of remembrance for all pets. Exhibits include Seeing Eye and police canine demonstrations, wolf education seminars, local kennel club meet and greet, and a variety of pet memorial vendors. This is a good opportunity to visit Abbey Glen, learn about the Sussex County dog community, or share your loving memories of a departed pet. Abbey Glen is in Lafayette at 187 Route 94. For more information, call 800-972-3118.

Ancient Egyptians worshipped dogs and when a dog died the family would go into mourning, shaving off their eyebrows as a sign of respect.

Sussex County Fairground Events

Several weekends each year, the best dogs in New Jersey and the surrounding states compete in obedience, conformation, and agility at the fairgrounds, from April to October. For a schedule, go to the off season events page at www.sussex-county-fair.org. Please note that dogs are welcome at some of the dog and horse events but are not allowed at the New Jersey State Fair. The entrance is on August Hill Road, just off Route 206 north of Newton. Follow signs.

Newton County Kennel Club. Held most years over Labor Day weekend in *September*, this AKC all-breed conformation show and obedience trial draws thousands of dogs. The two-day show also brings out the biggest vendors with the latest and greatest dog gear and dog lover gifts, clothes, and collectibles. Admission charged. Dogs not entered should not be on the site.

Garden State Australian Shepherd Club. This three-day agility trial is usually held on Labor Day weekend in *September*. This North American Dog Agility Council (NADAC) event is fun for competing dogs and dog spectators. Hosted by the Australian Shepherd Club, there are always lots of Australian Shepherds and NADAC is open to mixed-breed dogs, which means the variety of dogs spans the dog world. There are always two rings of agility action, food vendors are on site, and the trial runs rain or shine. Well-mannered dogs are welcome to come watch.

Ramapo Kennel Club. Held in mid-*October*, this AKC all-breed conformation show and obedience trial is another large show. This prestigious fall event often draws the best dogs in the tri-state area, who duke it out for Best in Show and High in Trial. It also draws some of the best vendors for woof-fabulous dog shopping. The club typically joins forces with the Palisades Kennel Club, which makes this a three-day event that goes on rain or shine. Admission charged. Dogs not entered should not be on the site.

Herding Trial

On the last full weekend in *October* the German Shepherd Dog Club holds a sheep-herding trial at the White Clover Sheep Farm in Sussex. The dogs work the sheep in an open field (versus a small ring) at this type of AKC trial. Dogs not entered should skip this event.

Overnights

Want to get outdoors for the whole weekend? Sussex County has several woof-wonderful campgrounds that are very dog-friendly. Policies change so remember to call ahead before planning your trip.

Panther Lake Camping Resort. In Andover just off Route 206, 973-347-4440, www.njcamping.com.

Kymer's Camping Resort. In Branchville off CR 519 on Kymer Road, 973-875-3167, www.njcamping.com.

Harmony Ridge Farm and Campground. In Branchville at 23 Risdon Drive, 973-948-4941, www.harmonyridge.com.

Cedar Ridge Campground. In Montague at 205 River Road, 973-293-3512, www.cedarridgecampground.com.

The Oxford English Dictionary suggests that "pup tents" were so named because they resembled dog kennels. Originally used in the military, the term pup tent *dates in writing from 1863, and it is likely that it was in use for some years prior to being written down.*

High Point Country Inn

You can also try this child- and pet-friendly bed and breakfast in Wantage. Located on seven acres, the inn has fifteen rooms, an outdoor swimming pool, and is close to all the state parks and forests. Always check current pet policy before booking a room. The inn is at 1328 Route 23 North in Wantage. For more information, call 973-702-1860.

You know you are a dog person when your dog has collars and leashes for different occasions.

Passaic County

Settled by Dutch farming families in the 1600s, Passaic County history is a microcosm of American history. The first European settlers, hard-working Dutch farmers, subsisted off the land for decades before iron ore was discovered in the area, which became critical to the Continental Army during the Revolutionary War. A century later a different material changed the county landscape. Many of the towns of Passaic, most notably Paterson, became cotton "boom" towns. While the southern end of the county was thriving through the Revolutionary War and the industrial revolution, the northern half remained a mostly rural area with farms and mines. And so it remains today. Passaic County has a diversity that visitors, both two-footed and four-footed, must see to appreciate.

Dog Day Out

Home to some of America's most famous four-footed creatures, this county is as dog-friendly as New Jersey can get. It was in the early 1900s that the collies of Sunnybank roamed the Terhune estate in Pompton Lakes. Immortalized in the stories of Albert Payson Terhune, the collies have become dog heroes for generations of children around the world. A delightful mix of pooch-friendly county parks and some of the state's best parks for rugged outdoor adventures await dog visitors and their human chauffeurs. For details on any of the county parks, go to the Passaic County website at www.passaiccountynj.org.

Barbour Pond Park

Located in Wayne Township, this small community park has Barbour Pond on one side and several large office buildings on the other. As such, it makes a great spot for the single women and baby stroller set of dog walkers. With a mile of paved paths around the ball fields, playground, and pond, you can count on company—especially at lunchtime—in this park. From Hamburg Turnpike, go north a short distance on Valley Road and then make a left onto Barbour Pond Road.

Goffle Brook Park

This 103-acre park is adjacent to Goffle Brook in Hawthorne. The southern section of the park contains numerous athletic fields, a playground, and picnic areas while the northern section contains a duck pond and a fenced *dog run.* Opened in August of 1998, this was New Jersey's first county dog park. It is just under an acre but has a very active user community. The park entrance is on Goffle Road; follow signs to the dog park.

In 1926, radio entrepreneur Donald May established the Technical Radio Laboratory in Midland Park and began operating the WTRL radio station. After just a short time in operation, the Federal Radio Commission (FRC) moved to revoke WTRL's license. Before its demise, however, WTRL did gain some brief notoriety when radio inspectors reported that its transmitter was located in a barn used to house puppies. A letter received by the FRC noted, "The gentleman who operates that station evidently has an eye for thrift if not an ear for harmony, for in all this broad land there probably is not another individual to whom it ever occurred to hitch a dog kennel to a radio station. Inasmuch as you have no jurisdiction over the kennel, but have over the station, it is probably wise for you to demand a separation of the two industries by stopping the station." Despite May's legal appeals, the "dog station" was shut down on September 1, 1928.

Friendship Park

This 8-acre county park is located in the lovely community of Bloomingdale. Having been left in its natural state, the park makes a growling good spot for some paws-ercise if you are in the area. The short hiking trails wind through the woods and a few picnic tables are scattered about. A small parking lot is located adjacent to the park on Glenwild Avenue. From Bloomingdale, go west on Hamburg Turnpike and then north onto Glenwild Avenue.

Garrett Mountain Reservation

With wide gravel hiking trails, a large pond, and huge green lawn for games, this county park is a woof-fabulous destination for you and your dog. The 568-acre reservation is situated more than 500 feet above sea level and provides sweeping views of northern New Jersey and the New York City skyline. So your fur-kid can meander along with the tourists and appreciate the smells, if not the view, or explore the woodland trails for different smells. Please note that dogs are not allowed on the grounds of Lambert Castle nor are they allowed in the adjacent Rifle Camp Park. Located in Little Falls, the reservation is also easy to get to. From I-80, take Squirrelwood Road east for a half mile to Rifle Camp Road. Follow park signs onto Mountain Avenue for the park entrance.

🐾 The great green lawn at the north end of the park is the fur-pect spot for a picnic. If you want to indulge yourself and your pooch, stop by My Sister's Gourmet Deli and Bake Shop at the corner of Rifle Camp and Mountain Roads for a delicious picnic spread.

Before billboards, TV commercials, and yellow pages, many businesses used unique signs as advertisements. One such trade sign is now a bit famous. In 1828, Horatio Moses fashioned a brass (actually gilded tin) dog to advertise himself as a tin and coppersmith. Today, this unusual "sign of the dog" can be seen at Lambert Castle.

High Mountain Preserve

Tails wag for this 1,154-acre township park. It has 10 miles of marked trails and, for those individuals energetic enough to hike to the top, the view of the New York City skyline is unsurpassed. Although I doubt your dog will be impressed with the view and he (and you) might be a bit winded from the 885-foot climb, he is sure to be happy romping around the large forest. This well hidden park is accessed from William Paterson University. Go to the top tier of Parking Lot 6 and look for the white *P*, which designates trail parking. Look for the red trail markers.

Longpond Ironworks State Park

Although the area is now dominated by the Monksville Reservoirs, the industrial ironworks, which date to the late 1700s, are within the state park boundaries. Longpond Ironworks Historic District is a four-paws-up park; dogs and their leash holders enjoy moseying about the ironworks just as much as trekking about on the forest paths. The historic site is on Greenwood Lake Turnpike, near the causeway at the north end of Monksville Reservoir in Hewitt. For more information on the area and special events (whether to avoid or attend), go to www.longpondironworks.org.

Morris Canal Park

Located in Little Falls, the park is in two pieces. The main park, with its lovely shaded walkway, is located behind the shops and restaurants on Main Street between Union and Stevens Avenues. Ample parking is available near town. The second, and smaller, canal park is located at Main Street and Long Hill Road, and is within walking distance from the larger park. Limited parking is available at the Long Hill Road location.

- Another section of the Morris Canal Park is in Clifton. It is located between the Garden State Parkway and Broad Street and provides a quiet haven for its visitors with ample parking, quiet-time spots, and an attractive setting.

Norvin Green State Forest

Within the undisturbed forests and rugged terrain of Norvin Green, there is a large trail system built on old logging and mining roads. Over a dozen different trails crisscross the park, varying in length from 1 to 6 miles. With hills ranging from 400 to 1,300 feet in elevation, Norvin Green provides avid hikers and their faithful hounds plenty of tail-wagging challenges. There are also old mines to explore and stream crossings to navigate. The Weis Ecology Center has trail maps for sale and provides the closest parking to the trail system. Continue on Ringwood Avenue through Wanaque and then go west on West Brook Road. Follow signs along Dale Road to Snake Den Road to the park entrance.

Ringwood State Park

Need to get away for the day? Located in the northeast corner of the county is Ringwood State Park. Famous for its beautiful Ringwood Manor, Skylands Manor, and the New Jersey Botanical Gardens, this park has an extensive trail system that elicits howls of delight from dog visitors. Since dogs are not allowed on the Manor grounds or in the botanical garden, head for the Shepherds Lake area for good dog walks. There are miles of trails around the lake and through the forests. From Memorial Day to Labor Day, dogs are not allowed on the beach but you can console them with ice cream from the concession stand. Trail maps are available at the visitor center, located on Sloatsburg Road. To reach this northern state park along the New York border, follow the signs along Skyline Drive to Sloatsburg Road to Morris Road. Follow signs in the park to reach the Shepherds Lake area.

- During the summer, boat rentals are available on Shepherds Lake. The rental company is private (not associated with the state park) and sets the rental policy, which is sometimes pet-friendly. Check it out and you might be able to take your hound out on the water in a rowboat or canoe.

Sterling Forest State Park (NY)

This New York state park comprises 17,953 acres and is a remarkable chunk of preserved woodland, a watershed for millions, and a tremendous outdoor recreation area. The unbroken deep-forest habitat borders Passaic County and connects to Wanaque WMA and Ringwood State Park. For adventuresome hounds that crave the outdoors, this is the park to find and explore. Start at the Frank R. Lautenberg Visitor Center, which overlooks Sterling Lake, and obtain a trail map. From Route 17 in Sloatsburg, go west on Sterling Mine Road and then right onto Long Meadow Rd. Follow signs.

❖ This is not really a "point of interest" but an unfortunate piece of information that readers should know. Many of the New York State parks closest to New Jersey are *not* dog-friendly. Many parks restrict dogs completely, others exclude them during the summer months, and the typical park rule states, "Dogs . . . must be *muzzled* and on a leash, not more than 6 feet. Not allowed in buildings, picnic or bathing areas, or on walkways." Geesh.

Terhune Memorial Park

Sunnybank overlooks Pompton Lake at the edge of the Ramapo Valley. It is a 9.5-acre tract of what was once the 40-acre estate of Albert Payson Terhune and his wife, Anice. The "spell" of Sunnybank can be felt underfoot as you walk along the lake or through the garden to visit one of the many memorial stones for Terhune's famous collies, including Wolf, Lad, and Bruce. With picnic tables and a gazebo along the water's edge, it is a beautiful place to stop and stretch some paws. The entrance, marked by a small blue sign, is off Terhune Road in Wayne Township.

The first dog to star in his own movie was a collie named Blair. The 1905 movie, Rescued by Rover, *was directed by Cecil Hepworth and starred members of his own family, including the dog. It is the story of a family dog, Rover, who saves a baby from gypsy thieves and is considered a classic of early British film.*

William Paterson University

Need a place to wander with your dog or do some canine-human socialization? Grab a big bag of treats and roam around this campus, just north of Paterson, with your dog or puppy. The campus offers lots of walking opportunities, without the threat of getting lost, and in winter the paths are well maintained. You are also guaranteed to meet lots of new people. For a campus wander, use entry 2 and park in the visitor center lot.

Tail-Wagging Training Facilities

Animal Action Pet Center

With training programs for basic off-leash and competition obedience, tracking, personal protection, and services for the physically impaired, this organization provides classes throughout Passaic County. Group classes are held in Hawthorne, Midland Park, Saddle Brook, and Clifton. For class information, go to www.dog-trainer.biz or call 973-742-5088.

Vince Rambala Dog Training

Puppy kindergarten and basic obedience classes are offered in Hillsdale, at Reigning Cats & Dogs, and in Bloomingdale, at the Bloomingdale Animal Shelter Society (BASS). Classes focus on teaching you to communicate effectively with your dog in a positive, fun way. Agility introduction classes are also offered during warm-weather months and are held at BASS. For details, go to www.vincerambaladogtraining.com or call 201-337-7299.

Paw-tacular Shopping

Allwood Pet Center

Shopping for your furry friend is simple at this store in Clifton. It is at 656 Allwood Road and you can pick up premium dog food, special treats, toys, and loads of cool canine accessories. 973-365-1300.

Mike's Feed Farm

For tail-wagging good shopping, check out Mike's Feed Farm. It is packed with dog furniture, holistic foods, fabulous treats, and the latest and greatest dog accessories, including designer coats, booties, dog sunglasses, and much more. The store is in Totowa at 142 Furlep Street, 973-256-8081.

Pequannock Feed & Pet Supply

With a knowledgeable staff and shelves loaded with the highest-quality dog food and treats, this store is sure to register on your dog's whisker radar. It is located at 85 Marshall Hill Road in West Milford, 800-834-6773.

While you are traveling around Passaic County, you can also get pet supplies at:

Petco. In Totowa at 1 Route 46 West, 973-256-9175.
Pet Smart. In Wayne on Route 57, 973-785-4479.
Pet Valu. In Pompton Lakes in Town Square on Wanaque Avenue, 973-616-1846.

Best-in-County Events

Bloomingdale Animal Shelter Society (BASS) Events

The Bloomingdale Animal Shelter Society is the local shelter for the communities of Butler, Bloomingdale, Pompton Lakes, Riverdale, Ringwood, and Wanaque. With a dedicated volunteer staff, BASS works hard to place stray and abandoned pets in new and loving homes and they host several fundraising events that are sure to appeal to your pooch. For more information, go to www.petfinder.com/shelters/bass.html.

Mutts at the Manor. Every spring—usually the first weekend in *May*—BASS hosts a picnic, dog walk, and an art exhibit in Ringwood State Park. Sporting a brand-new bandana, your dog can saunter about the park and make lots of new dog friends. Please note that pre-registration for the dog walk is required.

Annual Dog Show. In *September*, BASS holds a dog show at the shelter on Brandt Lane in Bloomingdale. The contests are all for fun, including obedience, agility, dog tricks, dog and owner look-alike, and best costumes. There are always lots of ribbons and awards for fun-loving people and their dogs.

Passaic County Fair

The Passaic County 4-H Fair, which has crafts, rides, 4-H and agricultural exhibits, and community organization displays and demonstrations, is held at Garrett Mountain Reservation. The fair is usually in *July*. For more information, go to www.njagfairs.com.

Walk for Homeless Paws

The Friends of Wayne Animal Shelter (FOWA) is a rescue organization, which operates the Wayne Township Municipal Animal Shelter. The Walk for Homeless Paws is FOWA's primary fundraiser. The annual dog walk and adoption fair is held in *September* at the Terhune Elementary School. You and your dog can mix and mingle with hundreds of other animal lovers and help raise awareness and money for homeless pets. For more information, go to the events page at www.waynetownship.com or call 973-616-0849.

Little Falls Street Fair and Craft Show

In the middle of *September*, you can "do" this street fair with your dog. Held on Main Street and Stevens Avenue, the event features arts, crafts, food, antiques, music, and special booths by local businesses and organizations. For more information, go to www.lfnj.com.

WMASS Walk-A-Dog-Athon

The West Milford Animal Shelter Society (WMASS) is an all-volunteer organization, formed in 1976 out of a desperate need to establish an adoption program at the West Milford Animal Shelter. One of the more popular events sponsored by the shelter is the Walk-A-Dog-Athon. It is held every *October* in Wawayanda State Park in Hewitt. For more information, go to www.westmilfordanimalshelter.org.

Hawthorne Street Fair

In early *October*, Hawthorne celebrates with a street fair on Warburton Avenue. Crafters join entertainers and food vendors to create a fun day for all. For details, go to www.hawthornenj.org.

You know you are a dog person when your dog gets a front row seat at every family wedding, especially your own.

Bergen County

The county was created in December of 1682 when the province of East Jersey was divided into the four counties of Essex, Middlesex, Monmouth, and Bergen. Situated in the northeast corner of the state with New York to the north and the Hudson River to the east, it is the most populous county, with a diverse culture and unique style. Historic mansions, beautifully landscaped homes, large townhouse communities, rugged county parks, extensive township parks, and acres of shopping malls coexist in relative harmony. For the dog traveler, there are quiet suburban parks with miles of paved walkways and surprisingly wild county parks to visit and plenty of interesting dog-friendly events and shops to keep those tails wagging.

Dog Day Out

With state, county, and township parks scattered about, members of the dog world can spend hours outdoors and never sniff the same tree twice. You can spoil your pet with long hikes along the Palisades or treat her to a social romp in a lovely dog park or simply stroll slowly around a pond on a warm spring day. All this and much more await canine visitors in Bergen County. Although much of the county is Fido-friendly, there are a number of townships, like West Englewood, that do not allow dogs in their parks. Read the signs to avoid the fines. For park specifics, go to the parks and recreation page at www.co.bergen.nj.us.

Campgaw Mountain Reservation

For a pup-pleasing day in the woods, this 1,300-acre county park gets four paws up. Trails vary in length from a half mile to almost 3 miles, all are well marked, and you can select the degree of difficulty. The flat Hemlock Trail loops around the pond while the steeper Old Cedar Trail loops around the mountain. Located in Mahwah, the reservation includes a downhill ski mountain, and therefore the area can be crowded on winter weekends. Conversely, summer weekends are quiet. To access the reservation trail system, take Darlington Avenue east from Route 206. After a quarter mile, turn right onto Campgaw Road and then make another right onto the park entrance road. The trailhead parking is the maintenance area on the left.

One of the newer dog sports is skijoring. In its simplest form, skijoring is dog-assisted cross-country skiing. A specially designed belt and tug line connect the skier to the dog or dogs, who wear comfortable harnesses for safe pulling, and away they go. If you ski and your dog loves a run, this might be your sport and your fellow dog lovers might even forgive you for constantly wishing for more snow!

DEMAREST FARMS

This 35-acre country farm is now operated by the fourth and fifth generations of Demarests. With 1,500 peach trees, 300 nectarine trees, 1,800 apple trees, plus a scattering of plum and cherry trees, there is always something in season and when it comes to vegetables, Demarest Farm grows it all. You can pick your own peaches, apples, and pumpkins and your dog is welcome to pick with you. The farm, which also has a deli and farm market, is at 244 Werimus Road, just off Route 71, in Hillsdale. For more information, call 201-666-0472 or go to www.demarestfarms.com.

NEW YORK ROAD TRIP

Got a free Saturday or Sunday for a road trip with your furry friend into New York State? Rockland County, which borders New Jersey, has two dog parks and, being dog-friendly, allows dogs in all its parks. I should note that dogs are not allowed in any township parks and the state park system in the vicinity is a tad unfriendly to dogs. For directions and details, go through the county website, www.co.rockland.ny.us, to the Parks page.

BUTTERMILK FALLS PARK. Located in West Nyack, this 75-acre park contains Buttermilk Falls, with its deep gorge and ravine. There are short, informal trails connecting the falls, stream, scenic overlooks, and parking area, which is on South Greenbush Road.

DATER MOUNTAIN NATURE PARK. This 350-acre county park, which is located in the New York/New Jersey Highlands, is heavily wooded with steep inclines and rocky slopes and is crisscrossed by several small streams. Adventure-loving hounds are sure to enjoy exploring the informal trails in this park. Parking is available at the end of Johnsontown Road in Sloatsburg.

KAKIAT PARK. This 376-acre county park borders Route 202 and the eastern edge of Harriman State Park in Suffern. Your dog is sure to enjoy hikes along the Kakiat Trail, a simple picnic, or just a stroll to one of the scenic lookouts. However, his favorite section of the park is bound to be the *dog park*. The dog run is 75 × 150 feet with chain link fencing and the area is mostly open with a few shade trees. The park entrance is on Route 202.

KENNEDY DELLS PARK. This 179-acre county park borders North Main Street and Crum Creek, along which winds a hiking trail that looks down at the stream below. There are also picnic grounds, ball fields, and the *dog park*. The dog run is 80 × 220 feet with chain link fencing in a large grassy area with very few trees. Located in New City, the park entrance is on North Main Street.

OVERPECK PARK

Of the four separate areas of Overpeck Park, the Henry Hoebel Area is guaranteed to provide a growling-good time throughout the year. Your first stop must be the *dog park*, which is in the southeast corner, near the bridge. A truly woof-wonderful dog spot, it is about a half acre with a wood chip base and sturdy chain link fence. There are several large trees for shade, several obstacles to encourage playing, and a large local dog community to ensure lots of playmates. Assuming your dog has some energy left, you can then use the 1.25-mile paved path for a long walk. The path forms a figure eight along the lake, loops around the huge green lawn, and passes the World Trade Center Memorial, which is impressive. The Henry Hoebel Area (Leonia North) of this county park is on Fort Lee Road in Leonia, less than a half mile from exit 68 on I-95.

PALISADES STATE PARK

The New Jersey Section of the Palisades State Park is part of the more than 100,000 acres of parklands and historic sites maintained by the Palisades Interstate Park Commission. Acquired in 1900 to protect the Palisades from stone quarries then in operation, the New Jersey Section is about 12 miles long and a half mile wide at its widest and contains 2,500 acres of wild Hudson River shorefront, including some of the most impressive sections of the Palisades. For rugged canines that crave the outdoors, this is a woof-wonderful park with over 30 miles of hiking trails. Navigators (aka you) will be thrilled to know that there are basically two trails: the Long Path, which runs along the cliff, and the Shore Trail, which hugs the base. Numerous connecting trails exist to create long and short loops and all are shown on the state park maps, along with the historic sites and parking areas, of which there are many along Henry Hudson Drive, which is readily accessible from Route 9. For the less energetic pooches, there are several picnic areas in which to enjoy the day together. Try the Ross Dock, Englewood, or Alpine picnic areas as starting points. Please note that dogs are not allowed in the Fort Lee Historic Park or Greenbrook Sanctuary. For driving directions and maps, go to www.njpalisades.org.

Pascack Brook Park

This small county park is tucked into the neighborhoods of Westwood. As in Wood Dale Park, the half-mile paved walking path loops around the pond and through the picnic area. If you are in the neighborhood, this park is a nice spot for a doggie break or a doggie picnic. There is a large parking area off Emerson Road.

Ramapo Valley Reservation

Exploring the wooded hillsides of this 2,145-acre park is guaranteed to bring out the hound in any dog. The rugged trails vary in length from 1 to 6 miles so you can wander for an hour or hike the entire day. The trail system in the reservation connects to the trails in Ringwood State Park, Ramapo Valley State Forest, and Camp Glen Gray. Trail maps are available and highly recommended for navigating these trails. For water-loving canines, use the Schuber Trail or go to Bear Swamp Lake, where the 2-mile Shore Trail loops around the lake and provides access to a dog "beach" near the dam. Access to Bear Swamp Lake is from Cannonball Road, while the main park entrance is on Route 202 in Mahwah.

A yip from Edward Hoagland, "In order to really enjoy a dog, one doesn't merely try to train him to be semi-human. The point of it is to open oneself to the possibility of becoming partly a dog."

Ridgewood Walkabout

With two tempting pet stores on the main street, a town park, and cute shops, this is a fabulous place to visit with your fur-kid. You can traipse about town with your pooch, getting in some window shopping or just caving in to the allure of a pet store for a toy or treat. There are also coffee shops, delicatessens, and bakeries for treats and snacks. Municipal parking lots are well marked in the downtown area. If you want more exercise, leave your car in the Wild Duck Pond Area, which is a mile east on Ridgewood Avenue, and walk into town.

Riverside County Park

Tucked into a curve of the Passaic River, this small county park has picnic areas and ball fields in both the north and south sections. What makes this park noteworthy is the *dog park* in the north section. Both parks are on Riverside Avenue in Lyndhurst.

Saddle River County Park

Ready for a long walk and endless doggie kisses? Saddle River is a delightful spot for dog visitors. Although frequently only a quarter mile wide and yet 6

3. A morning walk to the coffee shop.

miles long, this park has a paved path that stretches through all five sections: Rochelle Park, Otto Pehle Park, Dunkerhook, Glen Rock, and the Wild Duck Pond. All provide paw-tacular dog walks and are very popular with the dog-walking set. The path begins in the south at Rochelle Park, which has a large parking lot on Railroad Avenue, and there are paths on both sides of the river here, offering a very nice 2-mile loop. Just a bit north along Saddle River Road is Otto Pehle Park, which has another mile of path, a large playground area, and a medium-sized duck pond. If you are socializing a young dog, this is the best park to use. For woodland hounds or for longer walks, try the larger Dunkerhook Area, which is further north on Paramus Road in Paramus. The 2 miles of paths in Dunkerhook wind through deeper woods, and water-loving kids, two- or four-footed, can play in the stream at the north end of the park, near the double bridges. This is also where the connecting trail to Glen Rock meets the main north-south trail. Glen Rock, which makes a very nice starting point, is accessed from Prospect Avenue and it is a very nice 1.25-mile walk to the double bridges in Dunkerhook. All the way north in Ridgewood is Wild Duck Pond, which has a playground and picnic areas. If you just want a short stroll with your pooch, there is a paved path around the pond.

Van Saun County Park

Although your pup is not invited into the Bergen County Zoo, she is sure to vote paws-up for this park. Whether you just laze around the picnic area or hike the 1-mile paved path from the zoo south past the train and pony rides to the pond, this county park deserves a visit or two. This is also a superb park in which to socialize puppies or do a dog/stroller walk. There are plenty of parking areas but the roadway through the park is one-way and it can get very crowded on summer weekends. Use the entrance on Continental Avenue, which is off Spring Valley Road in River Edge.

Wood Dale Park

This is a small county park in Woodcliff Lake. There is a paved walking path around the pond, through the picnic area, and past the playground. Although the half-mile path is not long, it is a nice park for a doggie break if you are in the area. Please note that the majority of this park, which is to the south of Prospect Avenue, is undeveloped.

Paw-tacular Shopping

American Pedigree

This store has adorable dog clothing, designer collars and leashes, premium dog foods, all the basic supplies like feeders, bowls, supplements, and vitamins, and a nice range of treats and toys. The store is located at 76 Ridgewood Avenue in Ridgewood, 201-444-4415.

Mama's and Papa's

With two stores in Bergen County, you can pamper your pooch twice as much. Both stores carry a large selection of high-end foods and treats and have the best toys and accessories for dogs and their credit-card-toting humans. Store locations are 982 River Road in Edgewater, 201-969-1500, and 16 Engle Street in Englewood, 201-567-0010.

Wags & Wiggles

With wall-to-wall dog-pampering necessities, you might need to bring in your dog to help make the final selection, which is not a problem since dogs are always welcome to shop for themselves. From treats to toys to cards and gifts for your dog friends, you are sure to be tempted by one treasure or another. The store is at 196 Ridgewood Avenue in Ridgewood, 201-689-9247.

While traveling about in Bergen County, you can get pet supplies at:

Petco. In Paramus at 450 Route 17 North, 201-261-6306. In Ramsey at the Interstate Shopping Center, 201-327-5080.
Pet Goods. In Paramus at 651 Route 17 South, 201-670-6000.
Pet Smart. In Paramus at 60 Route 17 North, 201-843-0540.
Pet Value. In Dumont at 40 Washington Avenue, 201-385-3395. In Wycoff in Boulder Run on Franklin Avenue, 201-848-6070.

Tail-Wagging Training Facilities

First Dog Training Club

One of the first obedience-training clubs in America, First Dog offers obedience and breed show-handling classes at their training facility at 319 Knickerboker Avenue in Hillsdale. Classes for basic through competition obedience are held six days a week throughout the year. For more information, go to www.firstdog.org or call 201-722-0001.

Ramapo-Bergen Animal Refuge

The Ramapo-Bergen Animal Refuge (RBARI) offers a variety of training classes and programs, which are open to everyone. Group classes are not run continually; however, private instruction for basic obedience to behavior modification is available year-round and group classes for basic obedience are run on an "on demand" basis from spring to early fall. For more information, go to www.rbari.org.

Skyline Agility Club (NY)

Located in Garnerville, Rockland County, New York, this is an active agility club with classes, training sessions, and seminars held throughout the year. They also hold an AKC agility trial in October and a NADAC agility trial in May. Visit www.skylineagility.org for more information.

Best-in-County Events

Obedience Trial

First Dog Training Club hosts an all-breed, AKC obedience trial in *March* at Ramsey High School. This well-established obedience trial draws the best of the tri-state's competitive teams to Ramsey. Dogs compete at three levels throughout the day and the gymnasium bleachers offer visitors a spectacular view of the competition. Food is available. Dogs not entered in the trial cannot be in the building. For more information, go to www.firstdog.org.

Strut Your Mutt

Happy Tails Animal Rescue sponsors this dog walkathon. It is held in early *May* at Wood Dale County Park in Woodcliff Lake. All the animals that this rescue group handles are in foster homes and they often have smaller fundraising events for dog lovers throughout the year. For details, call 201-732-8842 or go to www.petfinder.org/shelters/htar.html.

Westwood Events

The one-day Crafts in the Park show is held every *May* and there is an Antiques in the Park event every *August*. Both events are free and are held in Veterans Park, which is on Broadway. For exact dates, check www.pjspromotions.com.

Art in the Park Show and Concert

This event attracts several thousand visitors to Van Saun County Park in Paramus every *June*. This long-standing juried art show also has performances from local bands and theater groups and exhibitions from more than a hundred elementary school children. Well-mannered dogs may attend.

Summer Concerts

On Thursday evenings through *July* and into *August*, your dog can enjoy the entertainment with you in Veteran's Memorial Park in Westwood. You can also enjoy an evening of entertainment in the park on Tuesday evenings. Concerts are held in Ramsey at Finch Park in *July* and *August*. Remember to bring chairs or blankets. Visit www.westwoodnj.gov for concert details.

Fall Craft Artists Festival

This craft, art, and antique show is held on East Ridgewood Avenue in Ridgewood in *September*. For more details, check www.pjspromotions.com.

FOCAS Dog Show

One of the oldest and largest shelters in New Jersey, the Bergen County Animal Shelter is assisted by FOCAS—Friends of the County Animal Shelter. This group holds some woof-wonderful dog events. One of the favorites is the "Dog Show," which has competitions for the funniest to the finest with prizes galore. The show is held every year in *September* at the shelter, which is at 100 United Lane in Teterboro. Registration is same-day, with refreshments and photos available all afternoon. FOCAS also runs a series of flea markets at the American Legion in Little Ferry, a Blessing of the Animals in May, and a photo session with Santa Claus in December. For event specifics, go to the events page at www.focasnews.org.

Dog Day in the Park

Held each *September* as part of National Dog Week, this celebration of the dog is held in Overpeck Park in Leonia and is sponsored by the Kennel Club of Northern New Jersey. The day's festivities include fly ball, agility, freestyle dog dance demonstrations, and obedience match shows. Spend a fun day with your canine friend! Admission and parking are free but you should pack your own lunches and plenty of water. Park entrance is on Fort Lee Road. For event details, go to www.kcnnj.org.

Ridgewood Fall Craft Festival

The town of Ridgewood holds its annual craft festival in late *September*. The main event is held on East Ridgewood Avenue.

Fair Lawn Street Fair and Craft Show

Half craft show and half street fair, this one-day event is held in *October* in Fair Lawn on River Road. The town also hosts summer concerts in Memorial Park every Sunday in July and August. For more information, go to www.fairlawn.org.

Metro Basset Bash and Howl-O-Ween Party

Held annually in *October* in Van Saun Park in Paramus, this basset hound event is a howling good time. If you are a basset lover, check out Tri-State Basset Rescue, who always have fun events on the calendar. The picnic is for members but basset wanna-be's and their people can come watch the events. Visit www.tristatebassets.org for more information.

Closter Street Fair

Every *October*, the borough of Closter celebrates with an old-fashioned street fair, including arts and craft vendors, food booths, and street entertainment.

Look for the Closter Animal Welfare Association booth and make a purchase to help the organization. For more information, go to www.closterboro.com or www.clawsadopt.org.

Ramapo-Bergen Animal Refuge Events

The Ramapo-Bergen Animal Refuge (RBARI) mission is to provide sanctuary for homeless pets while finding them a permanent, loving home. RBARI gets four paws up for having some of the best fundraising events in the state, which include wine-tasting parties, a casino night, golf outings, photos with the Easter Bunny and Santa, and their annual gala auction. The shelter is located at 2 Shelter Lane in Oakland. For event details, visit www.rbari.org or call 201-337-5180.

- Located in a turn-of-the-century farmhouse on the RBARI grounds, the Gift Shop sells unique handcrafted gifts and decorative items, including gift cards, stuffed animals, toys, party supplies, and glassware. The shop is open weekends. 201-337-9057.

You know you are a dog person when you actually own a sweater, raincoat, booties, or parka for your dog.

Warren County

The first Europeans to settle in the county were the Dutch, who came to Pahaquarry Township around 1650 to farm and dig for copper. It was not until 1825, however, that Warren County came into existence, separated from Sussex County by an act of the New Jersey legislature. Although he had no known association with the area, the county was named in honor of Dr. Joseph Warren, a war hero throughout the original thirteen states for his devotion to the revolutionary cause. Not much has changed since the 1800s; the county is a leader in milk, cattle, corn, and egg production in New Jersey and is one of the least densely populated counties. In Warren, you will find small towns full of friendly folks more than happy to share their parks and natural resources with your four-footed family member.

Dog Day Out

Warren County's western border is the Delaware River and its 362 square miles are hilly with low, steep mountains and fertile river valleys. Between its farms and towns, vast tracks of forest have been preserved for public use, which definitely includes dog jaunts through the woods. And your hound can roam for miles along, in, or even on the Delaware and Pequest Rivers. For pups that prefer civilization to water and woods, there are also quiet towns to explore, events to dress-up for, and hot dogs to munch down.

Allamuchy Mountain Natural Area

Located just north of Hackettstown, this 2,400-acre state forest has more than 14 miles of marked (I use this term loosely) trails. Crisscrossing the natural area and enhanced by unmarked mountain-biking trails, you and your hound can trek for hours and never encounter another human or dog. With literally dozens of paths heading in every direction, it is not uncommon for park users to get seriously lost in this natural area. Not being great woods folks and not trusting any of my dogs to lead me anywhere but the nearest food vendor, we enjoy the relatively tame hike up to and around Deer Park Pond. The length of the hike varies depending on the season and which parking area we use. If you want to explore, trail maps are available at Stephens State Park in Hackettstown. There are no signs for this park. The parking areas are on Deer Park Road, which is a small lane off CR 519.

Belvidere Walkabout

A charming Victorian town founded in 1845, Belvidere is on the banks of the Delaware and Pequest Rivers and is the county seat. A short amble around the downtown area is enough to absorb the feeling of a town lost in time, with a slower pace, and traditional American values. Mosey through the town square or slip through Riverside Park. Take a minute to pop into the Paradise Pet Center so your dog can get a treat and meet the "owner" dog, Toby. Or just study the architectural wonders, while your dog investigates all the old trees. There are several small delicatessens for snacks, lunches, or extra water. You can also wander across the bridge into Riverton, Pennsylvania.

Big Pocono State Park (PA)

Need a different kind of outdoor adventure? The steep hillsides and fantabulous views atop Camelback Mountain might be the solution. Located in Monroe County in northeastern Pennsylvania, Big Pocono State Park consists of 1,306 acres of rugged terrain on the summit and slopes of Camelback Mountain. Miles of maintained but often unmarked hiking trails meander about the park, providing an excellent opportunity for adventuresome dogs to explore. At the summit, you can enjoy the magnificent views of eastern Pennsylvania and, during the summer months, you can buy lunch or a snack at Cameltop Restaurant. The park facilities are maintained in cooperation with the Camelback Ski Corporation and the park is closed during the winter months. On I-80, go west to the Tannersville exit and follow signs for Camelback and the state park.

Pennsylvania adopted the Great Dane as their state dog with a most unusual vote. When the Speaker of the House called for a voice vote to designate the Great Dane, yips, growls, and barks assaulted his ears from every part of the chamber. With a rap of his gavel, the Speaker confirmed that the "arfs have it!" and the "Barking Dog Vote" entered the annals of legislative history on August 15, 1965.

Blairstown Walkabout

Start in Footbridge Park, admire the river, and then wander over the bridge into the tiny town of Blairstown. The two blocks comprising "downtown" have several small eateries and shops. Take time to explore the old mill, built by John Blair in 1889, and Blair Lake. If you want more paws-ercise, you can expand your walk by heading north or south from Footbridge Park on the Paulinskill Valley Trail. You can also treat your dog to lunch at the Doghouse Deli & Bagel Shop. This deli has outdoor tables and is on Route 94 across the street from the A&P shopping center, which is 3 miles south of town.

Delaware River Canoe Trips

Canoeing canines? Why sure, my dogs adore being out on the river, especially our sheltie, who prefers "on" to "in"! Many of the river outfitters have an open-boat policy with regards to dogs. Each outfitter has specific dog guidelines so please call ahead to confirm.

Pack Shack Adventures. In Pennsylvania at 88 Broad Street in Delaware Water Gap, 570-424-8533, www.packshack.com.

Portland Outfitters. In Pennsylvania at 428 Delaware Avenue in Portland, 570-897-6717.

Historic Bethlehem Walkabout (PA)

Spoil your pooch with a day trip to Bethlehem, Pennsylvania. The historic district, centered around Main Street, contains the Colonial Industrial Quarter, several historic sites, and the Bethlehem Visitors Center. Shops and cafés mingle with the historic homes and museums for a delightful stroll. If you want to extend your walk, head south a few blocks from downtown to Sand Island Park, which borders the Lehigh River. This park also connects to the Lehigh Canal towpath, which goes both east and west for several miles, should your dog be in the mood for some serious paws-ercise. Another way to extend your walk is to go several city blocks north along Main Street to Moravian College. While wandering about the campus, look for the two stone greyhounds perched in front of Johnston Hall. These are the Moravian Greyhounds—teams' namesake and mascot. There are several large municipal parking lots throughout the area.

Moravian College is not the only college to have a dog mascot. In fact, there are sixty-eight colleges and universities in the United States with dog mascots. By far the most popular breed is the bulldog, with forty institutions, which includes the Citadel and the University of Georgia. The husky is the next most popular with nine and the greyhound is a neck back with seven. Other mascot breeds include the setter, Scottie, Saluki, boxer, bloodhound, Great Dane, Chesapeake Bay retriever, and terriers.

Hot Dog Johnny's

One of the most famous hot dog spots in New Jersey is in Buttzville on Route 46, about a mile west of the Route 31 intersection. Hot Dog Johnny's is a historic landmark. Serving only hot dogs, French fries, soda, and ice cream, this little roadside restaurant draws huge crowds of loyal fans, which you and your furry pal will become after the first visit. With lots of picnic tables and plenty of grassy areas, you can enjoy your "dog" with your dog!

Jenny Jump State Forest

Set amid the rolling terrain of the Jenny Jump Mountain Range near Hope, this park offers hikers a variety of trail distances and difficulties. The moderate and well-marked Ghost Lake Trail ends at the Ghost Lake causeway, which is a good spot for a doggie dip, or your canine companion may find endless delight in sniffing all the rocky outcroppings and boulders along the Summit Trail. In all, there are about 6 miles of hiking trails, most of which begin at the park office. Like Allamuchy, this is a remote area in which you are as likely to encounter a black bear as another human, so wander with caution. From CR 519 in Hope, go east for a mile on Johnsonburg Road. Turn right onto Shiloh Road and follow signs to the park office.

Lakota Wolf Preserve

Once again the howl of the wolf echoes through the mountains of New Jersey. At this wildlife preserve, you can watch and listen to packs of Tundra, Timber, and Arctic wolves in a natural setting. Are you curious about your pet's wild cousins? A scenic walk through the preserve is fascinating and may help explain some of those odd behaviors displayed by your domesticated dog. There are also bobcats and foxes residing at the reserve, which is located in Knowlton Township. Reservations are not required but call ahead. No dogs are allowed on site. Admission is charged. For more information, go to www.lakotawolf.com.

All dogs—wild and domestic, extinct and living—belong to the Canid family. Canids have been around a long time and are the earliest known carnivores, appearing in the fossil record about 40 million years ago, well before other carnivore families like cats or bears. Currently, the Canid family tree includes thirty-five living species, including dogs, foxes, wolves, and coyotes. Fossil and genetic evidence confirms that all dogs are the descendants of wolves. However, thousands of years of selective breeding have separated the dog, from Chihuahua to deer hound, from the wolf in many more ways than just appearance.

Meadow Breeze Park

Warren County has miles of hiking trails through hilly terrain in isolated forests. This little park in Washington Township is a nice alternative. It has over a mile of paved walking paths that meander around the playground and ball fields and a short path along the creek. If you are socializing a young dog, there are plenty of families about. And the creek is shallow so even youngsters can play safely in the water. Unfortunately, the township does not plow the paths in winter. The main parking area is on Meadow Breeze Lane. From Route 57, west of Washington, go north on Brass Castle Road and follow signs.

Merrill Creek Reservoir

Situated on top of a mountain north of Stewartsville, this 290-acre environmental preserve is managed for low-maintenance recreational uses, which definitely includes dog hiking. A four-paws-up location, you are guaranteed to find other dog walkers during any season. Starting from the visitor center, there are 5 miles of well-marked, easy walking trails that hug the shoreline and cut through the woods. Looping and crossing, the trails can be used for short strolls for older dogs and puppies or for longer walks for more seasoned hikers. For a long excursion with your four-footed hiking partner or for a winter walk, try the 5.5-mile Perimeter Trail, which loops around the top of all the dams. Park personnel are friendly and helpful but very strict about the leash law. Maps are available. From Route 57, go north on Montana Road, which is a tiny little lane in New Village, for 2 miles. Follow the signs to the visitor center on Merrill Creek Road.

Oxford Furnace Lake Park

The Oxford furnace, owned and operated as part of the 4,000-acre Shippen family estate, was established in 1742 and remained in operation through the early 1800s. The nearby Shippen Manor, which is now a museum, and the furnace area are now owned by Warren County. The park area encompasses over 700 acres and includes ball fields and a small lake with boating and swimming facilities. Like most public beaches, this one does not allow dogs, but your furry pal can wander the informal trails and old roads with you. The park entrance is on Kauffman Drive. Follow signs from Route 31 in Oxford.

Paulinskill Valley Trail

For most of its 27 miles from Columbia to Warbasse Junction, the Paulinskill Valley Trail passes through rural landscapes, forests, and wetlands, and small towns in Warren and Sussex Counties. As with most rail-trails, it has a wide, firm cinder base and is popular with bikers, hikers, and horseback riders. Meandering back and forth across the Paulinskill River, it provides four-footed hikers loads of swimming holes and bunches of great smells in between. Being flat, this is also a terrific trail to use in the winter months. There are several easy spots to access this trail. If your fur-kid likes easy walks, start in Blairstown at Foot Bridge Park, which is on Route 94 and is also a good picnic spot. If your furry pal wants water, access the trail in Marksboro and head south. The parking area in Marksboro is on Spring Valley Road, a quarter mile north from Route 94. Trail maps are available from Kittatinny Valley State Park in Andover.

Pequest Trout Hatchery

Half way between Hackettstown and the Delaware River is the vast Pequest Wildlife Management Area. This 4,200-acre WMA contains 4 miles of the Pequest River, a trout hatchery, and wildlife education center. Although dogs are not allowed in the vicinity of the hatchery, throughout the surrounding area there are several miles of marked trails and miles of unmarked fishing paths along the Pequest River. This is a great place to park and explore. Trail maps are available at the main office. The entrance to Pequest is on Route 46, about 9 miles west of Hackettstown.

Stephens State Park

Tucked into the northern edge of Hackettstown, this small state park makes tails wag and paws prance. A lovely section of the Musconetcong River flows through this park, providing lots of swimming holes for water-loving canines, and there are 6 miles of marked hiking trails, which get steeper and rockier as you head away from the river. For a short nose-about, there is an easy walking path along the river, which is very popular with local dog walkers. If you just want a lazy afternoon with your furry friend, there are nicely shaded picnic areas all along the river. Trail maps are available at the office. From Route 46 in downtown Hackettstown, go north on Willow Grove Street for about 2 miles. The park entrance is well marked.

- If the day seems better suited to lazing about and wading with your dog in the river, you can pick up a picnic lunch on your way into the park at the Cozy Corner Deli, which is at 516 Willow Grove Street.

U-Cut Christmas Tree Farms

When the temperature chills and the leaves are gone, slip into a warm coat and load the pooch for the traditional tree cutting. Many of the tree farms are dog-friendly. Please do not let your dog "tag" the trees. For more information on tree farms, go to www.njchristmastrees.org.

Glenview Farm. In Blairstown at 2 Glenview Lane, 908-362-6904.

Hidden Hollow Farm. In Washington at 18 Spring Lane, off Brass Castle Road, 908-689-5678.

Mt. Bethel Christmas Tree Farm. In Port Murray at 41 Mt. Bethel Road, 908-852-5811.

Sunset Christmas Tree Farm. In Blairstown at 21 Frontage Road, 908-459-4048.

Worthington State Forest

Some of the most rugged terrain and splendid views of northern New Jersey are found in this vast 6,421-acre state forest, which is located along the Delaware River and adjacent to the Delaware Water Gap National Recreation Area. For fit hiking hounds and humans, one of the best hikes is to Sunfish Pond. Starting from the popular parking area on I-80, a rocky and steep trail follows Dunnfield Creek up Mount Tammany and then onto Sunfish Pond. Another trail circles the pond, with boulders and openings for resting humans and water-loving dogs. A long section of the Appalachian Trail runs through the same area and provides a convenient path back to your car. All the trails in the area have steep climbs and are in the 4- to 10-mile range but it does not get any better for trail hounds. For the map navigators, parking is available in two spots on I-80, just before the Gap and along Old Mine Road at Farview (Mile Marker 1) within the Delaware Water Gap National Recreation Area.

Paw-tacular Shopping

Canine Café

Once your dog discovers the delectable delights to be had at the Café, he may refuse to eat anything else! This little shop at 204 Main Street in Hackettstown has racks of homemade, healthy treats for dogs, and a fun selection of dog parent gifts as well. Dogs are encouraged to come in and select for themselves. 908-979-0040.

Cherrybrook Pet Supplies

Advertised as the ultimate spot for dog and cat supplies, the company store is worth visiting if you need supplies or just like to browse. Since the store caters to professional dog breeders, competitors, and groomers, you will find supplies here that local pet stores do not carry, like premium travel crates, an amazing wall of shampoos and conditioners for every type of coat, and another wall of scissors, combs, brushes, and clippers. Located at 2257 Route 57 in Broadway, the store is easy to find. For more information, call 800-524-0820 or go to www.cherrybrook.com.

Hackettstown Pet Supply

Whether you need a bag of premium dog food or a new crate or a fancy collar and leash set, this store has a knowledgeable staff and an old-fashioned pet store feeling. With an ever expanding selection of dog supplies, you may be surprised by this little store in Hackettstown at 141 Main Street. There is a municipal parking lot one block north. 908-852-3151.

North Warren Farm & Home Supply

With a little of this and a touch of that, this farm supply store in Blairstown makes a fun stop. Dog food, treats, basic supplies, and few specialty items make this store a good stop if you are in the area. It is located at the corner of Bridge Street and Route 94, just north of downtown Blairstown, 908-362-6177.

Paradise Pet Center

If you need supplies while out and about in northwest Warren County, try this local pet store. Dogs can shop for themselves or just snoop along the fish tanks (no pupkus, please). The store is in downtown Belvidere at 245 Waters Street, 908-475-1066.

Scrub-A-Dub Doggie

While not exactly my dog's favorite site (actually none of them would put this in the book if they got to vote), this grooming shop lets owners wash their own dogs using the comfort and convenience of a professional wash tub. Clean dogs. No mess. Definitely one of my favorites and the dog-loving human inhabitants are always "talking dog." The shop, which also has a great selection of doggie accessories and toys, is located at 126 Main Street in Hackettstown, 908-813-9990.

Tinkner's Farm Supply

As with most farm supply stores, this one has an excellent selection of pamper-your-pooch items. They carry a fabulous array of dog toys, including little squeaky toys for those canines that have mini-mouths, and a nice variety of high-end dog treats, bones, and foods. All the basics—from leashes to bowls to flea control—are always well stocked and well priced. The store is located at 90 Main Street in Hackettstown, 908-852-4707.

While traveling about Warren County, you can also get pet supplies at:

Pet Valu. In Hackettstown in Mansfield Commons on Route 57, 908-850-9922. In Phillipsburg in Pohatcong Plaza on Route 22, 908-454-3511.

Tail-Wagging Training Facilities

Hi-Hope Obedience School

Do you have an unruly dog? Located in Washington, with classes held throughout the year at the Washington Borough Hall, this local dog-training school has a friendly, dog-oriented staff that can help. Owned and operated by Peggy Swistack, the school offers classes in six-week sessions. Call 908-459-5561.

Pocono Mountain Kennel Club (PA)

Another choice for training classes in western Jersey is this well-established dog club in Pennsylvania. The club hires top trainers to run their obedience classes, which are offered once a week in the East Stroudsburg area. They also have show-handling classes on an as-needed basis. For more information, go to www.pmkc.org.

Positive Motivation Dog Training

From puppy kindergarten to therapy dog training to competitive sports, the trainers at this school cover it all. They have an eclectic selection of classes and a small, friendly staff headed by Pam Denison, author of *Complete Idiot's Guide to Positive Dog Training*. Classes are run year-round and are offered in six-week sessions. The facility is at 187 Route 94 (Fountain Mall) in Blairstown. For more information, call 908-362-9997 or go to www.positivedogs.com.

Sunrise Agility

Located in Stewartsville, Sunrise Agility offers daytime private and evening group classes for all levels of agility—puppy to competition. Owned and operated by well-known agility trainer Janet Seltzer, the school focuses on fun and training. Group classes are run year-round at an indoor facility in Pittstown. For more information, call 908-803-4360 or go to www.sunriseagility.com.

Best-in-County Events

Bethlehem Fine Arts & Craft Show (PA)

This large, two-day show is held in downtown Bethlehem, Pennsylvania. It is in early *May* and is sponsored by the Bethlehem Fine Arts Commission. For more information, go to www.bfac-lv.org.

All-Breed Show and Obedience Trial (PA)

The Pocono Mountain Kennel Club holds two AKC conformation shows and obedience trials each year at the West End Fairgrounds in Gilbert, Pennsylvania. Held on Fridays in *May* and again in *September*, these shows draw literally hundreds of dogs and kick off a full weekend of AKC events in the area. Admission charged. For more information, go to the club website at www.pmkc.org.

Summer Concerts

Enjoy free concerts at the Shippen Manor every Sunday evening from late June through August. Bring a chair, blanket, and your furry friend for some delightful performances. The schedule is available at www.wcchc.org.

Agility Trial (PA)

If you are in western Jersey, the Poodle Club of the Lehigh Valley agility trial makes a woof-wonderful day out. This two-day trial is held in early *July* at Northampton Community College in Bethlehem. This is a small, two-ring trial that draws a loyal local dog crowd—both to compete and watch. Admission is free and there is plenty of parking.

Sheep-Herding Trial (PA)

Every year in *July*, the American Tending Breeds Association hosts an AKC sheep-herding trial at Raspberry Ridge Sheep Farm in Bangor, Pennsylvania, which is just across the river in Northampton County. With multiple tests and courses offered, you are guaranteed to see all of the herding breeds represented at this trial. The dogs work in enclosures and in the open field. Only dogs entered should attend. For exact dates, check the event page at www.atba-herding.org.

Summer Concerts in the Park

The Belvidere Recreation Committee hosts free summer concerts in Belvidere's town square, Garrett Wall Park. Bring a lawn chair, blanket, and the entire family for an evening of music. Performances are given once a month. For exact dates and performers, go to www.belviderenj.com.

Knowlton Riverfest

Late in *August*, there is a three-day event along the Delaware River in Knowlton Township that celebrates music and nature. With performances all afternoon and well into the night, this event is for music lovers, whether they have two feet or four. Bring a chair or a big blanket and relax along the river while listening to performers from around the world. You, and your pooch, can cool off in the river or sample your way through the food vendors. The event is held at Hunter's Lodge Field, on Route 46 in Knowlton. For more information, go to www.knowlton-fest.com.

From 1969 to 1974, nobody had more Top 10 hits, moved more records, or sold more concert tickets than the band Three Dog Night. During this period Three Dog Night was undoubtedly the most popular band in America, with twenty-one consecutive Top 40 hits and twelve straight gold LPs. The band name was adopted from a phrase used by aborigines in the Australian outback to describe nighttime temperatures. A "three dog night" meant a very cold night that required "three dogs" for warmth.

Warren County Farmers' Fair and Balloon Festival

The Farmers' Fair began in 1937 and is now an annual event of note in Warren County. Where else can you thrill to a hot air balloon launch, tour the 4-H exhibit tents, watch traditional craftsmen at work, or cheer your neighbor on in a tractor pull? Being a traditional 4-H show, there are also Seeing Eye dog, obedience, and agility demonstrations, and the traditional Pet Show, which has an open registration and awards for dozens of categories from cutest puppy to most obedient. The Farmers' Fair is usually the first week of *August*. For an events schedule and contest rules, go to www.warrencountyfarmersfair.org.

Art Across the River

Held in late *September*, this outdoor art show is for students and professional artists. Knowlton Township celebrates the day with food, games, and live music. Well-mannered dogs can make lots of new friends as they wander about town with you. For specific details, go to www.artacrosstheriver.com.

Riverside Festival of the Arts

Held in the middle of *September* along the Delaware River, the art show is in Easton, Pennsylvania, and the craft show is in Phillipsburg. For specifics, go to www.phillipsburgnj.org.

Walk for Animals

Sponsored by Commonsense for Animals, this dog walk is held in late *September* at Warren Community College on Route 57 in Washington. The shelter is located at 2420 Route 57 in Broadway, at the same location as the Animal Health Center. For more information, go to www.commonsenseforanimals.org.

All-Breed Show and Obedience Trial (PA)

In *December*, the Lehigh Valley Kennel Club holds its AKC conformation show and obedience trial at the Rausch Field House at Lehigh University in Bethlehem, Pennsylvania. If you are interested in a quick road trip, this show site is lovely (even in December) and the trial draws quite a few entries from the local dog community. Show space is limited so your dog has to sit this one out. Admission charged. For more information, go to the club website at www.lvkc.org.

Overnights

Camp Taylor Campground

Camping trips with your pooch offer hours for long tummy rubs and quiet woodland hikes. Camp Taylor is in Columbia at 85 Mt. Pleasant Road. For more information, go to www.camptaylor.com or call 800-545-9662.

The Inn at Millrace Pond

This bed and breakfast in Hope is actually comprised of several historic buildings built round the first mill ever erected in the little village, which was founded in 1768 by Moravians. Superbly restored, the inn provides a serene location for a weekend getaway. The innkeeper must approve your dog's reservation but do not be afraid to call. This is one B&B that often says, "Yes." For more information, go to www.innatmillracepond.com or call 908-459-4884.

The Inn at Panther Valley

Located in beautiful Allamuchy just off I-80 and Route 46, this hotel has colonial New England–style cottages that can accommodate pets, so your weekend getaway can be fun for the entire family. For policy and reservation details, go to www.panthervalleyinn.com or call 908-852-6000.

You know you are a dog person when you meet someone with a dog and remember the dog's name, but cannot recall the person's first name (much less last) until you have met them two or three times.

Morris County

Created by an act of the state legislature in 1738, Morris County was separated from Hunterdon County and named after Colonel Lewis Morris, then governor of the Province of New Jersey. Today, Morris County is a history lover's dream. Every town has a deep historic heritage and the list of historic sites is long and lustrous. While dogs do not really do "history," they will have a woof-wonderful time visiting this county with its dog-friendly towns, dog events, great shops, country farms, wide variety of training facilities, and abundant parks.

Dog Day Out

Morris County gets triple woofs for outdoor sports and adventures. With national and state parks complementing a first-rate county park system, it is hard to find time to explore all the great township parks! Whether you want a leisurely stroll or a rocky climb, this county has a park for you and your pooch. The only county parks with dog restrictions are the Great Swamp National Wildlife Refuge and Outdoor Education Center, Wildwood Arboretum, Frelinghuysen Arboretum, and Historic Speedwell. For more information on any of the Morris County parks, go to www.morrisparks.net.

Alsteade Farm

Just west of Chester is Alsteade Farm, where folks stop to feed the farm animals, buy fresh fruits and vegetables, pick strawberries and pumpkins, and enjoy the special events. The farm owners are happy to have your four-footed friend come along and share in the shopping or take a hayride to the pumpkin field. If you are socializing a young dog or puppy, this is a great place to stop and visit. Alsteade Farm is directly across from Chubb Park on CR 513, about a half mile west of Chester.

Black River Wildlife Management Area

The dog-training and exercise area in the WMA is on the west side of Chester, just off CR 513 (old Route 24). The dog-training area runs parallel to Furnace Road. Trails are unmarked but well used by local dog walkers. The woodland paths are easy to find and fairly wide. The gravel parking lot is at the corner of Furnace and Tanners Brook Roads. Remember—hunting is allowed in all WMAs and seasons extend from September to March.

- The Black River WMA on the *east* side of Chester contains a 4-mile-long rail-trail. Tails wag for this trail, particularly if you hike in a pack. This lightly used rail-trail runs through the wetlands along the Black River so the smells are fur-fabulous, the terrain is level, and nobody gets lost (rail-trails go straight). Parking is available on Pleasant Hill Road. From downtown Chester, go east on CR 513. Make a left onto Hillside Road and then bear right onto Pleasant Hill Road. The trailhead is on the right.

Boulevard Trolley Line

Pads and feet enjoy this 2.1-mile paved path in Mountain Lakes. It runs from Crane Road to Fanny Road, along the Boulevard, and follows the exact route of a former trolley line operated by the Morris County Traction Company. Very much like a big sidewalk, this path provides an ideal walking surface, particularly when you combine dogs and strollers, and it serves as a history tour, with breathtaking views of the Colonial, Georgian, and Spanish-style homes along the Boulevard. The pathway is cool in the summer, courtesy of the shade trees, and is an excellent choice in winter, courtesy of the township snowplows. There is no dedicated parking area for the trail, but you can park along the side streets. From Route 46, go north on the Boulevard.

Burnham Park

With two large ponds and paved walkways, this little township park in Morristown is both a human and canine pleaser. If you need to stretch a few paws while in the area, this park is conveniently located on the west edge of town. It is visible from CR 510 but the parking area is on Burnham Parkway.

Central Park

For paws-ercise while touring the Parsippany/Hanover area, try this 40-acre park in Hanover Township. It has a short hiking trail through the woods along the south side of the Whippany River and a 13-acre section on the north side that holds a tot lot, gazebo, and a passive recreational area, perfect for a Frisbee game. Located northeast of Morristown, the park is 0.75 miles south along Jefferson Road from Route 10. The parking area is on Eden Lane.

Chester Walkabout

The small shops and eateries of historic Chester make a very nice dog out-and-about. My dogs enjoy window-shopping their way to Well Bred, a top-notch pet store and "barkery," and always beg for an ice cream at the Dairy Queen. If town gets crowded, there is a very nice spot of green at the east end for paw rests and tummy scratches. The town also holds festivals and art shows all summer and fall. Municipal parking lots are well marked and mostly down the side streets.

Chubb Park

Tired of hiking through the woods? Ready for a game of Frisbee? Chubb Park in Chester has plenty of fields to play in, a small pond to explore, and side trails lead to the Black River WMA trail system. This township park is worthy of many dog kisses. Park rangers are very strict about the leash rules. It is on CR 513, about half a mile west of Chester.

Columbia Trail

The Columbia Trail follows the South Branch of the Raritan River on an old railroad right-of-way, which runs from Flanders to High Bridge. Every section along the 8 miles in Morris County provides a quiet, flat, scenic dog walk and the wide paths make multiple dog walking easy. There are two easy access points in Morris County.

Flanders. For true solitude, use the rail-trail where it runs parallel to Bartley Road. This section allows you to ramble west for 3.5 miles to Long Valley and only cross two roads. From the parking lot, it is about 0.75 miles to Four Bridges Road, another 0.75 miles to Naughright Road, and then 2 miles into Long Valley. Use the fishing access parking area on Bartley Road. From Route 206, go west on Bartley Road. Go left after crossing the railroad tracks (Top Dog Obedience School is on the corner) and look for signs on your right.

Long Valley. For a quiet walk with your dogs, the trail on either side of Long Valley is fur-pect. Heading west toward Califon, it is about 4 miles to where the trail crosses CR 513, at the edge of Warren County. To use this trail section, park in Long Valley at the gravel lot on CR 517. Heading east toward Flanders, it is about 2 miles to Naughright Road and there are side trails through the woods for hounds that need to explore. Use the Gillette Trail parking area on Fairview Avenue, which is off CR 517 about a block north of CR 513.

Cooper Mill

Located in Chester, this restored gristmill on the Black River hosts a variety of demonstrations of life in the 1800s. While I do not suppose your dog is interested in an 1800s laundry day reenactment, there is a 3.5-mile hike that she will adore. The human half of the team is sure to appreciate the straight paths and conveniently placed trail signs. There are doggie swim spots at Kay Pond and along the Black River and the wide trail (for the first mile or so) makes multiple dog walking easy. Please note that the trail system connects to Wildwood Arboretum, where dogs are not allowed. The parking area is large and well marked. It is on CR 513, about a mile west of Chester.

Hacklebarney State Park

Some of the best dog hiking in the county is in this state park, just west of Chester. My dogs howl in anticipation through the parking process once we are at this park. They adore going "off path" to scramble through the boulders and crisscross Trout Brook as we journey down the hillside past the waterfalls and head for the river. For a calmer visit, there are 5 miles of trails, many of which are wide, with a packed gravel surface. Since this is a ravine, the trails do go up and down but most of the climbs and descents are smooth. The trails are not marked but it is easy to stay oriented as most trails loop back uphill to the parking area. This is a very popular park, particularly on summer weekends, when the hemlock forest in the ravine keeps temperatures deliciously cool. On the flip side, the trails tend to be very icy in early spring since the same system is at work and the thaw takes extra time. To find the park from Chester, go west on CR 513. Make a left onto State Park Road and follow the signs to the park.

- In the fall, stop at the Hacklebarney Farm Cider Mill on your way to the state park. This family-owned farm has home-baked pies, breads, cider donuts, and apple dumplings. Fresh cider, jams, and honey are always available. Dogs are welcome so long as it is not too crowded. Closed Mondays. The Cider Mill is at 104 State Park Road.

Hedden County Park

Tucked into the neighborhoods of Randolph, the centerpiece of this county park is the 6-acre Hedden Lake. For dog walkers seeking quiet and solitude, this is the right park, even on weekends. Although access to the lake is limited, there are multiple spots along Jackson and Wallace Brooks for some canine splish-splashing. Try the Indian Falls Trail for even more water encounters. For a dry paw walk, use the Hedden Circular Trail. Maps are posted in the parking area, which is on Reservoir Avenue. From Route 10, take Dover-Chester Road north to Quaker Church Road. Go right and then make a quick left onto Reservoir Avenue. The park entrance is well marked.

Horseshoe Lake Park

Located in Succasunna, this township park surrounds Horseshoe Lake. With a short walking trail and a 1.8-mile trail meandering around the park and lake, this is a great place to get some exercise with your dog. It is a local dog set favorite, so you are sure to have company. The Imagination Station playground, swimming area, and ball fields draw families and children to this park year-round so it is also a fur-pect place to socialize puppies. The park is visible from Route 10 but the parking lot is on Eyland Avenue.

Jockey Hollow

The Jockey Hollow Unit of the Morristown National Park makes a great dog day out. With over 27 miles of trails, there are a variety of distances for every canine fitness level and dogs vote paws-up for the hiking here. Trail maps are available at the visitor center and are posted at most parking areas. Try the Primrose Brook Trail for an easy 1.1-mile loop with lots of water access. For a longer 2.3-mile hike, try the Grand Parade Trail but keep in mind that dogs are not allowed in the Tempe Wick Farm, soldier huts, or visitor center. A quick caution—there are frequent encampments in the summer so check the events schedule if you want a quiet nature walk or your dog is gunshot-sensitive. For more information, go to www.nps.gov/morr/.

Lewis Morris Park

Named for Lewis Morris, the first governor of the State of New Jersey, this was the first park in Morris County. Over 1,100 acres and conveniently located between Morristown and Mendham, it is now one of the most popular county parks. If your hound craves woodland expeditions, there are well-marked trails, from 1 to 4 miles in length, and connecting paths to the Jockey Hollow trail system for truly long treks. Trail maps are posted in all the parking areas. If you are looking for a place to relax and munch hot dogs off the grill with your furry pal, there are extensive picnic areas with plenty of green lawns for a quick, waistline-reducing game of fetch. And, even better, tucked into the park is a temporary *dog run*. It was established with the help of the Morristown Area Responsible Dog Owners' Group (MARDOG), an organization of dog lovers promoting animal welfare and responsible dog ownership in Morris County. The dog run is a fenced section of two parking lots and is about half an acre. There is a grassy area at the far end, with trees surrounding most of the space. Follow the signs from the park entrance. For more information on new dog parks, special events, and activities in Morris County, go to www.mardog.org. The park entrance is on CR 510, just west of Morristown.

Loantaka Brook Reservation

Arguably the most popular county park, Loantaka begins just south of Morristown and runs south toward Madison. Encompassing the land around Loantaka Brook, the park has 5 miles of trails, most of which are paved and popular with bikers, roller-bladers, and stroller walkers. It is also a "hot spot" for local dog folks, so you are sure to have company, even during the week.

On weekends, this park can get downright busy. Casual dog walkers enjoy the smooth paved paths while outdoor enthusiasts find plenty of stream crossings for paw wading, geese to chase at Kitchell Pond, and fur-fabulous smells along the bridle paths for true woods hounds. Parking is available at South Street, Kitchell Avenue, and Loantaka Way, all of which are off Madison Avenue. The South Street parking area is a half mile south of Morristown and is well marked.

Mahlon Dickerson Reservation

Tails wag and paws scramble to get to this Morris County Park in Jefferson Township. With 3,042 acres and over 20 miles of truly fine canine hiking trails, you may have to travel long and far before encountering another two-footed visitor. The navigators should be happy to note that all the trails are well marked and maps are available at every parking area. For a canine expedition, try the Pine Swamp Loop Trail. With lots of rocks, small swamps, streams, and deep woods, this 3.8-mile trail is guaranteed to draw the "hound" out of every dog. For a more relaxing stroll with your pup, hike around Saffin Pond or mosey along the 2.5 miles of flat, smooth rail-trail. From Route 15, take the Weldon Road exit and head north. Follow the signs to the various parking areas.

Mount Hope Historical Park

Mining began in the early 1700s near Mount Hope, making it one of the oldest mining areas in Colonial America. The last mining area is now preserved in this county park in Rockaway Township. For pooches whose partners like history, there is a 2.7-mile loop possible using the Red and Orange Trails, which take you past several of the old mines. Please use the "safety before fun" rule and keep everyone on the trails since abandoned mines can be dangerous. All the trails start at the Teabo Road parking area. Trail maps are available. From Route 15 in Dover, go east on Richard Mine Road and then left onto Teabo Road.

Old Troy County Park

Snuggled into the suburban neighborhood of Parsippany, this 96-acre county park is a popular spot for weekday lunches and picnics. If you are in the area and need to stretch paws, there are several short walks that begin near the main parking area on Reynolds Avenue. Some of the paths are paved for easy walking and stroller pushing. Once in Parsippany, go south on Beverwyck Road to Reynolds Avenue.

Passaic River County Park

Located along the Passaic River just south of Chatham, this park is part of an effort to protect the river from development. Over 700 acres are available for picnics, fishing along the river, or leisurely hiking, although there is only a mile of formal trail. It is a good park to just nose around on the unmarked trails and let your pooch pick the path. Parking is available off River Road. From Route 124, go south on Fairmount Avenue. Make a left on Southern Boulevard and then an immediate right onto River Road.

Pyramid Mountain Natural Historic Area

Throughout this 1,300-acre county park, located in Montville, are mountains, streams, ponds, and narrow valleys. While the unusual geological attributes of Pyramid Mountain, such as Tripod Rock, may not impress your four-footed hiking partner, the variety of trails will get his tail wagging. This area has longer hikes (up to 19 miles), steeper climbs, and rocky, narrow paths, and, as such, should only be attempted with fit, trail-savvy dogs. The trail system is well marked in both the Pyramid Mountain and Turkey Mountain sections and maps are available at the visitor center on Boonton Avenue.

Randolph Dog Park

If you are a Randolph Township resident, you can take your canine pal to the Randolph Dog Park for a run and romp. Alas, this park is restricted to residents only. The dog park is located behind the Randolph Police Station.

Randolph Trails

Randolph Township has invested in an extensive trail system. The dirt and paved paths meander and loop for over 16 miles, connecting five parks. This trail system appeals to all sorts of dog visitors, from laid-back seniors looking for smooth pavement to boisterous balls of fur needing miles of exercise. With a variety of surfaces, a crisscrossing network of paths, and multiple starting points, it may take a few visits to find the fur-pect walk but your dog's tail is likely to wag off while you explore. Parking is available at the Randolph Town Hall and Freedom Park, both of which are on Millbrook Avenue just south of Route 10. An easy starting point is in Brundage Park, a 232-acre township park on Carrell Road, which is off Millbrook Avenue about 2.5 miles south of Rou 10. Trail maps are posted in the park and are available at www.randolph org/parks_and_recreation/.

Too hot to hike? For a quiet, relaxing day out, pick up a picnic lunc Burrini's Old World Market at 1204 Sussex Turnpike in Randolph on way to Brundage Park.

Riamede Farm

Roam the 50 acres and pick-your-own apples in this scenic old or Chester. The farm has cider all fall and offers free hayrides on weeke located at 122 Oakdale Road. For more information, call 908-879-5

Schooley's Mountain Park

Nestled among the hills of western Morris County, this park offers canine visitors (and their human chauffeurs) 797 acres of recreation facilities and fun. The floating bridge across the 8-acre lake gets pups wonderfully close to the geese and ducks and starts the short walk around the pond. For longer hikes follow the trail along the creek, which offers several nice swim holes, and loop around to the overlook at the top of the park. There are also acres of green grass if you just want to put down a blanket and snooze away the day. From Chester, go west on CR 513 to Long Valley. Make a right on CR 517 and follow the signs along Camp Washington Road to the park entrance.

Silas Condict County Park

A pristine lake and the historic Casino building are the focal points of this rugged and beautiful 265-acre park. For a quick paw stretch or just a bit of pooch time, this park has plenty of green grass, a few short walks, and offers picnic areas for everyone's pleasure—dogs included. From Boonton, go west on Main Street and then make a right onto Kinnelon Road. The access road to the park, William Lewis Arthur Drive, is on the left.

Tourne County Park

is 545-acre park, tucked away in the suburbs just north of Mountain Lakes, hort, easy hikes near the picnic areas and several longer hikes with steep for canine fitness buffs. Try the DeCamp Trail, which is a 1.3-mile loop de, gravel path, for multiple dog walks. For longer dog treks, use the the south side of the park. Trail maps are available at the parking areas. ville, go east on Route 46 into Mountain Lakes. Turn right onto the nd bear left onto Powerville Road. Take the first left, McCaffrey ess road to the park.

Traction Line Trail

recreation trail runs parallel to the New Jersey Transit Line town to Madison. It is popular with bikers, joggers, stroller se, dog walkers. For sound-sensitive dogs or puppies, be un close, very close, to the trail. Parking is available at lroad depot on Route 124.

stown, watch for guide dogs. Seeing Eye dog train- e streets around the Village Green. The Seeing Eye guide dog school. Founded in 1929 by Dorothy ched thousands of specially bred and trained en from across the United States and Canada. ing facility, and training grounds occupy a campus of almost 60 acres in the woods just outside Morristown. The Seeing Eye offers a two-hour informational seminar at the campus twice a week. The video, lecture, and training demonstration explain the breeding, training, and matching of a guide dog to a blind person. Please note that children must be nine years of age or older. For more information on the seminar, puppy raising, or dog adoptions, call 973-539-4425 or go to www.seeingeye.org.

If you are in Morristown on a Sunday morning, take your pup through the Morristown Farmers' Market. Running from the end of June through October, this open-air market is in the parking lot at Spring Street and Morris Avenue. Every other Sunday in July and August the market expands into a mini–street fair with music, health screenings, cooking demonstrations, and more.

Turkey Brook Park

On the hill above Flanders, this 267-acre park has a 9-acre pond, ball fields, soccer fields, and hiking areas. For a decent paw workout, try the 3-mile loop trail, which meanders through the woods at the southern end of the park. Access to the park is on Flanders-Netcong Road, about 2 miles west of Route 202.

U-Cut Christmas Tree Farms

Wandering through fields of pine and spruce trees is great fun for the dog half of the family too. So put on the hats and gloves, grab the fur ball, and go get a tree. Many of the tree farms are dog-friendly and will even allow well-mannered dogs on the hayrides. For directions and more information on tree farms, go to www.njchristmastrees.org.

Dixiedale Farm. In Chatham at Hillside Avenue and River Road, 973-635-2097.
Plut's Christmas Tree Farm. In Long Valley at 220 Flocktown Road, 908-852-6669.
Village Tree Farm. In Green Village at 8 Meyersville Road, 908-236-9202.

Quick—what is the dog's name in the cartoon classic The Grinch Who Stole Christmas? *And the answer is . . . Max!*

Paw-tacular Shopping

Bone Giorno

A store, a dog spa, and a training center—Bone Giorno has it all. Pick up some chicken-flavored microwave popcorn, a tower of treats, or a special dog birthday cake while you check out the dog spa or investigate the classes at Bone Giorno University. The store also has designer collars, leashes, and gifts to pamper your furry friend. Bone Giorno is at 583 Newark-Pompton Turnpike in Pequannock, 973-248-8440.

Canine Outfitters

While in the southeast corner of Morris County, check out the dog supplies, which range from gourmet food and treats to designer canine accessories, in this store in Gillette at 977 Valley Road. The store is associated with Carousel Outfitters, a large equine supply store. 908-626-1550.

Madison Feed & Pet Supply

For special diet or gourmet dog foods, exceptional treats, and other canine specialty items, check out this store at 262 Main Street in Madison, 973-377-8885.

Michael Wolf Studio

Located in Parsippany, professional photographer Michael Wolf can capture your dog (or your whole family) in a timeless portrait. This animal-loving studio donates 10–15 percent of their session fee to local animal shelters! Check out the gallery at www.michaelwolfstudio.com or call 973-599-1999.

Mike's Feed Farm

For tail-wagging good shopping, check out Mike's Feed Farm. It is packed with dog furniture, holistic foods, fabulous treats, and the latest and greatest dog accessories, including designer coats, booties, dog sunglasses, and much more. The store is located in Riverdale at 90 Hamburg Turnpike, just a block from I-287, 973-839-7747.

Morris-Passaic Pet Supply

This store, conveniently located at 590 Route 23 in Pompton Plains, has a huge selection of specialty dog foods, treats, and all the basics from leashes to doghouses. 973-616-0100.

Morris-Sussex Pet Supply

The big brown barn in Succasunna at 168 Route 10 has a barn full of specialty dog and cat foods, tasty treats, bones and chewies, and all the basic equipment for dog lovers and their dogs. 973-927-7777.

Pupcetera

Budgets beware! Browse the colorful collections of elegant dog coats and matching handbags. Buy a leather bomber jacket for your pooch. Shop for a pearl dog collar. Purchase matching designer collars and leashes. For dog lovers, this shop is truly "dangerous." Whether you are buying for your own pampered pet or selecting gifts, this shop is fur-fabulous. They also have a pet portrait studio with photo sessions scheduled monthly. The store is in Morristown at 28 Speedwell Avenue, 973-401-1131.

Well Bred

Located in downtown Chester at 15 Perry Street, this specialty store has "the thing" for your dog. From designer dog carry bags, dog sunglasses, and leather coats to great toys to fancy homemade treats, this shop has a woof-wonderful selection of great dog stuff. Bring your dog in to select her own treat. 908-879-6569.

While traveling about in Morris County, you can also get pet supplies at:

Pet Goods. In Succasunna at 10 Commerce Boulevard, 973-598-8882.
Pet Valu. In Parsippany in Westmount Plaza on Route 46 West, 973-257-2757.

Tail-Wagging Training Facilities

Bright and Beautiful Therapy Dogs

Not all dogs possess the special temperament that is necessary for them to become therapy dogs. However, if your dog has this potential, the volunteer staff at Bright and Beautiful can help you unlock and develop this wonderful talent. They understand the unequaled pleasure that comes from volunteering with your dog to help others. Located just north of Morristown, this wonderful organization can get you started. For more information, call 973-292-3316 or go to www.golden-dogs.org.

Dog Grooming School of New Jersey

One of only three dog-grooming schools in New Jersey, this one is located at 11 Townsquare in Chatham. For more information on a career as a groomer, call 973-635-0101.

Doggie Academy

This school offers a variety of fun and affordable training classes that will build the bond and strengthen your relationship with your dog. The staff knows what it is like to love a pet as much as a family member and they know how exhausting a rambunctious or undisciplined dog can be if his or her energy is not directed. A full class schedule is offered year-round with classes from puppy kindergarten to competition agility. The Doggie Academy is affiliated with the Mt. Pleasant Animal Shelter, which is at 194 Route 10 West in East Hanover. For more information, call 973-386-0590 and go to www.doggieacademy.org.

K-9 Campus

One of Morris County's largest canine training centers is in Randolph, just off Route 10. They cover the dog world from couch potato pet to professional athlete. The staff, headed by Anne Paul and Jean Owen, provides quality instruction for both dog and owner. Classes are offered for household obedience, puppy kindergarten, and competition agility, obedience, and rally. For a current class schedule, directions, or more information, go to www.thek9campus.com.

Somerset County Dog Obedience Club

This club conducts training classes during the week at the Long Hill Township Community Center, located in the southernmost corner of Morris County in Stirling. Classes include puppy kindergarten, novice obedience, and rally. They also sponsor special clinics including tattooing, microchip identification, and eye checks. For more information, go to the Community Center's webpage at www.lhcommunitycenter.org.

St. Hubert's Dog-Training School

With a firm belief that good training enhances the relationship between dog and owner and that a well-mannered dog quickly becomes a cherished family member, St. Hubert's offers puppy kindergarten through multiple levels of pet training, from which students (and their humans) can graduate into the sports training curriculum. It is located in downtown Madison at 22 Prospect Street. For current class schedules, visit www.sthuberts.org and go to the Pet Training School page or call 973-377-0116.

Therapy Dogs International (TDI)

Headquartered at 88 Bartley Road in Flanders, this volunteer group organizes therapy dogs for visitations to institutions, facilities, and any other place where therapy dogs are needed. TDI is a nonprofit organization. For therapy dog certification test requirements and locations or more information on TDI and their work, call 973-252-9800 or go to www.tdi-dog.org.

Top Dog Obedience School

This is arguably the "top dog" school in the state. The superb staff and owner, Betsy Scappichio, feel that the goal of training is to create a common language between dog and human so that both species can live together in harmony. At Top Dog, the lines of communication are opened for students and their humans each year in a wide variety of classes from puppy kindergarten to pet tricks to competitive sports. Classes are taught by a team of specialized trainers who focus on helping you build a strong bond with your dog. Located off Route 206 on Bartley Road in Flanders, the 5,000-square-foot indoor facility is home to some of the top dog trainers and competitors in New Jersey. For class schedules or information on UKC/ASCA trials, specialty shows, training clinics, behavior seminars, and other special events hosted by Top Dog, go to www.topdogobedience.com or call 973-252-3010.

Best-in-County Events

Dover Flea Market

Located in downtown Dover along Blackwell Street, this large flea market and street fair runs Sundays from April to December. For dog visits, attend early to avoid the foot crush that is typical at this popular flea market.

Poodle Club of New York—Obedience Specialty

The Poodle Club of New York frequently holds their AKC obedience specialty at the Long Hill Township Community Center, located in the southernmost corner of Morris County in Stirling. It is usually held the first week in *April.* For an exact date, go to www.lhcommunitycenter.org.

St. Hubert's Animal Welfare Events

Founded in 1939 by Geraldine R. Dodge, St. Hubert's serves animals and people with a wide variety of programs. This nonprofit, award-winning shelter provides safe refuge and compassionate care for thousands of lost, abandoned, abused, and unwanted dogs and cats every year. The welfare centers, located at 375 Woodland Avenue in Madison and at 3201 Route 22 East in North Branch, sponsor and host some of the best dog events in the area. For more information on any event, go to www.sthuberts.org or call 973-377-2295.

Canine Cotillion. People and their dogs enjoy an elegant evening of couture, catwalks, and cuisine at this annual event. Held each *April* at the Birchwood Manor in Whippany, the gala benefit helps raise funds for the nearly 4,500 animals that find safe refuge at St. Hubert's animal shelters each year. Although it is a bit pricey, the event is open to the public.

Bark Fest. Come stroll the beautiful grounds of Giralda Farms in *May* with your pup and other supporters of St. Hubert's. This noncompetitive walk is followed by activities and contests and, of course, there will be vendor and information booths.

Ice Cream Social. Summer evenings bring the entire family (dog included, of course) to enjoy the ice cream, doggie frozen treats, a short trail walk, or simply cool off by the baby pool at the Woodland Avenue shelter.

Pasta Night. Every *September* red checkered tablecloths, dripping candles, and music from the old country help set the mood as St. Hubert's Dog Training School in Madison is transformed into an Italian bistro. Dog lovers and their four-legged best friends enjoy an evening of pasta and fun, which includes a raffle and treats for the dogs.

Howl-O-Ween Hike. Every *October* the friends and supporters of St. Hubert's gather at North Branch Park in Bridgewater for a howling good time. The short walk is followed by furry-fun activities and contests.

Chester Events

The quaint town of Chester swells with visitors every *June* for the Spring Arts and Craft Show. Walk the streets and wander through the exhibits in the municipal field with your canine pal. If Chester becomes a favorite destination, come in early *August* for the Peach Festival, in *September* for the Fall Arts and Craft Show, and in *October* for the Apple Festival. For more information on the craft shows, go to www.chestercraftshow.com.

Doggone Purrfect Golf Classic

Held annually in *June* at the Skyview Golf Club in Sparta, the golf tournament is the primary fundraiser for Noah's Ark Animal Welfare Association. Although you cannot bring your dog, you can enjoy a fabulous day of golf and help out the shelter at the same time. The shelter is located in Netcong on Route 46. For more information, go to http://noahsarknj.hypermart.net.

Mount Pleasant Animal Shelter Events

This facility, founded in 1972, welcomes orphaned cats and dogs as space permits and holds fundraising and community service events throughout the year. The shelter is in East Hanover at 194 Route 10 West. For more event details, go to www.njshelter.org.

Mutts Marathon. By far the shelter's largest event, the one-mile walk around the beautiful Kraft campus in East Hanover is held annually in *September* in conjunction with the Shelter Showcase Expo, which highlights dozens of shelters from across New Jersey. The family- and pet-friendly afternoon event is filled with great dog entertainment, agility and Frisbee dog demonstrations, pet contests, therapy dog testing, raffles, prize giveaways, and informational exhibits. Admission charged.

Pet Photos with Santa. Held in late November, photo sessions are scheduled in advance for patrons' convenience.

Puppy Playground. Recognizing the importance of dog-to-dog interaction during their early years, the shelter hosts free play and socialization time in the evenings for puppies.

Benefit Concerts. The shelter also hosts several benefit concerts each year at parks or restaurants in the Denville-Boonton area. Your pooch has to pass on these but you will have a great time!

New Jersey Sheep Dog Trials

Every Labor Day weekend (*September*), the fields at Fosterfields Living History Farm look more like the fields of Scotland than a New Jersey farm. Located just west of Morristown, Fosterfields hosts the New Jersey Sheep Dog Trials. At this herding event, sponsored by the U.S. Border Collie Handlers Association, dogs compete for three days at four different levels. Watching these dogs work the sheep, some simply on a series of whistles from a handler hundreds of yards away, is absolutely fascinating. Only dogs entered in the trial are allowed on the grounds. For details, check the Morris County Parks calendar under www.morrisparks.net.

All-Breed Shows and Obedience Trials

On Labor Day weekend in *September* over a thousand dogs compete in the AKC conformation and obedience trials sponsored by the Schooley's Mountain Kennel Club, Sussex Hills Kennel Club, and Morris Hills Kennel Club. This three-day show is a great way to check out a new breed, find an obedience club or trainer, or shop for dog stuff at one of the vendor booths. Admission charged. Food is available on site. The obedience and rally trials are held outdoors and the conformation show is indoors. Dogs not entered should not attend these events. Previously held at Chubb Park, the show moved in 2005 to the Mennen Sports Arena in Morristown.

Hounds & Harriers Run

The Hounds & Harriers Run, sponsored by Rose City Runners, is held every *October*. It is a 3-mile race through Loantaka Park and the surrounding streets for people and their dogs (one dog per person, please) with proceeds going to St. Hubert's Welfare Centers. Dogs should be trained to run and provide proof of rabies vaccination. Entries are limited to 150 teams and unique prizes are offered every year. For more information, send an email to HoundsandHarriers@att.net.

Overnights

Mahlon Dickerson Reservation

You can take your dog camping at this Morris County Park. It has twenty-six campsites for tents and RVs that are open year-round. And dogs are welcome! For campsite rates and reservations, call 973-663-0200.

You know you are a dog person when your holiday cards feature your dogs, humans being optional.

Essex County

Established in 1682, Essex County was one of the four original counties of present-day New Jersey. For nearly two centuries, Essex experienced continuous industrial and urban growth and by the late 1800s, county leaders recognized the need to provide residents with parks and open space. The county park system was born in 1895 when Essex County purchased 60 acres from the city of Newark. This became America's first county park. In building their countywide park system, the town leaders had the foresight to retain Frederick Law Olmsted, the creator of New York's Central Park and the capital grounds in Washington, DC. His style, featuring winding roads, natural blended waterways, and open fields, is still evident in the Essex County parks. These unique and distinctive parks are a joy to visit and are wonderfully dog-friendly, as are the quaint towns of Essex County with their open-air markets, historic colleges, traditional holiday events, and stately old neighborhoods.

Dog Day Out

Today, Essex County sprawls over 127 square miles and the original 60-acre park has grown into 5,745 acres of green space. With miles of meandering paths through beautifully landscaped parklands, these enclaves are wonderful for quiet Sunday walks and the paved paths provide a good place to exercise your dog while pushing a baby stroller. And, during winter, many of the Essex County parks plow their paths. So, both you and your dog will vote four paws up for these parks and towns. For additional details on any of the Essex County parks, go to the Parks page at www.co.essex.nj.us.

Branch Brook Park

This 359-acre park is nearly 4 miles long, about a quarter mile in width, and was the first county park to be opened for public use in the United States. It is a beautiful greenway tucked away in Newark. Canine visitors and their human companions can stroll miles of paved paths bordering Branch Brook. And, in mid-April, over two thousand cherry trees bloom, marking the beginning of the New Jersey Cherry Blossom Festival, which is a wonderful time to plan your visit. For festival and park events, go to www.branchbrookpark.org. The visitor center is at the north end of the park on Mill Street, which is off Broadway Avenue. Bloomfield Avenue also cuts through the park.

Brookdale Park

Located in the northeast corner of the county north of Montclair, this 121-acre county park is like a little slice of dog heaven. With a pond and 7 miles of paved walking trails, which are in the open, threading through mature forests, along the road, and around the pound, this is a lovely location through every season. And, for the human chauffeurs, the park is well marked and has ample parking. From the Garden State Parkway, take Watchung Avenue west for a half mile and look for the park entrance on your right. There is also an entrance on the north end, off Bellevue Avenue.

Caldwell College

Founded in 1939 by the Sisters of Saint Dominic, this liberal arts college has beautiful old buildings and lovely grounds for a short stroll with your dog. If you want to socialize a puppy or young dog, visit the campus during lunch or late afternoon, when students are relaxed and have time to play with your pooch. The college is located on a 70-acre wooded campus in the small town of Caldwell. Although the paths are paved, they are narrow and there are occasional steps, so it is not a good place for a stroller. There is a large parking lot at the far end of the campus. From downtown Caldwell, go east on Bloomfield Avenue. The college entrance is on Ryerson Avenue, which is on the right.

Lord Byron, the famous British poet, was so devastated upon the death of his beloved Newfoundland, Boatswain, that he had the following inscribed on the dog's gravestone:
Beauty without vanity, strength without insolence, courage without ferocity, and all the virtues of man without his vices.

Eagle Rock Reservation

A 400-acre county park in West Orange, Eagle Rock gets a paws-up from canines for frolics and fun and thumbs-up from humans for convenience and easy access. Named for the mountaintop, with its excellent views of the New York City skyline, the park has 3 miles of relatively level trails, making this a great, low-impact afternoon hiking spot. There are also several miles of unmarked trails and picnic areas. From I-280, go north on Prospect Avenue and look for park signs on your right. There is also an entrance on Eagle Rock Avenue.

East Hills Dog Park

Located in Livingston on Shrewsbury Drive, this delightful *dog park* has separate runs for small and big dogs and is tucked into the woods at the edge of East Hills Park. Both enclosures have plenty of grass and trees for the dogs and chairs and benches for the humans. Dogs are also allowed on the 1.5-mile nature trail that winds through the park. Before using the dog park, however, you must purchase an annual park pass, which is available at the Livingston Township Building. For more information, go to www.livingstonnj.org/dogpark.htm.

Glen Ridge Walkabout

Need to get out on a winter morning? Want to wander slowly on a sultry summer evening? Glen Ridge grew to maturity during a period in which eclecticism was the predominant influence in American architecture. Homes here reflect all the major architectural styles from the mid-nineteenth century on. And a 2-mile loop, up Ridgewood Avenue to Bay Street and back down Essex Avenue, provides a unique opportunity to view some of these wonderfully restored mansions while your fur-kid checks out all the ancient trees. Park at the Glen Ridge Library on Ridgewood Avenue.

Take a short detour down Warren Street and treat yourself and your pup to an Italian pastry from the Gencarrelli Bakery, famous for their pastries, cookies, breads, and cakes. You will have no trouble finding a delicious treat and there are plenty of non-chocolate items to choose for your pooch too!

Grover Cleveland Park

This heavily wooded park of 41 acres borders Brookside Avenue in Caldwell. With well-manicured lawns and several miles of paved paths, this park encompasses Pine Brook Creek, which feeds a small pond at the lower end. For short dog walks or just a lovely stroll in the park, Grover Cleveland Park is absolutely terrific. Several stone footbridges connect the two areas of the park, divided by the creek. There are several municipal lots in Caldwell that are close enough to use for parking or there is a small parking area on Runnymeade Road at the south end of the park.

Maplewood Village

In the early 1800s, this small town was known as Jefferson Village, named in honor of Thomas Jefferson. When the first railroad station was built, the stop was called Maplewood after a large maple tree growing nearby. The town's name changed to Maplewood soon after. Today, this quaint village is very dog-friendly and a wonderful place to spend a day with your pooch. Pick up a gourmet lunch or snack in the village and then snag a bench for a lazy meal in Memorial Park. There are plenty of delis, coffee shops, and take-out restaurants within a few blocks of the park. While window shopping in the village, take your dog for a new toy or special treat at the Maplewood Pet Store, where dogs are always welcome to shop for themselves. Municipal parking lots are available.

Maplewood Memorial Park is a small township park in the heart of Maplewood, bordered by Valley Street and Dunnell Road. With its paved walkways, stone bridges, and open fields, it is canine "hot" spot. The *dog park* is an unfenced location on the north edge of the park, near the library and across from the railroad station, in which dogs may be off leash.

Mills Reservation

This 157-acre reservation is located in Upper Montclair and is largely undeveloped. With wide paths and deep forests, the 5 miles of trails are very popular with local canines and their human companions. Your hound is sure to find plenty of smells and "chat trees" as you wander through the woods. There is a small, unmarked parking area on Normal Avenue. Please note that there is no official off-leash area in this park. From Route 46 in Little Falls, go south about a mile on Valley Road. Make a right onto Normal Avenue and continue past the Montclair State University entrance. The parking area is on the left.

Montclair State University

Atop a hill in Upper Montclair, this college campus is an attractive setting for a pooch poke-about (kind of like a walkabout but with many more stops to sniff and poke with your nose). With broad lawns, classic landscaping, a natural stone amphitheater, and a mix of campus buildings, you can roam for hours with your roving nose on four feet, especially in winter, when the paths are sure to be shoveled. So, tie up those walking shoes and get some exercise with your pooch. Of course, large campuses are also fabulous for puppy socializing. The main entrance is on Normal Avenue off Valley Road. Follow signs from Route 46. Use the Red Hawk parking garage or Lot 4.

South Mountain Reservation

This county park covers over 2,000 acres, extending through the municipalities of West Orange, Maplewood, and Millburn. The tall trees surrounding streams, creeks, and ponds are sure to get that tail wagging! For hounds that crave long woodland hikes, this is the park to visit, as there are five marked trails covering over 15 miles. As you and your dog roam around the park, look for the old carriage roads and the equestrian paths. Local hikers, familiar with the park, frequently use them as connectors to other trails and to form convenient loops. As a starting point, lead your canine expedition on a section of the Lenape Trail. Start from the Locust Grove picnic area, which is in Millburn at the intersection of Lackawanna Place and Glen Avenue. For older dogs, cautious human companions, or families with strollers, try the walk down to the Rock Overlook on Crest Drive, which is closed to cars. Crest Drive is accessed from Wyoming Avenue and the park entrance is well marked. During the winter, Crest Drive is a popular dog-walking area so you are sure to have canine company. For lazy summer days, there are several picnic areas on Brookside Drive, which cuts through the park. Please note that dogs are not allowed in Turtleback Zoo.

- If you use the Locust Grove picnic area as your starting point, treat yourself and your pup to an ice cream before you go home. It is a short, three-block walk into downtown Millburn, where you will find excellent ice cream shops. There are also coffee shops and bakeries in the downtown area.

- Should you be in Millburn on a Friday (June to October), check out the farmers' market at the corner of Essex and Main Streets.

Verona Park

Dogs have trouble clapping but they can yowl their pleasure. And your dog will yowl once he knows about this enchanting park in Verona. Obviously designed by Olmsted, this 54-acre county park is landscaped around a beautiful 13-acre lake and has over 3 miles of paved walking paths. Meander along the paths for exercise or just sit on the grass and watch the boats. This park makes a terrific quality dog-time spot. It is also easy to find. From I-280, go north about 2.5 miles on Pleasant Valley Way and then make a right onto Bloomfield Avenue.

Watessing Park

Located on 70 acres in the eastern section of Essex County near Bloomfield, this long open park runs along Glenwood Avenue from Dodd to Broad Street. There are about 2 miles of paved walking paths. Second River, joined by Toney Brook, flows through the park, providing a nice background for a stroll with your dog. Parking is available on Glenwood Avenue or in one of the Bloomfield municipal lots.

- From July through the end of October, there is a farmers' market in the municipal parking lot just north of the park at Lackawanna and Glenwood Avenues. It is open Thursdays from 11 a.m. to 6 p.m.

Paw-tacular Shopping

Animal Instincts

At the north end of the Watsessing Park in downtown Bloomfield, there is a quaint little pet shop that carries premium foods, treats, and a fetching supply of toys. From the park, you can easily walk to the store for a special treat or new toy for your furry friend. The store is located on Lackawanna Place and is visible from the corner at Glenwood Avenue. 973-680-8000.

Montclair Feed & Pet Supply

Want the best for your dog? This store gets high-paws for dog food, treats, and travel gear. With a doggie deli, homemade treats, and a self-service dog wash, you and your dog may end up with more than just food. Owners Joel and Joan Tabor are always happy to have your dog come shop and can help you select the best products for your pooch. The store is located at 191 Glenridge Avenue in Montclair. There is a municipal parking lot conveniently across the street. 973-746-4799.

Paradise Pet

Established with a firm belief that dogs, cats, and birds should have a nutritious, well-balanced diet, this store sells only the highest-quality products on the market. Specializing in holistic and raw diets, the staff can help you select the best nutrition plan for your dog. The shop is located at 42 West Passaic Avenue in Bloomfield, 973-338-0795.

While traveling around in Essex County, you can also get pet supplies at:

Petco. In West Orange at 201 Prospect Avenue, 973-325-5040.

Tail-Wagging Training Facilities

Generation Pets

Located in Bloomfield, this dog-training school offers regular puppy kindergarten through basic and advanced obedience classes. Training is accomplished with modern techniques using gentle and balanced motivators to make everyday life with your canine enjoyable and fun. If needed, private instruction and behavior modification are also available. For more information, go to www.generationpets.com or call 973-779-3356.

Hal Wheeler's School for Dogs

With a training program directed at basic obedience and behavior modification, this school can shape your pet into a well-mannered, obedient companion in every situation. They offer group classes and private instruction at the training facility at 1126 Pompton Avenue in Cedar Grove. For more information, go to www.halwheelers.com or call 973-256-0694.

Best-in-County Events

Obedience Trial

Every *January* the top obedience dogs on the east coast slog through snow and ice to Verona for the K-9 Obedience Trial. This one-day AKC event is traditionally the start of the indoor winter circuit and draws some of the best dogs and handlers in the state. The trial is held at Verona High School. Dogs not entered should not be in the building.

Millburn Street Fair

Join the residents of Millburn as they celebrate spring at the annual street fair, which also has crafts. The fair is held each year in *April.* For more information, go to the calendar at www.twp.millburn.nj.us.

Art Shows

There are several art shows in township parks that provide a great opportunity for you to wander with your well-mannered dog. No leash tuggers or rowdy puppies, please. For exact dates for many of these shows, go to www.artsandcraftshows.net.

Art in the Park. In Upper Montclair in *May* at Anderson Park, off Bellevue Avenue.

Fine Arts and Crafts Show. In Verona in *May* at Verona Park.

Fine Arts and Crafts Festivals. In Montclair, twice a year, in *June* and again in *October*, artists and crafters converge on Brookdale Park for this expansive art festival.

Art at the Oval. In Livingston in late *September* at the Memorial Park Oval, off South Livingston Avenue.

Art Fair. In downtown Millburn in early *October.* Exhibitors set up along Millburn Avenue and from Main to Spring Streets. For more information, go to the calendar at www.twp.millburn.nj.us.

Bloomfield Harvest Festival. Bring your pooch out to view the arts and crafts, enjoy the live entertainment, and an eclectic assortment of activities and special events. This two-day festival is held in the middle of *September* on Broad Street from Bloomfield to Belleville Avenue.

Jersey Animal Coalition Events

This all-volunteer, not-for-profit organization has rescued and placed thousands of stray and abandoned pets since it was founded in 1989. With a new facility in the works, the Coalition hosts animal welfare events that are fun for the whole family. For more information, go to www.jaconline.org or call 973-763-7322.

Dog Walkathon. Held each *September* in Maplewood Memorial Park, the JAC walkathon brings out pet lovers from the community and beyond. And the walkathon is just the beginning! The JAC fair includes games, exhibits, food vendors, demonstrations, and celebrity guests. Fun for four- and two-legged creatures of all ages is guaranteed. The park is at Oakview Avenue and Valley Street in Maplewood.

Annual Gala. Held at Mayfair Farms in West Orange, this elegant evening honors the volunteers and tireless workers of JAC and focuses attention on the needs of homeless animals. Call the shelter for dates and ticket information.

July Fourth Pet Show. JAC helps the town of Maplewood run its pet show in conjunction with the annual Fourth of July festival. Open to all Maplewood residents. For more information, go to the event calendar at www.maplewoodonline.com.

Maplewood Halloween Parade

If you have a closet full of doggie costumes, check out the Maplewood Halloween Parade. Every *October*, the Village hosts a parade and lots of folks bring along the four-footed family member—in costume, of course! For more information, check out the event calendar at www.maplewoodonline.com.

PAWS—Montclair Events

Located at 77 North Willow Street in Montclair, this shelter was founded over twenty-eight years ago and has one of the highest adoption rates in the state. There are multiple fundraising events held in the area throughout the year. For more information, call 973-746-5212 or go to the events page for the shelter at www.petfinder.org/shelters/NJ07.html.

PAWS for a Bite. These fundraising events are held throughout the year at area restaurants. For the chosen evening, the host restaurant donates a portion of the receipts to the shelter. Come join fellow animal lovers for a good meal and help rescue a pet.

Bazaar and Craft Show. Held each November, this craft show has a wonderful selection of holiday and pet-related items. It is held at the Commonwealth Club, 26 Northview Avenue in Upper Montclair.

You know you are a dog person when your parents give up on grandchildren and start to refer to their "grand-dogs."

Hudson County

Around 1660, the Dutch designed and built an 800-foot-square walled town in what is today Jersey City. The site chosen was a former cornfield on the "heights" and it was given the name "Bergen," the Dutch word for hill. Only a handful of landmarks remain to connect contemporary Jersey City with its Dutch colonial and agricultural past and there is very little open space or parkland available in this largely urban and industrial area. However, there are a lot of dog lovers in the county and they have found and preserved space for their four-footed friends. They must also like to pamper their pets, since this area has some of the best pet shops in New Jersey.

Dog Day Out

In Hudson County, there are several great places to get out with your pup. The areas are all urban so be careful where you park and your dog may need to develop some quick "city smarts" to learn how to potty on cement. (Yeah, city dogs do this all the time. Especially since many towns allow them in the park but not on the grass. Weird.)

Liberty State Park

A green oasis in the sprawling metropolis of northeast New Jersey, this is one of the most dramatic and well-known state parks. While the Manhattan skyline, the Statue of Liberty, and Ellis Island will probably go unnoticed by your pooch, she is sure to enjoy walking the paved paths and there is plenty of grass to tempt any dog into a romp. The extensive playground and picnic areas draw families to the park from early spring to late fall, making this a great place to socialize puppies. And on warm days, you can almost always find an ice cream vendor for a delicious cool treat. Follow signs from the New Jersey Turnpike.

James Braddock Park

Known originally as North Hudson Park, this 167-acre county park in North Bergen contains Woodcliff Lake, which has two island bird sanctuaries, and the normal range of recreational facilities. You and your pooch can get some paws-ercise on the walkway around the lake or investigate some of the smaller wooded areas. There is also a small fenced *dog park* that has lights for twenty-four-hour use. The area is small and the local dogs seem to prefer a mud surface since they tear up the grass as soon as it grows. From Route 63, go east on Fairview Avenue.

It is ancient folk wisdom that "like cures like." And so, the remedy for a dog bite was to put hair from the dog that bit you on the wound. Thus, the phrase "hair of the dog" is part of the longer expression "the hair of the dog that bit you." The notion that a little bit of what pains you helps to heal the pain was extended to overindulgence in alcohol. So today, "the hair of the dog" refers to the practice of drinking an alcoholic beverage to ameliorate a hangover.

Hoboken Dog Parks

A vibrant community of old-timers and newcomers, of young and old, with a diverse culture and a long history, Hoboken is a unique metropolitan area. As with any largely urban area, open spaces and parks are rare commodities and yet, Hoboken has more dog parks than any other New Jersey town. This is partly due to the efforts of the Hoboken Dog Association (www.hobokendogs.org). There are also several small township parks that allow dogs on the walkways, although not on the grassy areas! Look for Pier A near First Street and Sinatra Park near Fourth and Sixth Streets. Please note that dogs are not allowed in Shipyard Park and its dog park is for residents only. Parking in Hoboken can be tricky but there is a public parking garage at 371 Fourth Street.

Church Square Park. This park is located between Fourth and Fifth Streets near Garden Street. It has large shade trees, benches, open areas, and a gazebo. Close to the downtown area, this is a great park to get your dog some exercise in the fenced *dog park* and then stroll around town for a bite to eat or simply show off your fancy friend.

Elysian Park. This park is located between Tenth and Eleventh Streets near Hudson Street. With wide, brick paths and large trees for shade, this picturesque park is a popular dog spot.

Stevens Park. This park is located between Fourth and Fifth Streets near Hudson Street. With paths winding between large trees, there are plenty of benches to rest on after your dog visits the fenced *dog park.*

Paw-tacular Shopping

Animal Pantry

Located at 320 Washington Street in Hoboken, this pet shop has a great selection of high-quality dog foods and all the doggie basics if you need supplies while in the area. 201-533-4454.

BeoWoof

Hoboken's premier pet boutique gets four paws up and is an absolute must visit. With a wide range of specialty dog items, from beds to bowls to carriers to toys, BeoWoof can be a wee bit dangerous for the dog lover's credit card. Located at 106 Fifth Street in Hoboken, this shop also has the healthiest, highest-quality pet foods and treats. 201-659-7387.

Cornerstone Pets

This eclectic shop has pet supplies, gifts for pets and their people, dog apparel, and home furnishings for both dogs and people. Located at 105 Ninth Street in Hoboken, you will not be sorry for taking time to visit this special little store. 201-232-7576.

Fetch-It Pet Supplies

The owners firmly believe that pets are members of the family and, as such, they deserve only the best food, treats, and supplies. When you shop this store, you will truly believe! From dog sunglasses (aka *doggles*) to parkas to pajamas, these guys have everything cool and cute for your pooch. And they carry a wide range of the healthiest dog foods and treats available. The original store is at 353 Second Street in Jersey City, 201-610-9405, and the new store, Fetch-It by the Park, is at 228 Seventh Street in Jersey City, 201-659-2880.

Paint My Best Friend

Hoboken artist Mark Davis has painted professionally for over a decade and draws on his life-long affair with dogs, cats, and birds to render affordable custom portraits of your best friend. The studio is located in the Monroe Center for the Arts at 720 Monroe Street in Hoboken. For more information about Mark Davis, go to www.paintmybestfriend.com or call 201-738-2267.

Best-in-County Events

Garden State Specialty

Every *February*, the best of America's show dogs arrive on the east coast, heading to the prestigious Westminster Dog Show in Madison Square Garden. However, in the week before Westminster, many breed organizations hold specialties (conformation shows and obedience trials for a specific breed) at the Meadowlands Exposition Center. This is a fabulous opportunity to view dozens of breeds and meet the biggest breeders. Your dog has to sit this one out. For more information and a current-year schedule, go to http://gsadogshows.org.

Hudson County Animal League (HCAL)

This all-volunteer organization, incorporated in 1993, continues to help stray, abandoned, and unwanted pets, thanks to generous donations from Hudson County residents. HCAL has a wide variety of fundraising events throughout the year, including the annual Hi-Hat Dinner Dance held every *March* in Bayonne. For more event information, go to www.hcalnj.org.

Purina Incredible Dog Challenge

Mark your calendars for late June. The Purina Incredible Dog Challenge is an invitational event, featuring some of the top dogs in their sport, and is a terrific weekend that your dog will not want to miss. This ultimate sporting event has woof-abulous dog competitions and events running for three full days. Many of the events are unique to the Incredible Dog Challenge. In the Jack Russell Steeplechase, for instance, little terriers race over a series of hay-bale jumps and into a tiny tunnel. First dog in the tunnel wins and the final scramble for the tunnel is pure terrier fun. In the Diving Dog competitions, water-loving dogs race to the end of a ramp and launch into a swimming pool. Furthest leap wins the day. Flying Disc dogs perform aerial maneuvers to music. And the agility competitors race through weaves, tunnels, and other obstacles in flat races and on relay teams. The qualifier and practice rounds are on the first day and the qualifying rounds for Diving Dogs and Flying Disc are open to the public. Of course, your dog does not have to compete to attend. All Purina Incredible Dog Challenges are open to the public, admission is free, and dogs are invited to attend. The third day of this event typically includes the Incredible Dog Walk, more demonstrations, and plenty of dog fun for everyone. This extravaganza is a regional event and, as such, is typically held every other year in Liberty State Park. For more information, visit http://events.purina.com/dogs/events/.

Hoboken Movies-under-the-Stars

Pier A Park, at First and River Streets, morphs into an open-air theater for Movies under the Stars, featuring popular movies each Wednesday evening from July through August 31.

Liberty Humane Society Dog Walk

The Liberty Humane Society (LHS) is a nonprofit organization that provides volunteers and financial support to Jersey City's Liberty Animal Shelter. LHS has a wide range of fundraising activities that you and your pup are sure to find fun. One of their biggest events is the Dog Walk, held at Liberty State Park in *October*. They also host a variety of fun dog events in the area and at the shelter. For the current events calendar, go to www.libertyhumane.org.

4. Greyhound extraordinaire, County, leaping to a third-place finish in 2005.

You know you are a dog person when you have more dog treat recipes than cookie recipes.

Hunterdon County

Some of New Jersey's first settlers put down roots in the heart of Hunterdon County and descendants of those original settlers are still living in the county today. Hunterdon's long history has been relatively peaceful, with a slow, orderly development, and much of the past is still mirrored in its present. With a rich history that residents work hard to preserve and an admirable commitment to maintaining open spaces and parks, this county gets four paws up from dog visitors. Packed with state, county, and township parks, the average canine mind boggles into a barking mass with all the possible choices for hiking, shopping, training, or spending the day with his favorite people. And, just across the river in Pennsylvania, there are growling good destinations for doggie road trips.

Dog Day Out

The diverse natural features of the county are preserved in dozens of parks, while the state parks offer even more opportunities for humans and canines to enjoy the outdoors. Selecting a location for a day out with your fur-kid is simple in this county and the welcome mat is out for dogs. For more information and trail maps, go to the county parks page at www.co.hunterdon.nj.us.

Bull's Island Recreation Area

Just north of Stockton along the Delaware River is an 80-acre state park that provides an excellent spot for dogs to splash about in the Delaware River or spend the day picnicking in the park. And, if that is not enough to get the paws prancing, the towpath for the Delaware & Raritan (D&R) Feeder Canal runs through the park so you can walk with your dog for miles, north or south. If your dog gets bored with the D&R, a footbridge spans the Delaware River here, so you can walk into Pennsylvania and wander on the towpath for the Delaware Canal. The park entrance is on Route 29, about 5 miles north of Stockton.

Carpoolong Creek Wildlife Management Area

This wildlife management area, tucked into the woods just north of Pittstown, contains a rail-trail that is a popular local dog walk. The unmaintained, mostly flat trail meanders along Carpoolong Creek and crosses a few quiet country roads as it heads northeast toward Clinton. Running through forests and along the creek, it is a delightful 1.75-mile dog walk, particularly for those looking for the extra space for multiple dogs. Trail access is provided by two unmarked, gravel pull-offs along Lower Kingston Road. From CR 513, make a left onto Kingston Road and bear left at the fork onto Lower Kingston Road.

The Carpoolong Creek rail-trail fades where it intersects the railroad tracks, a block south of Lower Landsdown Road. Follow the beaten-down path along the unused tracks for a short distance. This takes you to Lower Landsdown Road, at the beginning of the Landsdown Trail, which is a well-maintained county path that runs 1.8 miles north, ending in downtown Clinton. This is another excellent choice for an afternoon dog walk.

Clinton Wildlife Management Area

Located on the west side of Spruce Run Reservoir, the dog-training and exercise area has numerous trails crisscrossing the fields and forests, guaranteed to free the hound in any dog. Water-loving canines will quickly remember that the trails lead to the reservoir, where they can play in the water. Parking is on Van Syckel Road; the large gravel parking lot has one small sign. From Clinton, go west on Route 173 and then north on CR 635. Go right onto Van Syckel Road and look for the parking area on your right. Remember—hunting is allowed in all WMAs and seasons extend from September to March.

Clinton Walkabout

The little town of Clinton, where Beaver Brook meets the South Branch of the Raritan River, is a paw-tacular place to stroll with your pooch. Both Center and Main Streets are lined with delectable shops and cafés and many of the stores, like the Clinton Book Shop, are dog-friendly. Do not miss Fur Majesty, where your dog can select his own treat. The downtown area businesses also host a variety of special events, from garden shows to art festivals to pumpkin-carving contests. For details, go to www.clintonnj.com.

Columbia Trail

In the mid-1990s, the Columbia Gas Company constructed a gas line under the rail bed that was once the Central Railroad of New Jersey. The gas company then transferred rights to Hunterdon and Morris Counties to use the land as a recreational trail. The Hunterdon County section is 7 miles along the mountainside above the South Branch of the Raritan River. From Califon to

High Bridge is a 5-mile section passing through the Ken Lockwood Gorge that gets four paws up and a couple of yips as well. Being flat and with few road crossings, it is one of my favorite dog walks. For a walk closer to town, you can park at the old railroad station in Califon and walk 2 miles south to the start of the gorge. For playtime in the river, follow River Road south from Califon and park at the entrance to the gorge, where there is a small parking area.

Is it too hot to hike? You can drive through the Ken Lockwood Gorge. It is not an easy drive, with huge potholes and frequent narrow sections, but your dog will gladly sacrifice your car for the chance to play in the river here. The bottom of the gorge is a beautiful, cool, enchanting place on hot summer days. Your dog is sure to believe you "transported" him to a different part of the country!

Deer Path Park

Located in Readington Township, this 100-acre park of green fields has a 1-mile fitness trail and a 2-mile jog/walking path. There is a large pond, playground area, picnic areas, and several ball fields, which makes this a great place for puppies. The easy walking paths are all grass and loop around the fields. The park is on West Woodschurch Road, a short mile east of Route 31. Follow the signs.

Delaware & Raritan Feeder Canal

The Delaware & Raritan (D&R) Feeder Canal and the old Belvidere-Delaware rail line are part of the D&R Canal State Park. Running over 30 miles along the Delaware River from Milford to Trenton, these two old transportation systems are now very popular recreation areas and almost 20 miles are in Hunterdon County. For dog visits, I like to use the Kingston Fishing Access and Boat Launch, which is about a mile south of Frenchtown along Route 29. For a lovely stroll with your pal, meander north along the towpath into Frenchtown. For a serious doggie workout, leash up and go south toward Bull's Island State Park, which is a long 6.5 miles downstream. On busy weekends, keep leashes short (no flexi-leads) to avoid the avid bikers and your dog will howl with anticipation when he hears "canal walk." Parking is available in several spots along Route 29 and in Frenchtown on quiet weekends. For detailed maps and distances, go to www.dandrcanal.com.

Delaware River Canoe Rides

Spend the day on the river with your dog. There are multiple canoe liveries along the Delaware River in this section of New Jersey and Pennsylvania and many are very dog-friendly. Rules vary so always call ahead.

River Country. In Pennsylvania at 2 Walters Lane, Point Pleasant. For more information, go to www.rivercountry.net or call 215-297-5000.

Delaware River Tubing. In Frenchtown at 2998 Route 29. For more information, go to www.delawareriver.net or call 908-996-5386.

Should you be floating down the Delaware River south of Frenchtown, do not forget to stop at the Hot Dog Man. Located at the tip of Treasure Island, this floating hot dog vendor serves the best "dogs" on the river. Dogs are more than welcome to bob about in the river with their owners while everyone munches lunch.

Where did the term "hot dog" come from? The "hot" is obvious, but why "dog"? Since the late 1880s, the term "dog" has been a synonym for sausage and, going back to 1845, there are citations accusing butchers of using dog meat in sausages. A much nicer explanation comes from a link between the German sausage and the dachshund, which was imported to America by the Germans along with the sausage, or frankfurter. I must note that linguistic historians have debunked the idea that "hot dog" originated from a T.A. Dorgan cartoon. Whatever its origin, Americans now consume over a billion hot dogs each year.

Hoffman Park

A local favorite for four-footed splash experts, this county park in Union Township has a large lake with several well-worn dog swim spots and several smaller ponds scattered across the 353 acres. For paw workouts, there are also a couple of miles of trails, mostly old roads for easy walking. About half of the park is field and half is woods and all of it is flat except the hill behind the main parking area. From exit 11 on I-78, go south along Frontage Road a short distance to Baptist Church Road.

Hunterdon County Arboretum

Being a dog-friendly county, even the arboretum is open to dogs. The 105-acre park has several miles of marked trails through the lovely gardens and landscaped grounds. The Hunterdon County administrative offices are also here and you can get a trail map for the arboretum in the main office. The park is in Clinton Township on Route 31.

Hunterdon County Dog Park

Triple woofs and two whines translate in dog language to "Let's go to the *dog park* today." This off-leash area is located at the Hunterdon County Complex in Raritan Township. The 1.75-acre fenced space has benches for the people and a few trees scattered about for shade. As in most dog parks, grass has trouble growing in the middle but the large space makes for excellent doggie playtime. This dog park is on Route 12 about 3 miles west of the Flemington Circle.

5. Collar tag wrestling is a favorite of these two dog park buddies.

Lambertville Walkabout

This delightful little town has a carnival atmosphere on most summer and fall weekends and there are several events, including the annual Shad Festival in *May*, that your dog is sure to enjoy. The town also co-hosts, with New Hope, Pennsylvania, the Winter Festival, held the first full weekend in *February*. Whatever day you visit, your dog is sure to enjoy a stroll down the historic streets of Lambertville. The history, cultural diversity, and amazing architecture may not impress your hound, but he will appreciate an ice cream or deli treat from one of the many specialty shops. You can also extend your time outdoors with a walk along the D&R Feeder Canal or by crossing the bridge into Pennsylvania. For more information, go to www.lambertville.org.

Liberty Village

Although your furry friend cannot "shop" here, he is welcome to enjoy a day of window shopping, bench warming, or just a slow wander among the stores and outlets at Liberty Village and Turntable Junction. Of course, you can spoil him with a treat from one of cafés or sweet shops, many of which provide outdoor tables. With so many shops, there are plenty of signs from Routes 202 and 31 and parking is plentiful.

Musconetcong Gorge

If your hound needs to spend time in the woods with just the squirrels and the birds, take him to the Musconetcong Gorge. A wooded nature preserve totaling 425 acres, this remote county park has several miles of trails ranging from moderate to slightly difficult. There are a few steep areas but your dog probably will not notice those while he sniffs his way through the woods. A well-marked gravel parking lot is on Dennis Road, about a mile north of CR 519 in Riegelsville.

New Hope Walkabout (PA)

With over thirty restaurants and dozens of craft shops, specialty stores, and art galleries lining the quaint streets along the Delaware River and the Delaware Canal, this is a Fido-fabulous destination. You can enjoy a meal at one of the many outdoor restaurants or just share a snack as you meander the small alleys and back street shops. For a little peace and quiet, slip down to the canal and walk the towpath south. Please give the canal mules a wide berth. Stop in at the Information Center for town maps and historic site specifics. Additional information is also available at www.newhopepa.org.

Nockamixon State Park (PA)

The 5,283-acre Nockamixon State Park surrounds the 1,450-acre Lake Nockamixon. The park's forests and fields are a large green space in this rapidly developing area of southwestern Pennsylvania. Located in Bucks County, this park makes a delightful doggie day trip. Look for wineries, farm stands, and small-town events along the winding country roads as you zigzag west from Frenchtown or go south along Route 611 from Easton, Pennsylvania. In addition to the lake, there is a 2.8-mile paved path and miles of dirt trails for hikers and equestrians. The park trails are not open to mountain bikers so multiple dog walkers should definitely search this park out. The day use area gets crowded on summer weekends. The park entrance is on Route 563 in Kintnersville.

Peddler's Village (PA)

Tails wag happily for this village of shops and eateries in eastern Pennsylvania. The shady, paved path is a delightful spot for a dog stroll and you can treat your pooch to a treat along the way. Do not miss the Tails of the Village store, where you are sure to find a special doggie something. Parking is plentiful and they have a full calendar of outdoor events that your dog can enjoy. Go over the Delaware River on Route 202. Peddler's Village is in the center of Lahaska, Pennsylvania. For more information, go to www.peddlersvillage.com.

Point Mountain

Like the Musconetcong Gorge, Point Mountain is part of the Musconetcong Mountain Range. At 935 feet above sea level, the views from the top are as impressive as the steep climb up. This tough little hound-pleasing hike is tucked away in this 700-acre county park, located in the northern tip of the county. In addition to the 2-mile loop to the overlook, there are several miles of easy trails along the Musconetcong River, which provide woof-abulous spots for dog swims. Parking is available on Point Mountain Road, just a quarter mile south of Route 57 in Port Murray.

Ralph Stover State Park (PA)

Just west of Point Pleasant, Pennsylvania, is Ralph Stover State Park. Tohickon Creek flows through the 45-acre park, making it a howling good spot for a picnic and during high-water conditions you can watch local kayakers on the creek. The nearby High Rocks section of the park has an outstanding view of a horseshoe bend in Tohickon Creek and the surrounding forest. There is also a mile or so of easy walking paths for some paws-ercise. From Route 31 in Point Pleasant, go north on Tohickon Hill Road and then bear right onto State Park Road. Follow signs to the park entrance.

If your dog enjoys a "Sunday" drive, Route 32 in Pennsylvania is perfect. The road parallels the Delaware Canal and Delaware River for over 20 miles from just south of Easton to New Hope, Pennsylvania. Passing through quaint towns, there are several parks along the way that provide access to the towpath should you need to stretch paws.

Round Valley Recreation Area

The Round Valley Reservoir covers over 2,000 acres and is approximately 180 feet deep, making it the deepest lake in New Jersey. The park is over 3,600 acres. Unfortunately, dogs are not supposed to swim in the reservoir nor are they allowed on the beach. There are, however, trails for your dog to explore while he grumbles and growls at the no-swimming rule. For serious long distance hikers, there is the rugged, 9-mile Cushetunk Trail and for basic dog-ercise there is the 1-mile Pine Tree Trail. Both trails are accessed from the first parking lot. The park entrance is on Sand Hill Road, just 2 miles south of Route 22 in Lebanon.

Spruce Run Recreation Area

This park is primarily used for fishing, boating, swimming, and camping. There are no hiking trials. If you are looking to relax and spend the day feeding your pooch hot dogs "hot" off the grill, there are seven picnic areas overlooking the reservoir that will do just fine. The park, however, is popular and gets very crowded on summer weekends. The main entrance is on Van Syckels Corner Road, just off Route 31 in Clinton.

U-Cut Christmas Tree Farms

When the temperature chills and the leaves are gone, it is time to get out and cut your own tree, select a precut tree, or find a special holiday decoration. Many of the tree farms are dog-friendly. For directions and more information on tree farms, go to www.njchristmastrees.org.

Black Oak Farm. In Asbury at 9 Black Oak Farm, 908-537-4133.

Charlie Brown's Christmas Tree Farm. In Milford at 231 Adamic Hill Road, 908-995-4365.

Cherryville Farms. In Franklin Township on Quakertown/Cherryville Road, 908-806-4580.

Evergreen Farm. In Lebanon at 4 Bass Lane, 908-236-9550.

Jugtown Mountain Christmas Tree Farm. In Pattenburg at 10 Case Lane, just off CR 614, 908-735-5593.

Rosemont Tree Farm. In Rosemont on CR 519, www.rosemonttreefarm.com. 908-397-1809

Tewksbury Tree Farm. In Tewksbury at 50 Sawmill Road, 973-751-4662.

Voorhees State Park

Built by CCC units in 1933, this 1,000-acre park has seven trails that range from old gravel roads to narrow, steep paths. There are also picnic areas, several small ponds, and a playground area. Non-dog visitors are more likely to visit the New Jersey Astronomical Association observatory, which is located on the west side of the park. With few visitors, this quiet park makes an excellent location to wander with your hound and is a must-find for anyone walking in a pack. The park entrance is on CR 513 in High Bridge, just 2 miles east of Route 31.

The first living creature in space was Laika, a medium-sized brown dog. She was aboard Sputnik 2, which the Russians launched on November 3, 1957. Two different dogs, Belka and Strelka, were launched into space on board Sputnik 5 on August 19, 1960. They went on their historic flight accompanied by forty mice, two rats, and a number of plants. Both dogs were safely recovered after spending a day in orbit. Strelka eventually gave birth to a litter of healthy puppies, one of which was given to President Kennedy as a gift.

Paw-tacular Shopping

Country Pet Specialties

For premium dog food, treats, and a fur-fabulous selection of toys, this shop is worth a quick stop. Your dog has to let you shop for him here, since the owner's cat and parrot help attend to the shoppers' needs. The store is in Lebanon at 1271 Route 22 East, 908-236-8292.

Fifi Pet Boutique

A trendy shop for discriminating pooches and their people, Fifi's carries a unique collection of pet gifts, toys, uncommon accessories, and artwork inspired by our lovable four-legged friends. Located in downtown Frenchtown on Bridge Street, 908-996-0066.

Pets Pets Pets

A shop for the pet lover who has everything and yet needs more, this store has gifts for your dog and you. From treats to toys to food to dog games, the owners select only the best products for dogs and cats. The store is located at 438 CR 513 in Califon, 908-832-0533.

Fur Majesty

Arroooh! If people spoke dog, this shop would definitely get howls of joy. They supply customers with a grand selection of gifts, collectibles, toys, beds, and high-tech dog gear. And they have a dog "barkery" with delectable desserts for pampered pets. This doggone delightful store is in downtown Clinton, 908-730-7977.

While traveling about in Hunterdon County, you can also get pet supplies at:
Pet Valu. In Clinton in the Wal-Mart Plaza on CR 513, 908-238-0023.

Tail-Wagging Training Facilities

Barking Hills

With a unique collection of training classes, including pet therapy and entertainment preparation, this dog school offers owners more than just basic training. Classes run for eight weeks and instruction is available for puppies, family pets, and competition obedience, agility, flyball, and rally dogs. The indoor facility is located at the Lebanon Plaza shopping center on Route 22 in Lebanon. Several classes are held outdoors in Frenchtown. For more information, go to www.barkinghills.com or call 908-996-9911.

Training with Kindness

Located in Frenchtown, this well-known dog-training school offers classes from puppy kindergarten to competition obedience, agility, and rally. They also host dog chiropractic clinics and behavior modification seminars. For a class schedule or more information, call 908-479-4268.

Best-in-County Events

Winter Festival (PA)

On the first weekend in *February*, join the hearty folks of Lambertville, New Hope, and the surrounding Pennsylvania area in their celebration of winter. Cold, snow, and ice are given their due with concerts, chili cook-offs, special events, and an ice sculpture contest. There is also a snowfolk art contest with snowmen at the high school and in town. Sponsored by New Hope and Lambertville, this annual event is a lot of fun but you better potty your pooches before they get into town. This is one spot where yellow snow is a big no-no! For more information, go to www.winterfestival.net.

Lure Coursing

Truly a hound event, lure coursing is also a howl to watch, whether you have two feet or four. AKC-sanctioned lure-coursing trials are held by the Greater Valley Forge Rhodesian Ridgeback Club in *April* at the Hillsborough Country Club in Flemington. Come out to watch the hounds race each other across the open field and cheer on your personal favorite. For exact dates, go to www.gvfrrc.org.

Peddler's Village Events (PA)

The village is dog-friendly and there are several annual events that your dog is sure to enjoy. Peddler's Village is in Lahaska, Pennsylvania, just a few miles west along Route 202 once you cross the Delaware River. There are several large parking areas.

Obedience Match Show. The first full weekend in *April* and again on the first weekend in *October*, there is a three-ring dog obedience match (practice) in the open field at the east end of the village. Truly the dogs' day in the village, this popular event is a great time to visit.

Fine Art and Contemporary Crafts Show. Visit with your furry friend during the first full weekend in *June* and peruse the displays in and around the shops and open areas of the village.

Summer Concert Series. On Fridays in July, the village hosts a series of free two-hour concerts by local music groups. The performance is at the Gazebo, near the middle of town.

Bastille Day

In *July*, the people "take to the streets" to storm Frenchtown. The two-day festival includes races, fun walks, street sales, and special events. This usually quiet little town explodes with visitors as the town celebrates. For more information, go to www.frenchtown.com.

How do you say your favorite word, "dog," in other languages?

French	chien	*Spanish*	perro
Italian	cane	*German*	hund
Russian	собака	*Japanese*	inu
Hebrew	kehleb	*Navajo*	lha-cha-eh

Great Rubber Duck Race

During the Black Potato Festival, the little town of Clinton hosts the Great Rubber Duck Race on the second weekend in *July*. The race is held on the South Branch of the Raritan River at the Hunterdon County Museum in downtown Clinton and benefits go to the American Cancer Society. Sponsor a duck or two and bring out your furry friend to bark on your entries as they "race" down the river. For entry information, contact the Whitehouse Rotary or any of the shops in Clinton. You can also check www.clintonnj.com for event information.

Summer Concerts

Music concerts are held every Thursday, from late June to mid-August in Deer Path Park in Clinton Township. These county-sponsored events run for about two hours and well-behaved dogs are always welcome to come listen to the tunes. For an event calendar, call the park department or go to the parks and recreation page at www.co.hunterdon.nj.us.

All-Breed Show and Obedience Trial

On the first full weekend in *August*, the dogs in the tri-state area brave the heat and humidity to compete in the AKC-sanctioned Hunterdon County Kennel

Club conformation show and obedience trial. The one-day show is at the Hunterdon County Fairgrounds in Ringoes. All events are held outdoors, rain or shine. Admission charged. Only entered dogs are allowed on site.

Hunterdon County 4-H Fair

The last weekend of *August*, South County Park in Ringoes is host to the Hunterdon County 4-H & Agricultural Fair. Between the pet shows and the special events, this is a great place to show off your dog's special talent or great looks or just meet other canine lovers of all types. The fairgrounds are off Route 179. For event details and exact dates, go to www.co.hunterdon.nj.us/4hagfair.htm.

Bloomsbury Fine Art & Fine Craft Festival

For two days in late *September*, Bloomsbury hosts one of the largest arts and crafts festivals in the area. The art show is supplemented with children's events, food vendors, and a continuous round of entertainments. For details, call 908-479-6948 or go to www.bloomsburyartsfest.com.

Agility Trial (PA)

One of the larger agility trials, the Delaware Valley German Shepherd Dog Club event is held in late *September* at Maennerchor Field in Doylestown, Pennsylvania. With almost a thousand dogs competing on both Saturday and Sunday, you are sure to see your favorite breed racing (hopefully) from obstacle to obstacle regardless of the weather. The park is on Cold Spring Creamery Road in Buckingham Township.

Sheep and Fiber Festival

Held in *September* at the Hunterdon County Fairgrounds, this festival celebrates sheep and other "fiber" animals like llamas and Angora rabbits. Although your dog cannot attend this festival due to the health issues for her and the livestock, you can come out and watch the sheep-herding demonstrations. There is also delicious food, craft vendors, and livestock exhibits and competitions. For details, go to www.quintillion.com/gssb/.

Pooches and Polo Day (PA)

Polo matches are held every Saturday from mid-May through early October in Tinicum Park, which is located just south of Frenchtown in Pennsylvania. In *October*, the club also hosts a special Pooches and Polo Day, with doggy gift bags, costume contests, and a variety of people-pet contests. Come enjoy the polo season finale with your pal. Admission charged. For more information, go to www.tinicumpolo.org or call 908-996-3321. The park is easy to find on Route 611 in Erwinna, Pennsylvania.

Tracking Events

Just before the turkeys start hiding in *November*, the Lenape Tracking Club hosts two tracking events, one for beginners and one for advanced dogs. Watching these highly trained dogs follow a scent track across fields, streams, and through the woods is impressive, to say the least, and the variety of breeds participating guarantees fun and surprises. The location of the events varies a bit from year to year but most are held in Hunterdon or Warren County. Due to the scent discrimination issues, these are not good events for you to bring your dog. For tracking information and specific event details, go to www.lenapetrackingclub.org.

Overnights

Want to spend the night while visiting in Hunterdon County? Several historic bed and breakfast inns in Hunterdon and nearby Bucks County, Pennsylvania, allow dogs. In fact, a few are downright pet-friendly. Always call ahead for reservations and to verify the rules when traveling with your furry friend.

Black Bass Hotel. In Pennsylvania at 3774 River Road in Lumberville, 215-297-5770, www.blackbasshotel.com.

Golden Pheasant Inn. In Pennsylvania at 763 River Road in Erwinna, 610-294-9595, www.goldenpheasant.com.

Indian Rock Inn. In Pennsylvania at 2206 River Road in Upper Black Eddy, 610-982-9600, www.indianrockinn.com.

Riegelsville Inn. In Pennsylvania at 10-12 Delaware Avenue in Riegelsville, 610-749-0100, www.riegelsvilleinn.com.

Silver Maple Organic Farm and Bed & Breakfast. In Flemington at 483 Sergeantsville Road, 908-237-2192, www.silvermaplefarm.net.

Stone Ridge Farm B&B. In Hilltown at 956 Bypass Road, 215-249-9186, www.stoneridge-farm.com.

The Widow McCrea House. In Frenchtown at 53 Kingwood Avenue, 908-996-4999, www.widowmccrea.com

You know you are a dog person when your mail is primarily dog catalogs, dog magazines, premium lists, shelter newsletters, and vet reminder cards.

Somerset County

When it was founded in 1688, the County of Somerset was subject to the "jurisdiction of the County of Middlesex." But by 1714, Somerset had grown, needing its own court system, and by the Revolutionary War, the villages and towns in the county were large enough to support General Washington and his troops as they parried the moves of the British troops and raiding parties. Today, the 300 square miles of Somerset County are largely residential, with an eclectic mix of business complexes and small towns, and visitors, particularly those with four feet, are sure to find a new town or dog park to explore or a different dog sport or event to experience every time they journey through the county.

Dog Day Out

Whether your dog loves trees, gardens, ice cream shops, or rugged hiking trails, this county is a darling for dog visitors. It is also the land of dog parks. With plenty of pooch events, the Somerset County park system, and a half dozen dog parks, you may roam around this county for weeks without seeing the same tree twice. For park details, directions, and event schedules, go to www.somersetcountyparks.org.

Bedminster Township Dog Park

Tucked into the back of River Road Park, this half-acre *dog park* is grass with snow fencing and an active evening dog community. Although it is in the open, there are large trees along three sides that provide a bit of shade. The majority of the park is ball fields, but if you want to explore a smidge, there are trails into and through the wooded areas along the river. River Road Park is easily accessible from Route 202, just south of Bedminster, and the park entrance is well marked. To find the dog park, drive past all the ball fields to the end of the gravel road.

❖ The Bedminster trail system is also accessible from River Road Park. Look for the walking bridge over Route 202/206 to get in a dog walk while visiting this park. The Bedminster Hike & Bikeway is 2.8 miles long.

Bernards Township Dog Park

This 1-acre *dog park* has snow fencing and the usual mix of dirt and grass for a surface. There is a double-gate entry. Located across from Lord Stirling Stables in Basking Ridge, the dog park is in the War Memorial Athletic Field Complex on South Maple Avenue.

Colonial Park

The dog's choice award goes to this park. If you do not live close enough to visit frequently, your dog may actually request an address change once he knows about this park. Its 651 acres are all dog-friendly and it has paved walking paths, three ponds, access to the D&R Canal, a nature trail, acres of green lawn or blessedly white snow fields depending on the season, and a woof-abulous *dog park*. Truly one of the nicest dog parks in New Jersey, this 3-acre pooch park is all grass with chain link fence. There are trees along one edge and two separate sections, divided by snow fencing. The parking area is on the golf course maintenance road, but is well marked from Mettlers Road. Colonial Park also has a 1.4-mile paved fitness trail running from Mettlers Road to Elizabeth Avenue, should you or your dog need additional exercise, or you could amble through the woods on the nature trail. If it is the canal your canine wants to see or perhaps be in, you can meander over to the west side of the park to the D&R Canal. Each of these areas has a different parking lot but paved paths connect most of the facilities. Located in Franklin Township, Colonial Park is easy to find. From Route 206, take Amwell Road east and turn left onto Mettlers Road.

Delaware & Raritan Canal State Park

The Delaware & Raritan (D&R) Canal State Park contains two canal systems. On the west side of the state, there is the D&R Feeder Canal, which taps into the water supply of and then flows next to the Delaware River, eventually meeting the D&R Main Canal in Trenton. From Trenton, the Main Canal begins its 30-mile journey across the state to Landing Lane, in New Brunswick. The Main Canal crosses through Somerset, Middlesex, and Mercer Counties. Somerset County contains almost 19 miles of towpath so your choices for a dog day out along the canal are many. Easy starting points are at Griggstown and East Millstone. All of my dogs scramble frantically along the connecting trail to the towpath for one of their favorite canal walks south of Griggstown. It is also a delightful walk north from here or skip up to East Millstone for identically nice towpath sections. Towpath traffic is generally light so multiple dog walking is easy, although short leashes are always a good idea. For more canal details, go to www.dandrcanal.com.

Duke Island Park

Picnic with your pooch? With five huge picnic areas tucked into the woods and along the river, this park is purr-fect for lazy summer days spent nibbling hot dogs off the grill. It is also great for nosing about the trails and snuffling along the short canal towpath on crisp fall mornings. It is truly an "island" park, with the Raritan River on one side and the remnants of the Raritan Power Canal on the other. Dog walks are easy on the paved paths connecting all the park facilities or along the towpath. For water adventures, follow the paths to the west end of the park, to the dam on the Raritan River. This 332-acre county park is in Bridgewater and easy to find. From Route 202, take Milltown Road south to Old York Road. The park entrance is a half mile east and very well marked.

Montgomery Township Dog Park

Just off Route 206 behind the Montgomery Township municipal complex, this *dog park* is about a half acre with snow fencing. It has a grass surface and is mostly in the open. From Route 206, turn onto Covert Lane and drive to the end. Signs from the gravel parking area point to the dog park.

North Branch Park

A 185-acre county park, this is the workhorse of the Somerset County park system. An impressive array of events is held here annually, from dog and horse competitions to model airplane flying to the county fair. On off weekends, it is an appealing spot for a dog walk. Almost a mile of the park encompasses the North Branch of the Raritan River and there are streams meandering through most fields and wooded sections. There is no formal trail system. Located in Bridgewater Township, the main parking areas are on Milltown Road, but a small parking area for river access is on River Road.

Why "Fido"? It means "I am faithful" in Latin.

Six Mile Run Reservoir

Part of the D&R Canal State Park, this 3,037-acre park is for the dog that considers towpath walking too tame. Tempting your hound off the couch and into the woods is a biscuit-free task after he has been through this park. There are 6 miles of marked trails, and maps are available at the ranger station. Access to the trail system is at the D&R Park Office on Canal Road. Cross the river and canal in Blackwell Mills and make a right turn onto Canal Road. The office is visible on the left.

Sourland Mountain Preserve

The 2,870-acre county preserve stretches southwest across Hillsborough and Montgomery Townships. It is largely undeveloped but your dog is not likely to whine. With 6 miles of marked trails to meander on and a ducky little pond to explore, dogs and their human chauffeurs can make this a "regular." The Ridge Trail, at just over 3 miles, is the longest and covers the steepest terrain in the park. The pond loop or the Maple Flats trails are shorter and flatter for less energetic or time-constrained visits. From Route 206, take Belle Mead Road west for about a half mile to East Mountain Avenue. The park entrance is a mile north.

U-Cut Christmas Tree Farms

When the temperature chills and all the turkey leftovers are gone, it is time to get out and cut your own tree, and many of the tree farms are dog-friendly. For directions and more information, go to www.njchristmastrees.org.

Dower Tree Farm. In Peapack at 4 Todd Avenue, which is off Main Street, 908-781-5407.
McLaughlin Tree Farm. In Somerset at 289 Bennetts Lane, 609-259-8122.
Shadow Hill Farm. In Skillman at 213 Grandview Road, 609-466-3596.
Wolgast Tree Farm. In Somerset at 176 Bennett's Lane, 732-873-3206.

Washington Rock State Park

Situated on top of Watchung Mountain, this natural rock outcropping allowed General Washington to know when the British army, under General Howe, moved toward Westfield and to instruct the American troops to circle behind Howe's to cut off his retreat. Located in Green Brook Township, this state park is a popular site for dog families, and non-dog families, to picnic and relax. It makes a good spot for a paw stretch if you are in the area. From Route 22, go north about a mile on Washington Rock Road.

A small but notable instance of George Washington's steadfast adherence, even during war, to the gentleman's code of the eighteenth-century is apparent in a note written two days after the Battle of Germantown. The note said, "General Washington's compliments to General Howe. He does himself the pleasure to return him a dog, which accidentally fell into his hands, and by the inscription on the Collar appears to belong to General Howe." Neither the dog's name nor breed is known, nor the circumstances under which it was found, but history presumes that General Howe's dog was returned safely.

Washington Valley Park

Arwooh! Once your dog has roamed these woods, he is sure to howl for more. Hidden in the hills above the commercial and residential areas of Bridgewater Township, this gem of a forest is enchanting. For true woods hounds, the eastern half of the park—between Chimney Rock Road and Vosseller Avenue—is rugged and remote, while the western half—between Newmans Lane and Chimney Rock Road, containing the 21-acre reservoir, is popular with local fishermen and dog hikers. For water-loving canines, use the Middlebrook Trail, which tracks along the north side of the reservoir. In all, there are 7 miles of trails and parking is available on Newmans Lane and off Vosseller Avenue, at the end of Miller's Lane. Trail maps are available on the county park website.

Paw-tacular Shopping

Casey & Trixie's Pet Supply

Carrying all the premium dog food brands and a wide selection of basic supplies, this store in Hillsborough also has treats and toys to tempt you into pampering your pooch even more than usual. It is located at 434 Route 206 South, 908-359-5517.

Hungry Hound

With scrumptious homemade treats and an in-store pet photo studio, dogs and their people can get addicted to this store. From birthday cakes to designer carriers to dog jewelry, it is easy to find the perfect gift for a dog friend in this trendy little store in downtown Somerville at 94 West Main Street, 908-927-9663.

Pawsibility

Although mostly a grooming shop, this small store in downtown Basking Ridge has neat toys and cool canine accessories. You will find it at 25 South Finley Avenue, 908-221-9588.

While traveling around in Somerset County, you can get pet supplies at:

Petco. In Raritan at 300 Route 202, 908-203-8840. In Watchung at 101 Route 22 West, 908-322-2844.

Pet Smart. In Watchung at 1515 Route 22, 908-769-1250. In Bridgewater at 145 Promenade Boulevard, 732-748-7266.

Pet Valu. In Hillsborough at 601 Route 206, 908-281-9949.

Tail-Wagging Training Facilities

Best Friends

From boarding to grooming to training, Best Friends has it all. The training center offers a variety of group, private, or while-boarding training programs for pooches of all ages. Classes include puppy kindergarten and advanced positive training. For details go to www.bestfriendspetcare.com or call 908-822-9200. Best Friends is located at 825 Route 22 in North Plainfield.

Best-in-County Events

Intergroom Trade Show

Every *April*, dog groomers from around the world gather in New Jersey to compete, learn, and kibitz about dog grooming. In addition to the grooming competitions, the show features a large number of vendors who specialize in items for groomers, breeders/exhibitors, and kennel operators. Industry leaders demonstrate their products and show the public what is state-of-the-art in products, services, and techniques with special mini-grooming demonstrations, conducted by some of America's most celebrated groomers and contest title holders, in their booths. This three-day event is held at the Garden State Exhibit Center and is open to the public. An entry fee is charged and your dog has to sit this one out. The details for this year's event can be found at www.intergroom.com.

- The Wachung Mountain Poodle Club holds its annual AKC Poodle Specialty Show at Intergroom. The conformation show is typically held on Monday and is on the trade show floor.

Lure Coursing

Truly a hound event, lure coursing is a howl. AKC-sanctioned lure-coursing trials are held by the Irish Wolfhound Association of the Garden State in *April* and again in *December* in North Branch Park in Bridgewater. Bring your "hound" out to the park to watch the hounds race across the open field and cheer on your personal favorite. Visit the club website at www.iwags.org for more information.

- Want to see more? There are frequent lure-coursing trials in early November. These trials are hosted by the Northern New Jersey Irish Wolfhound Club and are also held at North Branch Park.

FOSRAS Dog Show

In early *May*, dogs, and their owners, come to Duke Island Park to compete in the annual dog show hosted by the Friends of the Somerset Regional Animal

Shelter (FOSRAS). Winning pooches in three different categories, Cutest, Best Groomed, and Best All Around, are awarded prizes and everyone gets to watch the fun and nibble on the baked goods! Check the FOSRAS website at www.fosras.com for details.

Lord Stirling Stables Family Fun Day

Sponsored by Lord Stirling Stables, Family Fun Day is held in *May* at the stable in Basking Ridge. While it is primarily a fun-competition day for Lord Stirling riding students, local rescue groups are on site with information and contests, and local dog organizations perform demonstrations and share information. Food, beverages, and various vendor booths are also on site. Pets are welcome to spectate or participate. For more information, call the stable at 908-766-5955.

Bonnie Brae Games

The Bonnie Brae Games, held in early *June* at the Bonnie Brae School in Millington, are a celebration of Scottish heritage and culture. With dancing, piping, folk singers, and athletic competitions throughout the day, visitors and clan members can be a wee bit Scottish for the day, although the organizers caution that the noise and excitement are usually too much for four-footed folks. While your dog rests at home, you can enjoy the dog show. Scotland is the country of origin of an amazing number of dog breeds, including the collie, Border collie, Shetland sheepdog, and golden retriever, and all are part of the Bonnie Brae event, as are sheep-herding demonstrations. For more information, call 610-825-7268 or go to www.eohebrides.com.

All the dogs portraying Lassie have been male. The original Lassie was a collie named Pal, owned by Rudd and Frank Weatherwax. Pal was hired to do the rapids stunt in the classic, Lassie Come Home, *and did so well he ended up playing the role in the movie. Weatherwax continued to use male collies for a good reason: both sexes shed their coat in the summer, when movies and TV shows are typically filmed, but since males have a thicker coat they do not look so scrawny during filming. Also, fans tend to think of Lassie as a big, heroic dog and females appear less impressive on film.*

North Plainfield Street Fair

Crafts, arts, fantastic foods, and entertainment are a pretty good summation of this afternoon event in North Plainfield. The fair is held the second Saturday in *June* and local rescue groups, like the Greyhound Friends, often have booths. For dog visitors, the organizers recommend being there early. For exact dates, go to www.npstreetfair.org.

Lord Stirling Stables Dog Walks

The trails in the Lord Stirling Park are reserved for equestrian use. However, the Friends of the Lord Stirling Stables sponsor a weekly dog walk. In the spring, the dog walk is held on Saturday morning, with registration beginning a half hour before the walk. During the warmer summer months, the walk is held on Saturday evenings. Distances vary depending on conditions and the make-up of the group. A small registration fee is charged, dogs must be leashed, and under control. All walks begin at the stable at 256 South Maple Avenue in Basking Ridge. Call 973-635-8672 or visit www.flssnj.org for more information.

Somerville Events

The downtown shops and businesses of Somerville sponsor a Street Fair, which includes artists, crafters, and food vendors, on the first Sunday in *June* and a Fall Festival, featuring musical performances, artists, and food vendors, on the first Sunday in *October*. Dogs are welcome to attend both events but bring plenty of water.

Englishtown Auction

Open weekends through much of the year, the auction and flea market are a county classic. With an indoor shopping area and an outdoor market on over 40 acres, you can indeed shop till you (or your dog) drops. Pets are welcome at the outdoor market. The auction is at 90 Wilson Avenue in Englishtown. For more information, call 732-446-9644 or go to www.englishtownauction.com.

Summer Concerts in the Park

Bring your furry pal out to Duke Island Park for the Somerset County Park's concert series. These free, family-friendly performances are on Sunday evenings through July and August. For a performance schedule, go to the parks department website, www.somersetcountyparks.org, or call 908-722-1200.

At the end of the Beatles' song "A Day in the Life," Paul McCartney recorded an ultrasonic whistle, audible only to dogs, for his Shetland sheepdog.

Movies in the Park

Families, and their dogs, are invited to old-fashioned "drive-in" movies, just without the drive-in part. So grab a blanket or a couple of chairs and head to Duke Island Park on Wednesday evenings in *August* for a large-screen movie showing in the park. Most of the movies are family-oriented, so your dog is sure to enjoy the films too. For movie listings, go to the parks department website at www.somersetcountyparks.org or call 908-722-1200.

Somerset County 4-H Fair

In the middle of *August* at North Branch Park, you can show off your dog's looks, talents, or charming nature at the dog show at the county fair. This three-day event has all the crafts, rides, and agricultural exhibits of a typical 4-H fair. Maps and schedules of daily events such as dog, horse, and livestock shows are available in the information tent. For exact dates, go to http://somerset.rce.rutgers.edu/.

All-Breed Show and Obedience Trial

In early *September*, the Somerset Hills Kennel Club combines with a dozen or more local breed clubs to hold an AKC conformation show and obedience trial. The one-day event is held at North Branch Park in Bridgewater. Admission charged. For more information, go to www.somersethillskc.org.

Gladstone Driving Event

Held in *September* at the United States Equestrian Team Center in Gladstone, this event brings the best horse driving teams from around the country to New Jersey. With single, pairs, and the impressive four-in-hand coaches racing through the fields and woods, this is a spectacular event to watch. And, being animal-friendly, well-mannered dogs are welcome to attend. A dog agility demonstration is also part of the weekend events. For exact dates, go to the Calendar of Events at www.horsenpony.com.

Agility Trial

One of the largest AKC agility events in the state is held on the second full weekend of *November* at North Branch Park. The Garden State Norwegian Elkhound Club trial draws close to a thousand of the best agility teams on the east coast to this county park. With up to four rings of competition, the excitement is endless during the two-day, and some years three-day, trial. Your dog can be in the park.

Craft Show and Pet Expo

Dedicated to the rescue, appreciation, and care of the greyhound dog, Greyhound Friends of New Jersey hold an annual Craft Show and Pet Expo the first full weekend in *December*. The show is held in the 4-H Building on Milltown Road in Bridgewater, across the street from North Branch Park. And the 4-H building is a pet-friendly place, so animals are welcome. For specifics, go to www.greyhoundfriendsnj.org.

You know you are a dog person when you can identify a dog's breed with just a glance and can discuss a mixed breed's possible parentage for hours.

Union County

Union County was officially formed by the state legislature in 1857. It was the last county created in New Jersey. Strangely, its county seat, Elizabethtown, was the leading settlement in the state in the mid-1600s and the first seat of government in New Jersey. It is the second smallest of the New Jersey counties but one of the most densely populated. With all these people and only a little bit of land, it is surprising to find so many dog-friendly parks and towns.

Dog Day Out

Union County may be small, but it gets a four-paw rating for its parks. From the heavily wooded Watchung Reservation to the tamer neighborhood parks to the suburban towns, this county and its townships offer a park for every mood. Many of the parks have wide paved paths, which are well used by the stroller contingent, and the county keeps the paths clear throughout the winter. It really does not matter what you feel like doing; this county has something for every day and every dog. For more information, go to the parks page at www.unioncountynj.org.

Briant Park

Centered around Briant Pond, this small county park in Springfield has a little over a mile of walking paths. The paved paths are wide and well maintained. Walk the dog. Jog the dog. Push the stroller. Throw the Frisbee. This little neighborhood park, with its small stream, pond, and open fields, is the perfect spot for some R&R with your dog. Park on Briant Parkway, which is just off Springfield Avenue.

Echo Lake Park

This popular county park in Mountainside has it all, starting with a fur-fabulous *dog park.* The 3-acre, fenced field is very popular with the tennis ball set. It has both open areas and woods but mud can be a problem. There are four gates to the park, which are rotated every few weeks, allowing for one "active gate." The active gate is marked by a golf flag. In addition to the dog park, there is Echo Lake, which is three dammed areas of the Nomahegan Brook, and there are paved paths winding along all three. It is a pleasant 2-mile, there-and-back walk. Another shorter path loops around the 9/11 Memorial, near Mill Lane. There are multiple parking lots along Park Drive, which is accessible from Route 22 northbound in Mountainside.

Kean University

Park your car and enter the 150-acre campus in Union dotted with woods, streams, and open space, an ideal environment for wandering slowly with your favorite pal. The campus is a delightful place to enjoy a canine morning out or to socialize a puppy. The main entrance is on Route 82, about 2 miles east of Route 22.

Lenape Park

One of the largest in the county, this park has several miles of walking paths, for a small doggie adventure, or the paths can be combined with the trails in Nomahegan Park for a truly long trek. Parking is available in Springfield on Kenilworth Boulevard. From Route 22, go south on Springfield Avenue and look for the park entrance on your left, near the target and skeet shoot facility.

Nomahegan Park

Come out and walk a couple of miles—any season, any time. You are guaranteed to see lots of other four-footed creatures on these popular dog-walking trails. Located in Cranford, this county park has ponds, paths, playgrounds, forests, and fields. For strolling about with your dog, alone or with a stroller, this park gets four paws up. There are short walks around the pond and longer walks to be found on the connecting trails. Many of the paved paths run through the woods along Springfield Avenue and Kenilworth Boulevard and are plowed in winter. From Route 22, go south on Springfield Avenue, which turns south at the edge of the park.

Summit Walkabout

Are you tired of trees and ready to take your dog window shopping? Downtown Summit is the place to go. With wide sidewalks, adorable stores with big windows, classic stone churches, and traffic-stopping mansions, you and your pup can wander the streets from Argyle Court to Morris Avenue and back again. You can also stop at one of the coffee shops or bakeries for a midmorning treat you can share with your favorite pal. The 1.5-mile-square area of downtown Summit has a bit of everything. Public parking is on DeForest Avenue.

Unami Park

Tucked into the neighborhoods of Garwood, this county park has a playground, ball fields, and paved walking trails. It is located in a quiet, suburban neighborhood. If you are in the area, this park is a refreshing spot for some pawsercise. There is a large parking lot at the north end, along Lexington Avenue. To find the park, go south on Central Avenue from Route 28. Make a left onto Massachusetts and another left onto Lexington.

Warinanco Park

With a skating rink, track, ball fields, and picnic grounds, this 204-acre county park draws large summer crowds; devoted park-goers, particularly those with four feet, use it throughout the year. For exercise-inclined hounds, there is a 1.25-mile paved walking path that meanders through the park and around the pond. On steamy summer days, the shaded picnic grounds provide the furpect spot for loafing around with your pooch. For a spectacular floral show, visit in late April or early May, when the tulips and dogwoods in the gardens typically bloom. Puppy socializers will find this a good park with lots of families and folks just out enjoying the fresh air. Paddleboats can be rented on the 8-acre lake and the rental company occasionally allows dogs to join in the fun. Rules seem to vary but it cannot hurt to ask. Parking is available at several large lots scattered around the loop road. The main park entrance is on Park Street. From Route 28 in Elizabeth, go south one block on CR 439 and then make a right onto Grand Avenue.

Why the name "dogwood"? One theory states that the name is a corruption of "dagwood," which referred to the slender stems of very hard trees used to make "dags" or daggers. Another theory has it that the tree got its name from its berries, which were called "dogberries" because they were worthless. "Dog" is commonly used among botanists to mean inferior quality or worthlessness.

Watchung Reservation

Paws go up and tails wag for this 2,002-acre preserve. With forests, picnic areas, streams, lakes, fields, 13 miles of marked hiking trails, and over 40 miles of unmarked trails, dog days out are easy in this county park. It is actually large enough to need multiple trips just to get oriented and find your dog's favorite spots. For woods hounds, start your hike near the lake in the middle of the park and explore outward. Many of the woodland paths are shared with the Watchung Stable, which is also located in the park. Shorter trails for easy meanders are available around the Trailside Nature Center, which has trail maps. The entrances, roads, and main facilities are all well marked and there are parking lots at the main trail intersections. Located near Scotch Plains, the reservation is between I-78 and Route 22. From I-78, take Glenside Avenue north into Summit and go south on Baltusrol Road, which becomes Summit Lane. Follow the signs to the park.

Paw-tacular Shopping

Best Friend Dog & Animal Adoption

This shelter runs a permanent resale shop, located at 1750 East Second Street in Scotch Plains. All the proceeds from the store are for the animals.

Just-4-Pooches

The retail store is located in historic downtown Cranford. Bring your pet in for treat sampling at this unique pet boutique. The selection of gourmet treats and unique gifts for pets and their parents is worth the hassles of parking. The store is at 8 Union Avenue in Cranford, 908-709-4364.

Pet Shanty

Need some supplies for your visit to the Watchung Reservation? With a complete line of pet supplies to choose from, you can find what your dog needs whether she is a puppy or a senior pooch. The store is conveniently located in Scotch Plains on Route 22, westbound side, 908-889-8262.

Village Pet Center

This small neighborhood store carries all the best dog food and a wide variety of pet supplies. They also carry a woof-wonderful selection of dog toys—a whole wall full of toys, actually. It is truly a dog dream come true! Located in Village Center off Springfield Avenue in New Providence, 908-464-8507.

While traveling about in Union County, you can also get pet supplies at:

Pet Smart. In Union at 2438 Route 22 East, 908-686-9333.
Pet Valu. In Garwood in Garwood Mall on South Avenue, 908-233-0722.

Tail-Wagging Training Facilities

Sit. Stay. Play!

Offering a variety of classes for all stages of your dog's life, this climate-controlled facility is on Route 22 West in Union. They also have doggie day care, where dogs socialize in a supervised environment, and private lessons. The trainers work with you to find the training program that is right for you and your pet. For more information and class details, go to www.sitstayplaytraining.com or call 908-688-3636.

Town & Country Dog Training Club

This club, organized to encourage obedience training for all dogs, is an active group of volunteers who love dogs and find great satisfaction in teaching others to help their dogs become better family members. Training classes for beginners to advanced obedience are offered at YMHA at 501 Green Lane in Union. Group classes are held once a week from September through May. For more information, go to www.dogobedience.org.

Best-in-County Events

Walk-for-Animals

People for Animals host a 2-mile walk-for-animals in Nomahegan Park each *May*. Following the dog walk, there are refreshments and dog contests. For more information, go to www.pfa.petfinder.org.

Cranford Street Fair & Craft Show

This one-day event is held in *May* on the streets of Cranford. Look for crafters, artists, food vendors, entertainers, and lots of family fun. The town holds another street fair in early *October*. For more information, go to www.cranford.com.

Pet Fair

Hosted by the Plainfield Area Humane Society (PAHS), the annual Pet Fair is held at the Trailside Nature Center in the Watchung Reservation in *May*. In *June*, the shelter also hosts the PAHS Golf Classic at Fiddler's Elbow Country Club, located in Bedminster. Although the day is pricey, the cause is noble and the golf outstanding, although your dog must sit this one out. PAHS also has photo sessions with Santa in *November* and has occasionally set up family portraits with pets. For more information, go to the event calendar at www.petfinder.org/shelters/NJ22.html.

Arts & Crafts Show

The county hosts a variety of special events at Nomahegan Park, including a fine arts and crafts show in *June* and again the first weekend in *October*. Check the Union County Parks calendar of events at www.unioncountynj.org for more information.

Obedience Trial

The Town & Country Dog Training Club hosts an all-breed AKC obedience trial every *July* at Warinanco Park in Roselle. The best-of-the-best obedience dogs on the east coast compete at three levels throughout the day. Food is available. Admission charged. Dogs not entered in the trial cannot be in the building but are allowed in the park.

Summer Concerts

Union County hosts concerts in *July* and *August* at Echo Lake Park. Bring a blanket and stretch out for some music under the Sirius star with your favorite canine. And, in mid-*September*, Union County holds a Music Festival at one of the county parks. For a concert schedule, check the Union County Parks website at www.unioncountynj.org.

The Sirius star, residing in the constellation Canis Major, is commonly called the Dog Star. In ancient Greek times the dawn rising of Sirius marked the hottest part of summer. This is the origin of the phrase "dog days of summer."

Springfield Street Fair

Crafters and vendors of all sorts join local restaurants in downtown Springfield for a fun-filled day in the middle of *September*. The fair is along Mountain Avenue.

Festifall

The annual street fair in Westfield is held in late *September*. This one-day fair takes place in the downtown area and is quite popular. Dog visitors should plan to go early, especially if the forecast is for warm weather. For more information, go to www.westfieldnj.com.

Dog Walk-a-Thon

Noah's Ark hosts a very popular dog walk-a-thon every *October* in Rahway Park in Rahway. The fundraiser features contests, music, raffles, and prizes. Noah's Ark is a nonprofit, all-foster-home animal rescue organization in Clark that assists homeless pets by finding them new homes. For more information, go to www.noahsark.petfinder.org.

Fanny Wood Day

This afternoon event is a celebration of Fanwood's history and Victorian heritage and combines a hometown celebration, complete with entertainment, contests, car show, poetry contest, and community organization booths, with a street fair, complete with food vendors and local artisans. It is held in early *October*. For more information, go to www.visitfanwood.com.

People for Animals Events

Founded in 1980, People for Animals is a state leader in animal welfare and hosts some very unique fundraisers, like the popular Casino Night held in *October* at the Union Elks Club in Union. In addition, they sponsor a variety of entertainment events sporadically throughout the year, including the popular Popovich's Comedy Pet Theatre in 2005. For more information, go to www.pfa.petfinder.org.

Overnights

The Pillars of Plainfield

Located in Plainfield, this is one of the few B&Bs in New Jersey that allows pets. The innkeepers of this beautiful Victorian mansion are very dog-friendly. The inn is at 922 Central Avenue. For more information, go to www.pillars2.com.

You know you are a dog person when getting invited to a dog's birthday party is perfectly normal.

Middlesex County

Middlesex was established in 1683 when the General Assembly, meeting in Elizabethtown, divided East New Jersey into four counties: Bergen, Essex, Monmouth, and Middlesex. Early settlers were drawn to the area because of its ideal location between New York and Philadelphia. This same advantage continues to draw people to the area, known as the "heart" of New Jersey. Middlesex County is located squarely in the center of New Jersey and is a hub of commerce and industry. Even though much of the county's 300 square miles is developed, the southern portion retains a somewhat rural atmosphere. So know matter what kind of event or type of park your dog prefers, you will find plenty to keep his tail wagging.

Dog Day Out

The Middlesex County Department of Parks and Recreation operates eighteen county parks encompassing 6,600 acres. Thirteen of these parks contain active recreational facilities, while others are conservation areas or are being held for future recreational development. Take a refreshing selection of county parks, supplement with a few excellent state parks, and voilà! You have a superb location for delightful day trips with which to spoil your furry friend. For county park information, go to the Department of Parks and Recreation page at http://co.middlesex.nj.us.

Cheesequake State Park

All the wonderful smells of open fields, marshes, swamps, and hardwood forests await your hound at this state park in Matawan. Your dog can sniffle and snuffle at will on any one of the five marked trails, with the longest being 3 miles. There are also several long boardwalks. Most of the trails are flat with a few inclines so travel is easy and many of the trails are hiking only. This four-paws-up park also has picnic groves and Hooks Creek Lake to explore. Follow the park signs from Route 34 in Matawan.

Davidson Mill Pond Park

Need some quiet time with your furry pal? The picturesque millpond in this county park may do the trick. Although the park has almost 500 acres, the developed area is small and peacefully quiet. You can use the open fields for a game of Frisbee or stroll slowly down to the waterfall. Just being in the park is good for the doggie soul in both of you. The park entrance is on Riva Avenue, a half mile east of Route 130 in South Brunswick.

Delaware & Raritan Canal State Park

The Delaware & Raritan (D&R) Canal State Park contains two canal systems, the Feeder Canal on the west side of the state and the Main Canal, which runs almost 30 miles across the state from Trenton to New Brunswick. Along the way, the canal crosses through Middlesex County. For a growling good outing, start at the Millstone Aqueduct, at the south end of Carnegie Lake, and go 2.2 miles north to Kingston. Through this section, the towpath travels between the lake and the canal. There are benches here and there, and there is a very nice spot to swim your dog at the north end of the lake, probably why my dogs like this walk so much. Parking is available at both ends. For more canal details, go to www.dandrcanal.com.

Donaldson Park

Tucked into a curve of the Raritan River, this county park, with its meandering paved paths, ball fields, picnic area, and grass lawns, draws a variety of visitors. If your dog needs acres of grass with lots of old trees to serve as "chat" posts, this is the fur-pect park. And best of all, there is a wide-open, fenced *dog park* just waiting to be explored by your furry pal. The well-hidden entrance is at the end of South Third Avenue in downtown Highland Park, just across the river from Rutgers University.

Edison Memorial Tower

Located in the Menlo Park section of Edison, the Thomas Edison Tower is located on the exact spot of the laboratory where Edison received over four hundred patents on inventions like the incandescent light bulb, the phonograph, and the electric railroad car. While the tower is fascinating, your dog will enjoy the Information Trail much more. The dirt path, on which Edison frequently walked while thinking over a problem, winds through the woods to a pond and picnic area. Parking is available at the tower, which is on Christie Street, two blocks north of Route 27.

Johnson Park

Home of the Middlesex County Parks Division, this showcase park along the Raritan River gets four paws up from dogs and their walking companions.

Running for over 2 miles between the river and River Road in Raritan, the park has ball fields, picnic areas, and a 2.5-mile paved path for hiking and biking. This paved path is an excellent choice for anyone who wants to combine the dog's day out with a baby-stroller walk or a roll on roller blades. In the middle of the park, you can cross the river and get on the D&R Canal towpath for an extended dog walk. The park also contains East Jersey Olde Towne. Pack a lunch and spend the day. The park entrance is on River Road in Piscataway.

One of the world's most recognized trademarks is the picture of a little white dog listening to a gramophone. The famous painting, His Master's Voice, *is of Nipper, a white fox terrier. Painted by Francis Barraud, the picture was eventually purchased and copyrighted in 1900 by Emile Berliner, the inventor of the flat disc record. The following year the copyright passed to the Victor Talking Machine Company, which was purchased itself in 1929 by the Radio Corporation of America (RCA). Nipper and Chipper, his new young pal, are still used in RCA advertisements.*

Old Bridge Waterfront Park

A little bit of beach and a little bit of boardwalk provide the fur-pect spot to hike your hound in this 52-acre county park in South Amboy. There are long piers, plenty of spots to get in the water, and convenient benches for resting all along the 1.3-mile walkway along Raritan Bay from Cheesequake Creek to Margaret's Creek. A large parking area is provided at the north end of the park, just past the drawbridge on Route 35.

Plainsboro Community Park Dog Run

This community park has a fenced dog run area. The half-acre dog run is in the open with more grass than dirt and has an active local dog group, particularly in the evening. Look for the dog park on the right side of the park. There are ball fields, playgrounds, and a few picnic areas in the park so it also makes a good place to socialize young dogs. The park is in Plainsboro on Scotts Corner Road, just north of Plainsboro Road.

Rocky Top Dog Park

This is a private, members-only *dog park* that features a 2-acre dog run, a swim pond, walking path, lots of huge trees for shade and a woodsy environment, lights for evening use, and a separate puppy play area. With a variety of membership plans to fit every dog family, this facility is the ultimate dog park and is open all year. It is in Kingston at 4106 Route 27. For more information, call 732-297-6527 or go to www.rockytopdogpark.com.

6. A beautiful morning at the bay for people watching.

Roosevelt County Park

"Walk the dog" takes on a whole new meaning in this 217-acre county park. Winding through the wooded areas and connecting the picnic groves, the dirt paths are woof-wonderful for dogs while the paved paths around the 8-acre lake provide a paw-tacular spot to show off your fancy pooch. The picnic areas and playgrounds are also lovely. Parking areas are scattered throughout the park, with the easiest access being off Route 1 at Lafayette Road in Edison Township.

The Scottish terrier who was the constant companion of President Franklin D. Roosevelt was a 1940 Christmas gift from Roosevelt's favorite cousin, Daisy. The little terrier's full name was Murray, the Outlaw of Falahill, which became Fala, and he is the only dog to appear on a Washington presidential memorial. It is considered good luck to rub Fala's nose, which is now shiny.

Spring Lake County Park

Very much like the elegant parks of Essex County, this park in South Plainfield centers around Spring Lake. It has about 2 miles of paved walking paths through the landscaped grounds. This is a popular spot for combining a stroller and a dog walk and the wide-open space draws people out all day long. Take your dog on a power walk around the lake or just collapse in the grass to watch the kids play soccer. With lovely stone bridges and lake views, you can also just grab a bench or a gazebo and relax. Parking areas on Maple and Sampton Avenues are well marked and easy to find.

Thompson Park

This is a 675-acre county park just south of Jamesburg in the southern corner of the county. Noses go up in a unanimous woof for this park, with its picnic groves, a variety of ball fields, and the 30-acre Manalapan Lake. The hiking trails are not marked but are well used and easy to locate. Not as easy to locate, but worth the effort, are the two *dog parks*! The two dog runs are behind the soccer fields and both offer shade for those blistering summer days. The main park entrance is on Forsgate Drive, which is just over a mile east of the Turnpike, exit 8.

U-Cut Christmas Tree Farms

When the temperature chills and the leaves are gone, it is time to get out and cut your own tree. Many of the tree farms are dog-friendly. For directions and more information on tree farms, go to www.njchristmastrees.org.

Barclay's Tree Farm. In Cranbury at 35 Orchardside Drive, 609-799-1855.
Habiak Tree Farm. In South Brunswick at 315 Dean's Rhode Hall Road, 732-297-2737.
Lantier Tree Farm. In Monroe Township at 145 Dey Grove Road, 732-446-9799.
Simonson Farms. In Cranbury at 260 Dey Raod, 609-799-0140.
W.V. Griffin Nurseries. In South Brunswick at 190 Fresh Ponds Road, 732-257-2484.

Paw-tacular Shopping

Pets Pets Pets

A shop for the pet lover who has everything and yet needs more, this store has gifts for your dog and special items for the dog chauffeur (aka you). From treats to toys to food to dog games, the owners select only the best products for dogs and cats. The store is located at 4095 Route 1 in Monmouth Junction, 732-855-8515.

While traveling about in Middlesex County, you can also get pet supplies at:

Petco. In Edison at 1025 Route 1 South, 732-516-0330. In Milltown at 300 Ryders Lane, 732-651-0260. In Old Bridge at 1060 Route 9, 732-721-9610.
Pet Smart. In Woodbridge at 83 St. George Avenue, 732-750-1090. In East Brunswick at 269 Route 18 South, 732-651-0700.
Pet Valu. In Edison at 775 Route 1 South, 732-339-1233.

Tail-Wagging Training Facilities

Leader of the Pack

Located in New York, this organization offers semi-private and private agility classes in the Dayton area. This organization also hosts several USDAA and CPE agility trials each year. For more information, go to www.lotp.com or call 607-627-6360.

Best-in-County Events

Super Pet Expo

Held every *February* at the New Jersey Convention and Exposition Center in Edison, the Super Pet Expo crams every corner with foods, supplies, rescue information, and pet-related services from the tri-state area and beyond. Specialty events, like auditions for the Letterman Stupid Pet Tricks, are also frequently held at Pet Expos. Admission is charged for humans. Your dog is free. The Expo promotes responsible pet ownership and helps draw attention to abandoned pets. In addition to all the rescue and shelter organizations, exhibitors cover every aspect of pet care, including specialty foods and treats, toys, dog services, therapy practitioners, and animal photographers. The events schedule grows each year but usually includes agility and fly-ball demonstrations. For dates and details, go to www.superpetexpo.com.

All-Breed Conformation Show and Obedience Trial

For two days in late *March*, the New Jersey Convention and Exposition Center in Edison goes to the dogs, lots of dogs. The New Brunswick Kennel Club joins forces with the Twin Brooks Kennel Club to hold a three-day, AKC-sanctioned conformation show and obedience trial. The conformation shows draws over two thousand dogs and nearly two hundred dogs compete in the obedience trials. Unentered dogs cannot attend. Admission charged. For details, go to www.nbkc.org.

New Jersey State 4-H Dog Show

The State 4-H Dog Show is the annual event where 4-H Dog Care & Training and Seeing Eye Puppy project members demonstrate their accomplishments in a competitive format. It is held in conjunction with the Ag Field Day, which is Cook College's annual spring festival. 4-H'ers and their dogs compete in several divisions: Obedience, Seeing Eye, Junior Showmanship, Agility, and Grooming. This event is held every *April.* For more information, go to www.nj4h.rutgers.edu.

Thompson Park Concerts

Musically inclined pooches will appreciate attending one (or all) of the county's outdoor concerts, held in *July* and *August* in Thompson Park. The concerts are staged in the gazebo every Wednesday afternoon and feature an array of musical performances. For more information, call 732-745-3900.

Highland Park Events

Held in the middle of *May*, the annual Highland Park Street Fair has local crafters and artists, a wide variety of food vendors, and continuous live music. Combine the street fair with a visit to Donaldson Park and you have the perfect doggie day out. The fair is held along Raritan Avenue between Second and Fifth Avenue, which is a half mile north and a bit uphill from the park.

Every Saturday evening in *July* and *August*, Highland Park has an outdoor movie presentation on the Highland Park High School grounds. Bring chairs and blankets. There is also a Farmer's' Market on Raritan Avenue, between Second and Third Avenue, every Friday from July through early November. In *September*, you can enjoy the Art in the Park Festival, which is a juried outdoor art show with live music and shopping in the Main Street/Raritan Avenue retail district. In *October*, your dog may enjoy the Harvest Festival. For more information on events, go to www.mainstreethp.org.

Because Your Dog Is Worth It Too Day

L'Oreal Paris hosts this annual event to celebrate the dogs in our lives and to showcase local rescue groups. A full day of events, including dog beauty contests (of course), dog hay maze, agility training, and a dog wash, combines with artists, dog product vendors, and local rescue groups to provide a fun day out for everyone. All proceeds benefit the Breast Cancer Foundation. The event is held in early *August* at the L'Oreal facility in Cranbury at 35 Broadway Road, just off Route 130.

- Look for the Greyhound Friends of New Jersey at this event. This active group also holds group walks in several parks in northern New Jersey. Visit their website at www.greyhoundfriendsnj.org for more information.

Middlesex County Fair

Open every weeknight and all day on the weekend, this country fair has rides, food vendors, 4-H shows, and free entertainment. It typically runs through the first week of *August*. Although dogs are not allowed at the fair, they can come if they are entered in the Animal Show, which has contests for dogs, puppies, and best animal costume. The fair is held in East Brunswick. For details on this year's fair, go to www.njagfairs.com.

Dog Days at the Museum of Agriculture

The New Jersey Museum of Agriculture hosts a one-day event for dogs. Vendors, doggie projects, and information await you and your dog at this special event, held in late *August*. Dogs must be spayed/neutered and have current tags on their collars. Admission charged. The museum is centrally located off U.S. Route 1 South and College Farm Road in North Brunswick, on the campus of Cook College–Rutgers University. For more information, call 732-249-2077 or go to www.agriculturemusem.org.

Art on the Green

This local art show is held in downtown Dunellen in early *September*. Well-mannered dogs are welcome to peruse the works with their leash-line holders.

Paw Pals Dog Walkathon

Round up the dog, tie on the sneakers, and come meet other animal lovers while raising money for a good cause. This dog walk, held in Sabella Park, is sponsored by the North Brunswick Township Parks Department to raise money for local animal organizations. It is held in the middle of *September*. For specifics, go to www.northbrunswickonline.com.

Princeton Dog Training Club Events

Every *September*, the Princeton Dog Training Club, one of the larger performance dog clubs in the state, holds its fall agility trial at Thompson Park in Jamesburg. This two-day event is outdoors, rain or shine, and your dog can be in the park. This club also holds its annual obedience trial, one of the most prestigious events in the area, at the Athletic Center at Rutgers University in the middle of *January*. Due to space limitations, please do not bring your dog to the obedience trial. The club's spring agility trial is held in mid-*May* at the Middletown Grange Fairgrounds in Wrightstown, Pennsylvania. For details, go to www.princetondogtrainingclub.com.

Metuchen Country Fair

This township fair is held the first weekend in *October* in downtown Metuchen. A full day of crafters, street entertainment, and vendors awaits you and your pooch at this street fair. Look for the Animal Rescue Force (ARF) exhibit. For details, go to the calendar at www.metuchenchamber.com.

- Metuchen Farmers' Market brings New Jersey fresh produce to downtown Metuchen on Saturdays from mid-June through September. The market is located at the corner of Central and Middlesex Avenues.

Tri-State Pet Expo

The primary purpose of the New Jersey Tri-State Pet Expo is to promote responsible pet ownership and care at a family event. Held annually in late *October* at the New Jersey Convention Center, the Expo has something for every animal lover and is a fun family day with a petting zoo, pony rides, demonstrations, special attractions, and much more to appeal to every animal lover. Educational seminars and demonstrations are offered throughout the weekend. Admission charged. Alas, due to the large number of animal exhibits, your dog cannot attend this event. For dates and details, go to www.horseandpetexpo.com.

You know you are a dog person when you have your dog's hair styled at a grooming spa but get your hair cut at the nearest barber shop.

Mercer County

Many argue that it was the arrival of the College of New Jersey (now Princeton University) from Newark in 1756 that shaped the county's early history. It was, however, the historic battles at Trenton and Princeton that shaped the history of an entire nation. Named in honor of General Hugh Mercer, who died from wounds inflicted during the Battle of Princeton, the county was not officially founded until 1838 when it was carved out of the four surrounding counties. One hundred years later, another "battle" was fought on Mercer County soil. In 1938, in what has become one of the most famous radio addresses of all time, Orson Welles acted out his *War of the Worlds* invasion, landing his imaginary Martians in what is now West Windsor Township. With all this history, county residents are used to visitors (of all kinds) and they have parks and towns worth visiting.

Dog Day Out

The Mercer County Park Commission has several large parks and there are state parks as well as large, well-managed township parks in both Princeton and Trenton. For such a small area, the doggie day trip options are endless. Furthermore, the area is basically flat so walking is easy and lakes are abundant. There are also quaint, historic towns and the D&R Canal to explore. For more information on the county parks or for a calendar of events, go to the parks page at www.mercercounty.org.

Banchoff Park Dog Run

Located in Ewing Township, this 70-acre township park has tennis courts, a pond, picnic area, and an informal trail system. The fenced dog run is a short walk from the parking area. The park entrance is on Mountain View Road, just south of Bear Tavern Road. From exit 2 on I-95, it is less than a mile to the park.

Core Creek Park (PA)

Located in Middletown Township in southern Bucks County, Pennsylvania, Core Creek Park gets a triple tail-wag rating. There are paved paths around Lake Luxembourg and miles of dirt hiking trails through the woods, fields, and along the quiet streams throughout the 1,200 acres. Spend the morning or the day; your dog's tail will not stop wagging and his doggie grins will last all evening. The park is located just south of Newtown, between CR 413, Woodbourne Road, and Yardley-Langhorne Road. The entrance is 1.5 miles south along CR 413 from Newtown. Turn left onto Tollgate Road.

Delaware & Raritan Canal State Park

The Delaware & Raritan (D&R) Main Canal runs almost 30 miles from Trenton to New Brunswick and the first 6 miles travel through Mercer County. For a lovely stroll with your dog, start at the parking area off Alexander Road and go 2.6 miles south to Port Mercer. This section of the towpath travels through the woods to the east of Princeton Battlefield State Park, providing a very nice canine-walking corridor. Another option is to point your hound north and walk 1.6 miles to the Millstone Aqueduct, near the south end of Carnegie Lake. For more canal details, go to www.dandrcanal.com.

Garden Walks

Spring blooms beautifully in the parks and gardens of Mercer County. While your furry friend may not appreciate the landscaping the way you do, he is sure to enjoy the walk and the time spent with you.

Kuser Farm. Enjoy a trip back in time to the summer country home of Fred Kuser. The mansion and estate grounds are open to the public. Located just east of I-295 on Kuser Road in Trenton.

Marquand Park. Just blocks from downtown Princeton, this beautiful 17-acre tract includes woodlands, forest glades, and open parkland, which provide a magnificent setting for a grand variety of trees and shrubs. In fact, eleven of the trees located here are the largest of their kind in the state of New Jersey. Most of the walks are paved and a map is posted near the parking lot on Lovers Lane.

Pettoranello Gardens. Part of Community Park North in Princeton, this 13-acre park was dedicated in 1992 to Pettoranello, Italy, to honor the Pettoranello artisans, many of whom helped build Princeton University. All the paths are paved. Parking is available off Mountain Avenue.

Princeton University. This charming campus has lovely, landscaped grounds. A visit to Prospect Gardens, which date to the mid-1850s, is worth the parking hassles. The grounds surrounding the house present an array of trees, bushes, plants, and flowers from the commonplace to the exotic. The flower garden was designed by Mrs. Woodrow Wilson and, viewed from above, the paths outline the University seal. A longer stroll around Princeton University is also a wonderful way to spend time outdoors, surrounded by the historic buildings, mature landscaping, and sculpture collection.

SAYEN GARDENS. This 30-acre botanical showplace has become widely known; the property has elaborate gardens accented by gazebos, ponds, streams, and the historic Sayen House. Located at the corner of Hughes Drive and Mercer Street in Hamilton.

HAMILTON VETERANS MEMORIAL PARK

Four woofs and a whole-body wiggle is a good description of this park in Hamilton Square. Built in honor of Hamilton's veterans in 1977, this magnificent 333-acre park has ribbons of walking paths winding through wooded areas, picnic grounds, and around the lake. All the paths are paved and many of the lawns are beautifully landscaped. And, best of all, the park has a fenced *dog park* on the north side. There are big and small dog enclosures with double gates. It can get muddy so bring clean-up supplies. Well-marked entrances for the park are on Klockner Road and White Horse-Hamilton Square Road.

HISTORIC FALLSINGTON (PA)

In 1971, the Village of Fallsington in Bucks County, Pennsylvania, was placed on the National Register of Historic Places and today there are more than ninety preserved structures in this wonderful three-hundred-year-old village. Stroll with your pooch through the streets and slide back in time to Colonial America. The village is Fido-friendly and there are plenty of special events throughout the year. For more information, go to www.historicfallsington.org.

LAWRENCEVILLE VILLAGE DOG PARK

Spoil your dog with a morning romp and roll at the Lawrenceville *dog park*. It is medium-sized with a pea-gravel base but is surrounded by trees and has chairs for the people part of the family. The park also contains ball fields, a playground, and a paved bike path for additional doggie exercise. The park entrance is on Yeger Drive. From exit 5 on I-95, go north on Federal City Road. Cross Pennington-Lawrenceville Road and make the first right onto Yeger Drive.

MERCER COUNTY PARK

Encompassing over 2,500 acres, the park is a growling good time! With a dog-friendly atmosphere and excellent facilities, like 3 miles of paved paths, picnic areas, and plenty of parking, this park is bound to become a favorite. Water-loving canines will truly enjoy Lake Mercer and you can watch national-level regattas and rowing races together. The paths loop and meander, connecting all the major park facilities, including the ice rink, picnic area, marina, tennis center, and ball fields. In this park, you can sit and watch some very good baseball games—with your dog! And there are huge grassy areas if you just want to be lazy. Best of all, the park contains the Bark Park. This is a very nice *dog park* with big and small dog enclosures, double gates, benches, and a few trees for shade. The Bark Park has its own parking area and it is easy to find by following the signs throughout the park. Main park entrances are located on Hughes Drive, Edinburg Road, and South Post Road in Princeton Junction.

In 1893, two brothers, Fred and Louis Ruekheim, conceived the idea of covering popcorn with molasses. After a few false starts, Louis cooked up the formula that is still a company secret. The words "cracker jack" were a slang expression in those days, meaning something very pleasing. The brothers loved the phrase and had it copyrighted for their product, Cracker Jacks. And the little dog that appeared on boxes in 1918? His name was Bingo and he belonged to Fred Ruekheim's grandson, who is the little boy in the sailor suit.

Mountain Lakes Nature Preserve

Once an active farm, this 74-acre tract is reverting to a natural state. Providing a great place for paws-ercise in the Princeton area, this park has about 7 miles of paved and dirt paths. A short, unpaved trail named in honor of James Sayen, a leader in acquiring open space for public use, loops the lakes and provides a rewarding way to tour the Preserve. For longer walks, the trail system connects to several neighboring parks. The preserve is on the north edge of Princeton. From Route 206, turn west onto Mountain Avenue.

Princeton Battlefield State Park

On January 3, 1777, the peaceful winter fields and woods of Princeton were transformed into a war zone by the fiercest battle of its size during the American Revolution. The Clarke House, which witnessed the fight and served as sanctuary for General Mercer, who died there nine days after the battle, serves as the center point for this state park. If you want a nice doggie stroll, the paved paths link all the historic sites in the park. If you want a long walk, this park is the southern end of the Princeton trail system. There are also trails to the D&R Canal and the Institute for Advanced Study Woods. The parking lot on Route 206 is well marked.

Rosedale Park

Encompassing 472 acres, this large county park in Pennington includes a 38-acre lake stocked with trout. Situated along the lake, the large picnic area is a lovely spot for some healthy, healing dog time. There is also a huge green grass field that begs for a picnic on a blanket. Very few trails exist in this park, but Curlis Lake Woods to the west and Pole Farm Park to the south offer long, flat walks should your dog need exercise instead of a snooze. Located on Blackwell Road, a mile east of Route 31 in Pennington. Closed in the winter.

❀ For long canine treks, there are two county parks in the area worth sniffing out. First, behind the Mercer County Equestrian Center (MCEC) on Federal City Road is Curlis Lake Woods. This park has several miles of wide, easy-to-follow trails along the lake or through the woods. Some of the trails are used as riding trails so remember to yield to horses and keep leashes short. There are three marked trails that crisscross the park but all pass the lake and the fields behind MCEC. The trail system connects to Rosedale Park in the northwest corner, along Blackwell Road. Parking is available on the road along South Main Street, just east of Route 31, or at MCEC. A second park is Pole Farm Park. For a tranquil, quiet walk with your furry friend, use the broad, easy trails around the fields and meadows of this park. Located just south of Rosedale Park, this 813-acre park contains two marked trails. The main loop, which is mostly farm roads and mowed paths, is about 3.5 miles. Look for the trail along Blackwell Road, directly across from the Rosedale Park entrance. Parking is also available on the unmarked road at the corner of Keefe and Cold Soil Roads.

U-Cut Christmas Tree Farms

When the temperature chills and the leaves are gone, it is time to get out and cut your own tree and many of the tree farms are Fido-friendly. For directions and more information on tree farms, go to www.njchristmastrees.org.

Bear Swamp Tree Farm. In Trenton at 300 Basin Road, 609-587-1411.

Washington Crossing State Park

This 2,000-acre park preserves the landing site of the Continental Army on Christmas Eve in 1776, prior to the Battle of Trenton. With 15 miles of trails and several large picnic areas, you and your pooch can hike or relax or both. Maps are available at the Interpretive Center. The main park entrance is on Washington Crossing-Pennington Road in Titusville. It is also possible to park along River Drive, just west of Route 29. This area of the park provides access to the D&R Feeder Canal towpath and another large picnic area. You can walk the towpath north or south or you can wander over the bridge into Pennsylvania. There are several locations for doggie swims in the Delaware River. From exit 2 on I-95, take Bear Tavern Road north and follow signs to the park.

❀ Washington Crossing Historic Park is on the Pennsylvania side of the Delaware River. It is a Pennsylvania state park and dogs are welcome to wander around the historic site, explore the river area, or take a walk along the Delaware Canal towpath. A few weekends a year there are encampments in the park, which put all kinds of new smells into the air for your pooch to experience.

Paw-tacular Shopping

Hazel and Hannah's Pawtisserie

Spoiled your pooch yet this week? Wiggle your way into downtown Princeton and treat your pet to homemade treats, elegant dog wear, or a stylish canine accessory. This small, exclusive shop is located at 16 Witherspoon Street, 609-921-7387.

Pets Pets Pets

A shop for the pet lover who has everything and yet needs more, this store has gifts for your dog and special items for the dog chauffeur (aka, you). From treats to toys to food to dog games, the owners select only the best products for dogs and cats. The store is located at 2 John F. Kennedy Boulevard in Somerset, 732-545-6675.

Rosedale Mills

The ultimate in farm supply stores, the big barn has an astounding selection of outdoor, farm, and pet supplies. Browsing through the premium garden tools, fancy ferret food, and wild bird food may keep you busy for a bit before you even get to the dog section, where they have premium dog treats, heated dog beds, stylish food bowls, and more. Located at 101 Route 31, the large complex is easy to find just north of Pennington, 609-737-2008.

While traveling in Mercer County, you can get pet supplies at:

Petco. In Princeton at 301 Harrison Street, 609-252-0294.
Pet Smart. In Princeton at 111 Nassau Park Boulevard, 609-520-9200. In Hamilton at 170 Marketplace Boulevard, 609-585-4418.
Pet Valu. In East Windsor in Town Center Plaza on Route 130, 609-371-7010.

Tail-Wagging Training Facilities

Princeton Dog Training Club

This well-established club hosts a variety of training classes from obedience to agility. Classes are held throughout the year, in and around the Princeton area. For more information, call the club at 908-431-0460 or go to www.princetondogtrainingclub.com.

Best-in-County Events

Middletown Grange Fairgrounds (PA)

If you are in central New Jersey or want to take a fur-fabulous road trip, keep this site on your whisker radar. Throughout the spring, summer, and fall, the

Middletown Grange Fairgrounds host a variety of dog events, including conformation shows, obedience trials, and agility competitions. All of the events are outdoors, rain or shine, and there is plenty of parking. The entrance is on Penns Park Road in Wrightstown, Pennsylvania. Unentered dogs should not attend these events.

Lower Bucks Dog Training Club. In the middle of *April*, you will find the tri-states' obedience and rally dogs at the fairgrounds for this club's AKC trial, which typically draws almost a hundred competitors to the one-day trial.

Kruisin' Kanines Agility Club. This Pennsylvania-based club holds their annual AKC agility trial here in late *April*. With dogs competing all weekend, you are sure to see awesome dogs challenge the course with true grit and gusto. For more information, go to www.kruisinkanines.com.

Princeton Dog Training Club. For a dog-licious spring day trip, come out and watch this AKC-sanctioned agility trial in late *May*. It is three rings of action and excitement and the Princeton Club usually teams up with the Lower Camden Dog Training Club to make this a two-day event. For exact dates, go to www.princetondogtrainingclub.com.

Greater Philadelphia Dog Fanciers Association. Held the first Friday in *June*, this show is part of a three-day event. The AKC-sanctioned conformation show and obedience trial are held on Friday and draw over a thousand entries.

Huntingdon Valley Kennel Club. Held the first Saturday in *June*, this show draws over 1,500 entries. It is AKC-sanctioned and part of the three-day event.

Burlington County Kennel Club. Held the first Sunday in *June*, this AKC show draws almost 1,500 entries in conformation and obedience and generally supports four or more specialties (breed-specific competitions). This is just one of many AKC events sponsored by the very active Burlington County Kennel Club.

Hatboro Kennel Club. In early *October*, this club holds its AKC conformation show and obedience trial at this site. There are usually four or five designated specialties and sweepstakes. Admission charged.

All-Breed Show and Obedience Trial

Every spring, Mercer County Park goes to the dogs! On the first full weekend of *May*, the Trenton Kennel Club joins forces with several breed clubs to hold an AKC conformation show and obedience trial in the park. And, before the Trenton show on Sunday, there are two days of conformation and obedience trials held by breed clubs, making this a three-day event. The lovely setting and wonderful facilities draw the dog set from across the east coast. Some of the larger breed clubs that help host this annual event are: Afghan Hound Club of Northern New Jersey, Delaware Valley Toy Dog Fanciers Association, and the Garden State Terrier Club. There is plenty of parking. Admission charged.

SAVE Events

Founded in 1941, SAVE is a nonprofit shelter dedicated to protecting the health and welfare of companion animals in the Princeton area. This organization has some splendid annual events for dog and cat folks. For more information, go to www.save-animals.org.

Pet Jet Set. This annual benefit is held in *May* at the Princeton Airport on Route 206. The glamorous evening features a gourmet dinner, music, and a fashion show featuring couture for pooches. Tickets are pricey but the cause is worthy.

Walk-a-thon. Held in *June* at Rosedale Park in Pennington, the annual walk-a-thon fundraiser is open to all and to all of their four-footed friends.

Halloween Parade. Strut your mutt's stuff at the woof-abulous, tail-wagging SAVE parade in *October*.

Hamilton Township Events

This Hamilton Township municipal park has an annual Civil War reenactment in the middle of *July*, which runs for three days, and a Septemberfest in *September*. Both events are held in Veterans Park. Well-mannered dogs that can handle the noise and crowd are welcome. For exact dates and a schedule, go to the Residents page at www.hamiltonnj.com.

Music-in-the-Park

Every Saturday evening through *July* and *August*, Mercer County hosts a Music-in-the-Park concert, covering a diverse range of music from blues and rock to jazz and symphonic. Get your doggie blanket, chairs, and a picnic and come out and enjoy the music with your furry friend. The concert stage is located near the ice rink in Mercer County Park. For a concert schedule, go to the Cultural and Heritage Commission page at www.mercercounty.org.

Ride for the Animals

Sponsored by the New Jersey Veterinary Foundation, the annual bike-a-thon is held in Mercer County Park in the middle of *September*. There are two different bike rides and two walk and jog routes. Dogs are welcome. For more information, go to the special events page at www.njvma.org/public/foundation/index.asp.

Tails on the Trails (PA)

The Tails of the Tundra Siberian Husky Rescue holds an annual Tails on the Trails day, which is much more than a group hike. Frequently held at Core

Creek Park in Langhorne, Pennsylvania, the hikes are 1 mile and 2 miles and every dog, every size, and every shape is welcome. There are merchandise booths, foster dogs to visit and/or take on the hike, sled dog demonstrations to watch, and other fundraiser events in which to participate. The dog walk is held in late *September*, rain or shine. This nonprofit group has a busy schedule with events in New York City, New Jersey, and eastern Pennsylvania. For more information, go to www.siberescue.com.

Kuser Farm Events

Hamilton Township hosts several events at this municipal park each year. In the middle of *October*, the township has a Fall Country Harvest. The afternoon event includes food, music, costume parade, and hayrides. In early *December*, the Winter Wonderland event runs for four days, beginning with a tree-lighting ceremony and continuing through the weekend with Santa visits, music, and food. For exact dates and a schedule, go to the Residents page at www.hamiltonnj.com.

You know you are a dog person when your closet contains a special section of clothes decorated in dog, with an emphasis on your favorite breed.

Monmouth County

Formed in 1683 by the Proprietary Assembly, Monmouth County was named after Monmouthshire, England. It is located on the Atlantic Coastal Plain of central New Jersey and is the sixth largest county in the state, occupying 471 square miles. This figure includes land only. No exact figure is available for water but it is estimated at approximately 59 square miles. First settled by migrant New Englanders in 1664, Monmouth County has been a desirable place to live for centuries. And dogs have "the run of the county." Whether you and your dog crave the beach, fancy a Frisbee game, or pant for long walks through the Pinelands, you are sure to find a bounty of parks and events to keep you both grinning all year long.

Dog Day Out

Monmouth County has a woof-wonderful county park system, 27 miles of Atlantic Ocean beaches, miles of boardwalk, and some of the best wildlife management areas for dogs in the state. There are also state and national parks to explore. For details and excellent maps of all the county parks, go to www.monmouthcountyparks.com.

Allaire State Park

Known for its historic nineteenth-century iron-making town, Allaire Village, and the Pine Creek Railroad, this state park has over 3,000 acres of pine and oak forests, a long section of the Manasquan River, first-rate picnic grounds, and a network of trails, which wind through the park, providing opportunities for day strollers or long-distance hikers. Dogs are welcome to join you for an outdoor lunch in the picnic area and they are cordially invited to mosey around Allaire Village, though they are not allowed in the buildings. For woodland wanders, try the 1.5-mile red trail or the 4.5-mile green trail, both of which are easy hikes restricted to pedestrians, of the two- or four-footed variety. If your hound needs a long hike, use the orange trail, which, at 16.5 miles, offers a bit more challenge. Most of the trails start in the main parking lot for Allaire Village. Take exit 31 on I-195. Go north on CR 547 for a short distance and then make a right onto CR 524. The park entrance is on the right.

❖ Allaire Village also hosts numerous special events throughout the year that your dog may enjoy attending. To find an event to make his day a special occasion, go to www.allairevillage.org.

Assunpink Wildlife Management Area

The dog-training and exercise area is roughly in the middle of the WMA, south of the little town of Roosevelt. With three lakes and multiple parking access areas, this is one of the more popular WMAs. The dog-training area is deep in the park at a small lake, just north of CR 524. From Imlaystown go north to CR 524 and continue for about 2 miles. Roosevelt Road, which is a small gravel road on the left, provides access to the dog-training area. Remember—hunting is allowed in all WMAs and seasons extend from September to March.

Bayshore Waterfront Park

Located next to Monmouth Cover Marina, this 197-acre county park in Port Monmouth has a fishing pier and a long stretch of beachfront along Raritan Bay, providing beautiful views of the New York City skyline, which will not impress your pooch at all. The smells along the water will have his full attention, assuming, of course, he is not in the water. Your dog is sure to enjoy this park through every season so navigators can rejoice that it is easy to find. From Route 36 in Middletown, take Main Street east to Port Monmouth. From Main Street, make a left onto Wilson Avenue. At the end, turn left onto Port Monmouth Road and look for the park on your right.

Beaches and Boardwalks

The beach towns of Monmouth County all have their own rules for dogs on the beach. And, as township policy changes frequently, it is always wise to read the signs and avoid the beach areas in summer. Many beach communities do not allow dogs on the beach or boardwalk. Thankfully, there are a few that do.

Avon-by-the-Sea. Dogs are allowed on the beach from October 2 to April 30. Dogs are not allowed on the boardwalk.

Belmar. Dogs that are wearing a valid and current license tag issued by the Borough of Belmar are permitted on the beach in the area south of the Belmar Fishing Club pier at First Avenue and extending south to the border of Spring Lake, which is at North Lake Drive, from October 1 to April 30. Dogs are not allowed on the boardwalk, except when accessing the beach.

Bradley Beach. Dogs are never allowed on the boardwalk or promenade along

Ocean Avenue, except when directly accessing the beach. Dogs are allowed on the beach and may be off leash (but under control) from October 15 to April 15.

Monmouth Beach. Dogs are allowed on the beach from mid-September to mid-May.

Manasquan. Dogs are allowed on the township beach from November 1 to March 31.

Ocean Grove. Dogs are allowed on the beach from October 1 to April 30.

Sea Girt. Dogs are never allowed on the boardwalk but are allowed on the beach from October 1 to April 30.

Spring Lake. Dogs are allowed on the beach and boardwalk from October 1 through May 14.

Clayton Park

Tucked into the rolling farmland of western Monmouth County, this rustic 421-acre site in rural Upper Freehold is a popular destination for dog walkers. One of the most beautiful parks in the county system, the property is known for its stately forest. There are 8 miles of trails, with short loops and longer walks of 2 to 3 miles. The entrance is on Emley's Hill Road, which is off Imlaystown Road.

When you are in the area, stop by the quaint town of Imlaystown. Visitors with two feet or four will enjoy the town with its historic landmark, Saltar's Mill, and picturesque Imlaystown Lake.

Dorbrook Recreation Area

A paved trail winds its way around and through the north side of this 535-acre county park in Colts Neck, providing a lovely dog walk. The 2.4-mile trail has two loops, which border the forest to the north and are easy to access from any parking area. The smooth pavement makes easy going for dog walkers pushing a stroller or anyone brave enough to roller blade with their dog. With an in-line skating rink, athletic fields, playgrounds, tennis courts, two swimming pools, and open fields, this park gets busy with families and fitness buffs, making this a good stop on the puppy socialization tour. From Route 18, go north on Route 34 and then east on CR 537.

Edgar Felix Bike Path

This paved path is very popular with the local dog set throughout the year. It sneaks between neighborhoods and through coastal forests, avoiding most roads in a very congested area, very much like Patriot's Path in Morristown. The map shows this trail crossing multiple roads but a bridge across the Garden State Parkway and underpasses at Routes 34 and 35 eliminated the big ones, leaving only a few small roads to cross in Allenwood. Wheel, foot, and paw

7. A moment of rest between Frisbee games.

traffic is heavy on the trail, however, and we were often forced to use a short leash. The easiest trail access point is in downtown Manasquan, where the trail is well marked on Main Street, across from the municipal parking lot.

HARTSHORNE WOODS PARK

As you follow your dog's wildly wagging tail down the trail, you feel miles away from civilization and yet, you are less than half a mile from the coast. With 741 acres in the three sections, Rocky Point, Buttermilk Valley, and Monmouth Hills, your dog can explore for days and never sniff the same tree twice. And, with 15 miles of trails crisscrossing the three sections, the map reader can pick from a variety of trail types and lengths to get just the right mix for the day's adventure. In the Rocky Point Section, there are 3 miles of paved paths and a network of connecting sand paths, which loop around and through the old naval installations. Although paved, these trails are steep, particularly the trail down to the Navesink River Pier, which has a small beach area perfect for doggie swims. In the Monmouth Hills Section, hardy hikers and their hounds can make an expedition out of the Cuesta Ridge, Laurel Ridge, and Grand Loop trails, while easier woodland walks are available in the Buttermilk Valley Section. This is a quiet park with few visitors so multiple dog walkers should make this a "regular," though several of the trails in the old missile barracks and batteries area are popular with mountain bikers. Trail maps are available in the park. The park entrance for Rocky Point is at the end of Portland Road while the Buttermilk Valley parking area is on Navesink Road. Both roads are easy to find from Route 36 in Atlantic Highlands.

- The United States War Dogs Association is a nonprofit organization of former and current United States Military Dog Handlers. Its members are committed to establishing a permanent war dog memorial and seek to educate the public about the invaluable service of military canines to our country. In New Jersey, the group's efforts are focused on adding a war dog memorial to the New Jersey Vietnam Veterans' Memorial at the PNC Bank Arts Center in Holmdel. This memorial honors all who served during the Vietnam War, especially the 1,557 New Jerseyans who did not return home. As for the dogs, they served in all four branches of the military in Vietnam. It is estimated that 4,900 dogs were used during the course of the war. (Exact numbers are not known since records of the dogs in Vietnam were not maintained by the military until 1968.) A model of the war dog memorial is on display at the Education Center and the site has been approved. Dogs continue in service today at military bases around the world, and the War Dogs Association works hard to provide them with extra supplies and is determined to gain these wonderful animals recognition and continued support. Their website, at www.uswardogs.org, has excellent information, photos of current dogs on duty, and moving stories of past heroes.

Holmdel Park

Home of Longstreet Farm, Holmdel Park gets an enthusiastic paws-up from canine visitors. Hiking hounds will find nose-pleasing trails winding through the shady woods and rolling hills, while strolling pooches will find the smooth path that loops leisurely around the pond and through the arboretum a joy. And picnic groves offer fur-pect spots for those lazy days in the park when hiking and walking are not necessary. Besides the 6 miles of marked trails, this 564-acre county park also has tennis courts, playgrounds, a fitness trail, sledding hill, and the Longstreet living history farm, which your dog must skip. Around the pond, farm, and picnic groves you are sure to have company but the majority of the trails are in the north end of the park, where you and your hiking hound can get away from the crowds for a solitary trek in the woods on many days. The rolling terrain offers a few challenges and multi-dog walkers will be happy to note that cyclists and equestrians must remain on the roads at this popular county park. The entrance is on Longstreet Road. From Route 34 in Holmdel, go north to Roberts Road and follow signs to the park.

Huber Woods

Another good place to escape the beach crowds and get some serious exercise for your pooch is at this county park in Atlantic Highlands. Huber Woods has 6 miles of trails to explore. The majority of the multi-use trails are east of Brown's Dock Road but for a strenuous trek try the Many Log Run trail on the west side. Good dog sounds and smells are everywhere so almost any trail will make your pal happy. Trail maps are available at the parking area, which is on Brown's Dock Road. From Route 35 in Middletown, go east about 3 miles on Navesink River Road'. Turn left onto Brown's Dock Road and look for the park entrance on the left.

Manasquan Dog Beach

Although dogs are not allowed on the main township beach until winter, they are allowed on the inlet beach all year. Unofficially known as the "dog beach," this natural beach is along the Manasquan River Inlet, at the southern end of Third Avenue. Officially known as Fisherman's Cove Conservation Area, it is a 52-acre county park. This undeveloped tract on the Manasquan Inlet is a great place to fish, walk along the Manasquan River beach, or just laze about in the sun. Parking is available in the municipal lot. From Route 35, go north on Route 71 into Manasquan and then go east on Frisk Avenue, which turns into Brielle Road. Go right onto Third Avenue and park along the street or in the municipal lot.

Manasquan Reservoir

Canine fitness buffs adore this park. The 5-mile perimeter trail has panoramic views of the reservoir, crosses no roads, and provides a great trail experience for all users. Although it is popular with joggers, cyclists, and equestrians, the wide gravel path offers plenty of space and there are easy-to-find paths cutting through the woods that lead to all the good dog swim spots. The Manasquan Reservoir is a 1,200-acre preserve in Howell Township. The entrance is on Windeler Road. From Route 9, go east on Georgia Tavern Road and follow signs to the parking area.

MONMOUTH BATTLEFIELD STATE PARK

One of the largest battles of the American Revolution took place in the fields and forests that now make up the park, and today's visitors can amble about the preserved rural eighteenth-century landscape of hilly farmland and hedgerows. Miles of hiking trails crisscross the 2,764 acres, linking the battlefield, historic areas, and picnic groves. For multi-dog walks or just a bit more solitude, use the parking area on Route 9 rather than the main park area on Business Route 33, just west of Freehold. Follow signs from Route 9.

- Cannons roar and musket volleys rumble through the woods as American and British troops engage in a mock battle every June. It is an impressive display but many dogs find the "sounds of battle" nerve-wracking. If your dog is not sound-sensitive, he may just become a history buff at this event.

- Just around the corner from the state park is Battleview Orchards. This well-established orchard and farm market has fruits, vegetables, homemade pies, and a huge selection of delicious treats. Select a dessert for yourself and your pooch. Picnic tables are provided. The farm market is on Wemrock Road, just north of Business Route 33.

MOUNT MITCHELL SCENIC OVERLOOK

At 266 feet above sea level, this 12-acre county park in Atlantic Highlands is the highest point on the entire Atlantic seaboard. Take your dog up and let him snuffle the breeze while you enjoy the scenic views of Sandy Hook, Raritan Bay, and the New York City skyline. This park also offers picnic tables and the Monmouth County 9/11 Memorial. From exit 117 on the Parkway, go east on Route 36 about 13 miles and look for signs for Red Bank/Scenic Road. Follow signs to the park.

SANDY HOOK AND FORT HANCOCK

Part of the Gateway National Recreation Area, the Sandy Hook section of this national park is a favorite of my pooches. The park is very dog-friendly, with canines allowed on the bay beaches year-round and permitted on the ocean beaches from the middle of September to the middle of May. Our four-footed pals are also welcome on all the trails. Once she knows about this park your dog is sure to beg for frequent visits. We use the park all year but late fall and spring are fur-fabulous times to visit with your dog, when the beaches are virtually empty. Stroller families will find the 5-mile paved path, connecting the beach access areas and Fort Hancock, excellent for getting both children and dogs out. For relaxing rambles, walk the paths and sidewalks of Fort Hancock or explore the old missile batteries. There are also plenty of trails through the coastal forests but watch out for cactus. Trail maps are available at the visitor center. For more information on the park, go to www.nps.gov/gate/.

Seven Presidents Oceanfront Beach

Alas, this is the one exception to the overall dog-friendly rule of the Monmouth County park system. Dogs are never allowed on the beach in this park, although they can be in the park, which is located in Long Branch at Ocean Avenue North.

Shark River

Located in Neptune and Wall Townships, this 588-acre county park contains a popular fishing lake and a large picnic grove in the woods. Your dog can mosey about the lake for some paw stretches or you can wander across the street to the trailhead, where hiking hounds can snuffle their way along 7 miles of trails. For water-loving pups, use the Rivers Edge trail to find swim holes along the Shark River. The park is easy to find on Schoolhouse Road. Follow signs from Route 33.

Spring Lake Walkabout

The picturesque seaside town of Spring Lake offers visitors an unhurried atmosphere of gracious living that has made it a unique resort on the Jersey Shore for more than one hundred years. Turn-of-the-century architecture borders the wide tree-lined streets around Spring Lake, while small shops, elegant hotels, and delectable restaurants compete for your attention in the downtown area. Keep this town on the whisker radar whenever you are in the area whether you need to window shop or just saunter around town looking good with your favorite pal.

There seven states that officially recognize a breed as their state dog.

Louisiana	*Catahoula Leopard Dog adopted in 1979*
Maryland	*Chesapeake Bay Retriever adopted in 1964*
Massachusetts	*Boston Terrier adopted in 1979*
North Carolina	*Plott Hound adopted in 1989*
Pennsylvania	*Great Dane adopted in 1965*
Virginia	*American Foxhound adopted in 1966*
Wisconsin	*American Water Spaniel adopted in 1986*

At this time, New Jersey does not have a state dog. Any suggestions?

Tatum Park

With 368 acres of woods and fields, this county park in Middletown is an appealing spot for some doggie exercise. There are no other facilities here, so the 4 miles of trails are generally quiet, making multi-dog walks easy. Picnic tables offer a relaxing place to lunch. Trail maps are posted at the parking areas, which are on Holland Avenue and Red Hill Road. From Route 35 in Holmdel, go 1.5 miles south on Laurel Avenue and then make a left onto Holland Avenue. The park entrance is on the right.

Thompson Park

Home to the Monmouth County Park System administrative office, this park was once Brookdale Farm, a premier thoroughbred breeding/training facility. Today, it offers recreational facilities for almost every interest, dogs included. The *off-leash dog area* is near the summer theater and craft center and is accessed from the west entrance. It is a large grassy area with plenty of space for dogs to play and romp. There are no trees or shade so in summer the local dog community uses the park only in the early morning and late evening. There are also old farm roads and a former horse exercise track in this 665-acre county park, both of which are popular with fitness buffs so you are sure to have company. For longer wanders, there is a 1.8-mile paved path that can be accessed near the tennis courts and your pal can get his paws wet in Marlu Lake. The park has plenty of ball fields and playground areas to draw families so this also makes a very good place to socialize young dogs. From the Garden State Parkway, go 2 miles west on CR 520. The park entrances are well marked.

Turkey Swamp

Tails wag right off for this county park! With a 17-acre lake, 4 miles of easy hiking paths, and multiple picnic areas, a dog day out is just plumb wonderful here. Located in Freehold Township, this popular park has relatively level hiking trails with plenty of paths meandering around the lake and through the day-use areas. If you are not in the mood for hiking, plan a day on the water. Dogs are usually allowed on the rental boats and canoes in this dog-friendly park. From Route 9 take CR 524 west to Georgia Road. Proceed 1.7 miles to the main park entrance.

Turkey Swamp Wildlife Management Area borders the west edge of the county park. If your dog needs an expedition into the "wilds," there are numerous unmarked hiking trails through the WMA.

New evidence suggests that turkey skin can cause acute pancreatitis in dogs. So make sure you give your dog the meat (no bones either) at Thanksgiving.

U-Cut Christmas Tree Farms

When the temperature chills and the leaves are gone, it is time to get out and cut your tree. Many of the tree farms are Fido-friendly and will even allow well-mannered dogs on the hayride to the field. It is always wise to ask first. For directions and more information on tree farms, go to www.njchristmastrees.org.

Anne Ellen Christmas Tree Farm. In Manalapan Township at 114 Daum Road, 732-786-9277.

Keris Tree Farm & Christmas Shop. In Allentown at 848 CR 524, 609-259-0720.

Lincroft Christmas Tree Farm. In Lincroft at 523 Newman Springs Road, 732-747-4381.

Woodfield Christmas Tree Plantation. In Colts Neck at 164 CR 537, 732-542-6692.

Paw-tacular Shopping

B. C. Woof

Carrying a full line of Dr. Harvey's all-natural premium food and treats, this store also has a fur-fabulous selection of collars, beds, toys, and this-and-that for cats and birds. The store is in Manasquan at 104 Main Street, 732-223-1218.

Cosmopawlitan Pet Boutique

The best in pet supplies is available in this store, including a full line-up of premium foods, beds, dog apparel, treats, and toys. The store is at the intersection of Route 34 and CR 537 in Colts Neck, 732-683-1985.

Dill's Feed & Supply

For premium dog food, treats, and those hard-to-find supplies, try this store in Freehold. It is west of town at 263 Throckmorton Street, just before Route 9, 732-431-4114.

Hungry Puppy

Budgets beware! This store is jammed with great stuff for dogs and their people. They carry a full line of premium pet foods and high-end supplies. The store is at 1288 Route 33 in Farmingdale, 732-938-4470.

Pets Ahoy

If you are at the beach and in need of supplies, stop by this store in Bradley Beach. They carry all the main dog food brands, treats, toys, and a bit of everything else. It is located at 100 Main Street, 732-988-0707.

While traveling about in Monmouth County, you can also get pet supplies at:

Petco. In Freehold at 4345 Route 9 South, 732-866-0517. In Howell at 4755 Route 9, 732-942-7364.
Pet Smart. In Manalapan at 7 Route 9, 732-683-1119. In Holmdel at 2101 Route 35, 732-615-9770. In West Long Branch at 310 Route 36, 732-544-8970.
Pet Valu. In Cliffwood at 319 Route 35, 732-765-0818.

Tail-Wagging Training Facilities

Jersey AGility

Formed in 2000, Jersey AGility (JAG) brings together agility lovers in Monmouth and Ocean Counties and across central New Jersey. JAG provides training classes, a place to practice, and regularly scheduled agility trials. If your dog wants to do agility, this is where to go. With some of the best trainers in the state and an excellent facility, your dog is sure to have fun. For more information, go to www.jagdogs.com.

Purr'n Pooch

Purr'n Pooch is a full-service pet care facility, offering boarding, grooming, and training classes. They also have a doggie daycare with daily play and socialization sessions. Training classes focus on positive reinforcement and are available for boarded dogs, in group sessions, and in private instruction. There are two locations: 80 Gilbert Street in Tinton Falls, 732-842-4949, and 2424 Route 35 in Wall Township, 732-528-8100. For more information, go to www.purr-n-pooch.com.

Shelly's School for Dogs

The training program, designed by owner Shelly Liebowitz, covers everything from behavioral problems to basic obedience and aggressive behavior, as well as specialized applications, such as tracking, drug detection, and preparation for AKC and Schutzhund competitions. Classes run year-round. The school is located in Freehold at 179 South Street. For more information, call 732-845-3787 or go to www.shellysschoolfordogs.com.

Dog-Ease Daycare

Residents of Monmouth County can spoil their furry friends at Dog-Ease Daycare. The dog-loving folks at Dog-Ease provide all-day care and continuous fun for your dog, whether she is a youngster or just plain rambunctious. They have two convenient locations: Shrewsbury and Marlboro. For more information, call 877-717-DOGS or go to www.dog-ease.com.

Best-in-County Events

First Saturday Events

Asbury Park shops and restaurants keep their doors open from 6 to 10 p.m. on the "First Saturday" of the month. Indulge your special furry friend with some window shopping, snacking, and local musical entertainment, as you amble about town. Each day has a theme, like the Dog Days of Summer event in August. For details, call 732-775-7676 or go to www.firstsaturdayasburypark.com.

❀ If you are in Asbury Park on a Saturday morning, stop by the UEZ Farmer's Market. This hugely successful and very popular farmer's market is open every Saturday during the summer months (weather permitting). It runs from 7 a.m. to 1 p.m. in Firemen's Park at the corner of Sunset Avenue and Main Street in Asbury Park.

East Freehold Park Events

For a howling good time with your furry pal, stop by East Freehold Park in Colts Neck to watch an agility trial. This park is home to several large agility trials hosted by AKC and NADAC clubs. Events are held once or twice a month at this park from March to late October and almost every breed has representatives competing in agility. Your dog may be in the park.

Afghan Hound and Central Jersey Hound Association. These clubs brave the elements and combine to hold the first AKC outdoor trial in the area on the last weekend in *March* or early April.

Agility Association of Central New Jersey (JAG). AKC trials are held in the middle of *April* and again in *June*.

Agility Association of Central New Jersey (JAG). NADAC trial is held in late *June*.

Bayshore Companion Dog Club. AKC trials are held in early *June* and early *October*.

Fast Pawz. NADAC trials are held the first full weekend in *November*.

Hunt Tests

Once or twice a year the Eastern German Shorthaired Pointer Club hosts an AKC hunt test at the Assunpink Wildlife Management Area. With almost all the hunting breeds represented, you are guaranteed to see some high-class performances and some funny bloopers as the younger and less experienced dogs get their start. Your dog may be in the park but leave sound-sensitive or gun-shy dogs at home. The trial is held in early *April* and some years the club hosts another event in late *October*. For details, go to the club website at www.easterngspc.org.

All-Breed Show and Obedience Trial

Every Memorial Day weekend in *May*, the dogs of New Jersey (and many other states) go to East Freehold Park in Colts Neck for a three-day extravaganza. Three large kennel clubs, including Staten Island, Plainfield, and Monmouth County, combine their efforts to host this AKC conformation show and obedience trial. The best of the best always attend these outdoor trials. Unentered dogs may not attend. Admission charged.

Asbury Park Pet Parade

Open to everyone, this pet parade is sponsored by the Asbury Park Homeowners. It is held in late *June*. With the parade, there are prizes, awards, and plenty of pooch and people fun. Prize categories include best dancer, highest jumper, softest fur, best-groomed, biggest nose, longest tail, best owner-pet look-alike, and best trick. The parade starts at Kennedy Park on Cookman Avenue in Asbury Park and the entry fee goes directly to the SPCA shelter. For details, go to www.monmouthcountyspca.org/events.htm.

Dream Stables Charity Dog Walk

Sponsored by Dream Stables, this early *June* dog walk is held on a Sunday in Dorbrook Park in Colts Neck. All benefits go to the Monmouth County SPCA. For details, go to the events calendar at www.monmouthcountyspca.org.

- Monmouth County SPCA operates the Cats and Dogs thrift shop. It is open Wednesday to Saturday and is located adjacent to the shelter in Eatontown at 260 Wall Street. Call 732-542-5342 for more information.

Red Bank Jazz & Blues Festival

The annual Red Bank Jazz & Blues Festival, which takes place in Marine Park by the gentle and beautiful Navesink River, offers three full days and nights of jazz, blues, food, crafts, and plenty of family fun. It is held the first full weekend in *June* and over 100,000 attendees enjoy some of the best jazz and blues music around. Well-behaved dogs are welcome but go early to avoid the foot crush. For more information, go to www.redbankfestival.com.

Belmar Music Events

On Monday evenings in the summer, Belmar hosts a series of summer concerts at the Huisman Gazebo, located at Fifth and Ocean Avenues. On Thursday and Friday nights in June, July, and August, outdoor concerts are held at the Pyanoe Plaza on Main Street. All the concerts begin around 7 p.m. and are free. So grab the pooch and a chair and enjoy the music.

Monmouth County Fair

With free entertainment, a horse show, 4-H shows and exhibits, daily demonstrations and competitions, and a large variety of food vendors, you are sure to enjoy the Monmouth County Fair, whether your dog competes in the pet show or not. Stop at the Monmouth County SPCA booth for the latest shelter information and fall event schedule. Dogs are not allowed on the show grounds unless they are competing in the pet show. The fair is held every year in late *July* at East Freehold Park in Freehold. For more information, look for the Fair page at www.monmouthcountyparks.com.

Clearwater Festival

In *August* in Asbury Park, your dog can enjoy the Clearwater Festival with you. It is an open-air music and arts festival celebrating the spirit of people working and singing together for the environment. The finest in music and dance combines with environmental activism to celebrate our waterways. Clearwater, through its volunteers, seeks to protect the Raritan Bay, surrounding waterways, and New Jersey coast. For more information, go to www.clearwatermc.org.

Brielle Day

The major annual event of the Borough of Brielle, Brielle Day was established in 1972 and is held each *September* on the first Saturday after Labor Day. The majority of the day is devoted to shopping for crafts, with over two hundred artisans displaying their wares in booths set up in the park. Nonprofit groups and local businesses provide entertainment and food. During the summer, there are also concerts every Monday at the Green Acres Park gazebo. For more information, visit www.briellenj.com.

Festival of the Sea

The Festival of the Sea has become one of Point Pleasant Beach's top events. Beginning in *September* of 1975 as an end-of-summer gathering, the festival has grown into a major event. It is held downtown on both Arnold and Bay Avenues. Local restaurants and vendors provide the large crowds with seafood delicacies and a variety of nonseafood fare. There are also craft vendors, shop sales, and local musicians on hand to entertain the crowd. For more information, go to the events calendar at www.pointpleasantbeach.com.

Skyhoundz Event—Dog Frisbee

Held each *September* at Stevenson Park in Middletown Township, the fur truly flies at the annual Middletown Canine Frisbee Competition hosted by the Yankee Flyers Disc Dog Club. Come see first-timers and world finalists competing. Got a dog that can catch a Frisbee? You are more than welcome to enter. Just want to watch? That is just fine too. Stevenson Park is at 940 West Front Street in Middletown. For more information, go to www.skyhoundz.com.

Red Bank Pet Walk and Fair

Animal lovers from near and far join their dogs for a walk in the park and surrounding Red Bank every *October* to raise funds for shelter animals. Held in Marine Park, this large pet walk and shelter fair typically draws over a thousand participants and their pooches. The dog walk is about a mile and is followed by contests and ceremonies. The event is sponsored by local businesses and is the Monmouth County SPCA's largest fundraiser. For details, go to the events calendar at www.monmouthcountyspca.org.

Thompson Park Day

This *October* day of fun and games is for the whole family, dog included! Visitors enjoy free entertainment, kids' rides, an arts and crafts sale, food festival, pony and wagon rides, and other activities, which include a dog costume contest at the *dog park*. For details on this annual event, go to the events calendar at www.monmouthcountyparks.com.

Garden State Sighthound Association

The Garden State Sighthound Association (GSSA) began in the lovely horse-country region of Monmouth County, brought together by a group of sighthound owners and breeders (predominantly Borzoi fanciers) who were dedicated to preserving the natural and inherent talents of their dogs. In cooperation with other area clubs, GSSA began to host field trials under the auspices of the American Sighthound Field Association (ASFA) and now hosts other performance events, in addition to its lure-coursing field trials, organized practices, and demonstrations. The club uses several locations in Monmouth County for events, and has hosted events in Hunterdon and Burlington Counties. Probably considered the club "home turf" is Bucks Mill Recreation Area, located in Colts Neck on Bucks Mill Road. GSSA uses this park for monthly practice sessions, training clinics, and multiple race meets. They also hold multiple race meets at Twin Gate Farm, located in Englishtown on Sweetmans Lane. For more information and event details, go to www.gardenstatesighthounds.org.

Horse Park of New Jersey

The 147-acre Horse Park of New Jersey in Stone Tavern, Monmouth County, is the result of a unique state and private partnership, working together to create a world-class equine exhibition facility. Throughout the year, equine events are scheduled for most weekends and many weekdays, including frequent multi-day events. Food vendors are on site during show days. And, as horse folks are all animal-friendly, dogs are welcome to come watch. If your dog is comfortable around horses, you can have a lot of fun at these events, which include Arabian, Quarter Horse, and Palomino shows as well as dressage, show jumping, and driving events. For an events calendar and directions, go to www.horseparkofnewjersey.com.

Overnights

Turkey Swamp Park Campground

Dogs are allowed at this county park and can even enjoy camping with you. With more than sixty-four wooded campsites, your dog is sure to find one that has just the right combination of trees. The campground is open from mid-April to November and is located at 66 Nomoco Road in Freehold Township. For more information, go to www.monmouthcountypark.com or call 732-462-7286.

You know you are a dog person when your spouse wants to come back in the next life as one of your dogs.

Burlington County

When American independence was declared in 1776, Burlington County was nearly one hundred years old. During the preceding century, it had grown from tiny hamlets along the Delaware River to the largest county in the state, covering 827 square miles. With more than three hundred years of development and growth, Burlington County offers a glimpse of the founding of our nation, its war for independence, its growth through the industrial revolution, and its struggle in the twenty-first century to preserve its history, farms, and natural resources. With an unmatched variety of towns, from the historic to the artistic to the good ole farming town, several large rivers, a large county park system, huge state forests, and dog-friendly events, Burlington County is a delight to explore.

Dog Day Out

Bordering the Delaware River on the west with a flat, wide-open terrain through to the Pinelands in the east, Burlington County is dotted with quaint riverfront towns, farms, and huge tracts of undeveloped state forests. Dog visitors and their human chauffeurs can enjoy a wide variety of activities. There are plenty of lakes for swimming, miles of trails to explore, and delightful little towns through which to stroll. For details on the county parks, go to the parks page at www.co.burlington.nj.us.

Amico Island

Located on a 55-acre peninsula, this county park gets tail wags and wiggles for its woods, ponds, and, especially, the river shoreline where Rancocas Creek enters the Delaware River. This little park is worth sniffing out for the 2 miles of hiking trails, picnic areas near the pond, and the river beaches. A trail map is posted in the parking area, which is well hidden at the end of Norman Avenue, off Saint Mihel Drive in Riverside.

Batsto Village

For a peaceful day out with your pup, visit Batsto Village, which is a former bog iron and glassmaking industrial center that operated from 1766 to 1867. Wide sand roads meander about the restored village and there are several very nice doggie swim spots near the dam. The village is very dog-friendly. The Batsto Natural Area, which includes Batsto Village, is 8 miles east of Hammonton on CR 542. For more information, go to www.batstovillage.org.

Bordentown Walkabout

A quaint riverfront town located in the northwest corner of the county, Bordentown is the perfect spot for a dog day out. Wide sidewalks, small shops and cafés, gorgeous restored homes, and unique historic sites are just a few of the highlights. Wander the streets and parks before heading back down Farnsworth Avenue for a treat at the bakery or in one of the cafés. For more information, go to www.downtownbordentown.com.

Brendan T. Byrne State Forest

You can follow your dog's wagging tail on 25 miles or more of sandy trails and roads crisscrossing this state forest. Pure, iron-rich streams flow through acres of swampy land covered with dense stands of Atlantic white cedar. A large section of the Batona Trail cuts through the park with plenty of trail intersections that provide 6- to 14-mile loops for super-hound hikes. Near the forest office, there are shorter loops on wide, easy-walking paths, including the 1-mile Pakim Pond loop. If it is just too darn hot to hike, there are several picnic areas with table and grills located throughout the park. Trail maps are available at the park office, which is a mile south of the Routes 70 and 72 intersection.

The Batona Trail is almost 50 miles in length and links Brendan T. Byrne, Wharton, and Bass River State Forests. Although dogs may not use the trail for overnights (all the camping areas are in state parks or forests), the Batona Trail is well maintained by the New Jersey State Park Service and the Batona Hiking Club and makes an excellent dog hike. Additional information can be found at http://members.aol.com/batona/.

Canoe Trips

Escape for the day to the Pinelands and treat your pooch to a canoe trip down one of the many rivers, including the Bass, Oswego, Wading, Batsto, and Mullica. Many of the canoe rental companies are dog-friendly and offer a variety of trips from two-hour easy paddles to all-day excursions. Kayak policies vary. Please remember to call ahead and check current policy.

Adams Canoe Rental. In Vincetown at 1005 Atsion Road, 609-268-0189.

Bel Haven Canoes. In Green Bank at 1227 CR 542, 609-965-2205, www.belhavencanoe.com.

Pine Barrens Canoe and Kayak. In Chatsworth at 3260 CR 563, 609-726-1515, www.pinebarrenscanoe.com.

Freedom Park

Four paws up! This Medford Township park has ball fields, playgrounds, and a paved walking path but your dog is going to zoom directly to the *dog run*. With acres of running space, a creek, and a nature trail in the fenced area, this is probably one of the nicest dog parks in the state. The park is on Union Street, across from Allen Road in Medford. From exit 34 on I-295, go east about 8.5 miles on Route 70. Make a right onto Jones Road and then a left on Union Street. The dog park is near the Pinelands Library.

Mount Laurel Acres Park

Located on the walking path in the middle of the park, the Mount Laurel Township *dog park* has two fenced areas, one for small dogs and one for large. The park also has a paved path for addition paws-ercise. Mount Laurel Acres Park has entrances on Church Street and Union Mills Road.

Mount Holly Walkabout

Originally named "Bridgetown," back when travelers used multiple bridges to cross the Rancocas Creek, this quaint town is a lovely place for a pup stroll. With wide sidewalks, historic sites, small shops and cafés, and long tree-lined streets dotted with beautifully restored mansions, it is a pleasure just to wander slowly with your furry friend. The town also hosts special events that vary every year. Parking is available in municipal lots scattered about town. For more information, go to www.mainstreetmountholly.com.

One of the permanent events is held on the fourth Saturday of every month. Local artisans gather in Mount Holly for the Rancocas Craft Show. Displays are set up in the Park Drive municipal lot. Well-mannered dogs are always welcome to come browse.

Neshaminy State Park (PA)

Just across the Delaware River in Pennsylvania, this 330-acre state park is along the Delaware River in lower Bucks County and gets its name from Neshaminy Creek, which joins the Delaware at this point. The park has swimming pools, picnic pavilions, two boat launches, and a marina. Your dog may appreciate checking out the 4 miles of marked trails. Try the River Walk Trail. At the intersection of State Road and Dunks Ferry Road, the park is easily reached from Route 13.

Penn State Forest

Located on the east side of Wharton State Forest, this lesser-known park has miles of sand roads for easy, long hikes and the 92-acre Lake Oswego for variety. Dog visitors find this park, with over 3,000 acres of undeveloped forest, well worth the drive, particularly on crisp winter days. The easiest access to the park is at Lake Oswego. From Route 206 in Vincentown, go east on CR 532 for 11 miles and then south on New Gretna-Chatsworth Road. Follow signs to Lake Oswego.

Rancocas State Park

The Rancocas Creek area is a popular spot for local dog walkers. There are marked and unmarked hiking trails throughout the 1,200-acre park. Please do not enter or hike through the New Jersey Audubon Society lands since dogs are not allowed in the nature preserve. From exit 45 on I-295, go a mile east on Rancocas Road. Access is at the gravel lot near the entrance to the Powhaten Indian Reservation or from a small township park along Rancocas Boulevard on the south side of the park.

Riverfront Promenade

The historic city of Burlington has a woof-wonderful dog walk along the Delaware River. Known as the Riverfront Promenade, the brick and paved path runs along the river from the bridge to the west end of town. With a cool breeze blowing off the water, lots of river traffic, and plenty of large trees, your dog can stroll in the summer heat or strut his stuff on a brisk winter day. Then for pooch pampering, go into town a few blocks to High Street and buy your pal an ice cream treat or a more substantial snack from one of cafés. There is a large gravel parking lot at the end of High Street.

One of the most common creatures in folklore and legend is the black dog. This fearsome animal is usually encountered along lonely tracks, at ancient crossroads, in churchyards, or at old bridges. Occasionally, the black dog is helpful and friendly, but most often a chilling portent of bad luck, ill health, and death. One such legend surrounds the city of Burlington and the pirate Blackbeard. According to local lore, Blackbeard hauled his crew ashore one dark, stormy night to dig a deep pit under a black walnut tree in which to hide his treasure. Once the deed was done, Blackbeard shot a hapless crewman and buried him upright along with a black dog to guard the chests. The black dog, it is said, was unhappy with the assigned task and haunted the area on stormy nights for many, many years. Blackbeard never returned for his treasure but Robert Louis Stevenson used much of the story in a little book called Treasure Island.

- From May through October, look for the farmers market at High Street and Pearl Boulevard for a seasonal selection of homegrown fruits, vegetables, and flowers. Baked goods are also available.

Silver Lake County Park (PA)

Just a few miles into Pennsylvania is Silver Lake County Park. Easy to find from Route 13 in Bristol, this 460-acre Bucks County park has miles of paved walking trails around the lake and picnic areas scattered about. With so much to explore, your dog is sure to vote paws-up for a jaunt across the river. The closest park entrance is on Bath Road in Bristol.

Smithville Park

This park is the centerpiece of the Burlington County Parks System and gets four paws up from dog visitors. With an intriguing past preserved in Historic Smithville, this 280-acre park also has picnic areas, the 22-acre Smithville Lake, and 4.4 miles of wonderful trails, including a 600-foot floating trail on the lake, which either confounds or delights most dogs. Growing from a typical, small mill operation on the Rancocas Creek to a major industrial plant employing hundreds of workers in its shops and yards, Smithville was also a model industrial town, with advanced town planning, sustainability, and a focus on workers' rights and welfare. Today, this picture-perfect park offers hours of dog adventures whether your pup needs to swim, run, hike, or just laze about begging for grilled hot dogs. Park maps are available at all parking areas. Entrances are located on Railroad Road and Smithville Road, just east of Mount Holly.

Sculpture Garden

The Burlington County College Sculpture Garden at the Pemberton Campus has been in existence since 1988. Supported by the college and several Burlington County organizations, the Sculpture Garden was originally intended to showcase the works of local artists, but in recent years its scope has expanded. Sculptors are invited to submit works for the annual competition and approximately eight works are selected for each show. The Pemberton Campus is a dog-lightful spot for a stroll with your pooch. It is located at the intersection of Pemberton Parkway and CR 530 and is easily accessible from Routes 38 and 206.

U-Cut Christmas Tree Farms

When the temperature chills and the colors of the day are green and red, it is time to get out and cut your tree or select a special holiday decoration. Many of the tree farms are dog-friendly. For directions and more information on tree farms, go to www.njchristmastrees.org.

Bush Christmas Tree Farm. In Pemberton Township at 312 Magnolia Road.

Chesterfield Christmas Trees. In Bordentown at 193 Chesterfield-Crosswicks Road, 609-298-3234.

Croshaw's Christmas Tree Farm. In Columbus at 26815 Mt. Pleasant Road, 609-298-0477.

Indian Acres Tree Farm. In Medford on Tuckerton Road, 609-953-0087. They also host a craft show in *September* and have pumpkin-picking hayrides in *October*. For more information, go to their website at www.indianacrestreefarm.com.

Jim Alexander's Tree Farm. In Edgewater Park at 1131 Railroad Avenue, 609-877-7976.

Sandy Creek Tree Farm. In Columbus on Route 206, 609-587-1411.

Spruce Goose Tree Farm. In Chesterfield at 194 Bordentown-Georgetown Road, 609-298-2498.

Wading River Christmas Tree Farm. In Washington Township at 12 Turtle Creek Road, 609-965-1601.

Wharton State Forest

Wharton State Forest is the largest single tract of land within the New Jersey State Park System. Throughout Wharton are rivers and streams for canoeing; hiking trails, including a major section of the Batona Trail; miles of unpaved roads; and numerous lakes, ponds, and swamps. With abundant wildlife and miles of uninhabited forest, this is a unique spot in New Jersey. With almost 500 miles of trails and dirt roads, you can explore with your dog for months and never take the same path twice. To get started, use the trails around the park offices in Batsto Village and Atsion. The Batsto Natural Area, which includes Batsto Village, is 8 miles east of Hammonton on CR 542. The Atsion Recreation Area is 8 miles north of Hammonton on Route 206.

Whitesbog

Once a thriving town and one of the largest cranberry farms in the state, the now silent village stands as testimony to a time when agriculture was changing dramatically across the state. Miles of sand roads, streams, ponds, and old cranberry bogs await your hound with lush smells and fascinating new vegetation to explore. Easy walking and a very Fido-friendly staff make this a popular choice for winter walks. The site is undergoing restoration and is leased to the Whitesbog Preservation Trust, which holds several events and fundraisers throughout the year, many of which are dog-friendly. For more information on the village and events sponsored by the Trust, call 609-893-4646 or go to www.whitesbog.org.

One of the fundraisers is a monthly or bimonthly group dog walk. Open to everyone and their dog, the group meets at the General Store before heading off on a morning trek through the park. Distances vary depending on the make-up of each group. Donation requested. Use the Whitesbog calendar for details.

Paw-tacular Shopping

Competition Dog

A unique company that knows the true prize in training dogs is not how many ribbons you win or how many birds you bag but the relationship that develops between you and your dog. This retail store has a wide range of hunting, tracking, and outdoor sports gear for humans and hounds along with a huge selection of specialty treats and holistic foods. The store is located at 703 Stokes Road in Medford. For more information, call 609-654-9950.

Jake's Dog House

This store should come with a warning label for all credit-card-carrying dog owners! An unmatched selection of luscious homemade treats at the Barkery is complimented by a woof-wonderful selection of toys, cool canine accessories, and plenty of dog-people gift items. One of several stores in New Jersey, the Burlington County location is in the Promenade Shops at Sagemore, which is on Route 73 in Marlton. For more information, call 856-797-9944.

While traveling about in Burlington County, you can get pet supplies at:

Petco. In Cinnaminson on Route 130 South, 856-303-0944. In Willingboro at 4318 Route 130 North, 609-877-9711.

Pet Smart. In Mount Laurel at 62 Centerton Road, 856-802-9949. In Moorestown at 1331 Nixon Drive, 856-439-9899.

Pet Valu. In Marlton at Evesham Plaza on Route 70, 856-810-9595. In Mount Holly in Lumberton Plaza on Route 38, 609-702-7228.

Tail-Wagging Training Facilities

Allen's Kennels

This training facility is well known in the Jersey dog community. Classes and seminars are offered in household and competition obedience, agility, rally, and conformation showing. Whether you want to become a competing team or just want to be best pals for life, the staff at Allen's can help. For class schedules and special events, call 856-235-0196 or go to www.allenskennels.com.

Dog Days Camp for Canines

While not exactly a training school, this state-of-the-art dog daycare facility is certainly noteworthy. Open long hours during the week, the staff offers otherwise stuck-at-home pets a chance to run and play all day while their owners are working. The facility is at 19 North Maple Avenue in Marlton. For more information call 856-985-7086 or go to www.dogdaysinc.net.

- On weekends, the building is used for classes held by the Jersey Dog Trainer, who holds puppy and basic obedience classes. Call 856-767-6307 for details.

K-9 Basics (PA)

At their facility located at the Peticote Animal Clinic & Farm in Southampton, Pennsylvania, this dog-training school offers classes and instruction in puppy socialization, basic obedience, agility, and high-end police work including narcotics, tracking, explosives detection, and search and rescue. Courses focus on challenging your dog's mind and body so he can become the relaxed, calm, attentive dog you always wanted. They also have paw-tastic special events throughout the year, like a canine first-aid seminar hosted by American Red Cross instructors. To get class or event schedules, go to www.k9basics.com or call 609-820-3564.

Village Green Farm

Do you have a terrier or dachshund at home that needs a positive outlet for all that pent-up energy? Village Green Farm Earthdog Center, located in Crosswicks, offers a variety of opportunities for you and your dog to discover the fun of working together in the earthdog sport. Terriers and dachshunds have deep-seated hunting instincts that can be validated and shaped in a safe, constructive way in the organized practice and competition of earthdog tests. Earthdog classes are offered at all levels and visitors are welcome to attend. Dogs not competing or practicing should not attend, since the noise and excitement often turns the best-behaved pooch into a lunatic. For class information, go to http://members.aol.com/_ht_a/digm2/homepage.htm.

Best-in-County Events

Mill Race Village Festivals

A variety of small shops and cafés make up this unique village in downtown Mount Holly. Besides strolling through the artisans' shops with your pooch, mark your calendar for one of the special events. In early *May*, the Village holds a Fantasy Tea & Art Faire, turning an ordinary day into the extraordinary. In *October*, you can dust off your dog's favorite costume and take your furry pal to the Witches Ball, the area's best Halloween costume ball. And in *January* you can bring your hound to the Fire & Ice Festival to view the ice carvings. Your dog should probably pass on the chili! For details, go to www.millraceshops.com.

Agility Trial

Burlington County has some of the largest agility trials in the state and the Delaware County Kennel Club hosts one of them at the Lumberton Fair Grounds in Lumberton. It is typically on the second weekend in *April.* Held rain or shine, this two-day event draws almost a thousand agility dogs, so you are sure to see your favorite breed flying over the jumps or zipping through the weave poles. For exact dates, go to www.dckc.org.

Burlington County Animal Alliance Events

Although not directly affiliated with the Burlington County Animal Shelter Center, this private, nonprofit animal advocacy group works to promote adoption of shelter animals and to raise public awareness of the problems. With so many animals to rescue, the volunteers often hold fundraisers, like the annual Doggie Easter Egg Hunt. Usually in *April,* this doggone good fun event is held at the shelter and includes Easter Bunny photos. They also participate in the Burlington County Earth Fair in Mount Holly. This one-day event is held in *April* at historic Smithville Park on Rancocas Creek. Come out and socialize with the foster dogs and cats, visit the K-9 kissing booth, do some shopping, and have a whole lot of fun. Another local favorite is the *October* Howl-o-ween Day, which includes a pet costume contest and photos. The Burlington County Shelter is located at 35 Academy Drive in Westhampton. For a calendar of events, call 609-265-5073 or go to www.bcaaofnj.org.

From the very young to the very old, pets bring joy to our lives. They offer unconditional love, warmth, trust, and friendship. Unfortunately, there are still more animals than homes. A small way to help is by purchasing animal welfare license plates. These special plates support the animal population control program run by the state. For more information call 888-486-3339 or go to www.state.nj.us/mvc/cit_plates/ani_friendly.htm.

Burlington County Kennel Club Events

One of the largest and most active dog-training clubs in the state, it holds fourteen events a year, including conformation, obedience, agility, herding, and tracking trials. All events are held in Burlington County or just over the river in Pennsylvania. The club also offers show-handling classes and has club member events throughout the year. For membership information or an event calendar, go to www.bckc.org.

Agility Trials. On the last weekend in *April,* this club hosts a two-day AKC agility trial at the Lumberton Fairgrounds on the CR 541 Bypass in

Lumberton. In *October*, the agility community joins the Burlington Kennel Club at their annual, two-day trial held at Mill Creek Park in Willingboro. Both events are outdoors.

Herding Trials. Held twice a year, in the middle of *May* and the middle of *September*, these two-day AKC events test dogs on ducks or sheep and are open to all AKC-recognized herding breeds. The events are held at Dog Hollow, 67 Springs Brook Road in Shamong.

All-Breed Show and Obedience Trial. The club's AKC all-breed conformation show and obedience trial are held in early *June* (or late May) at the Middletown Grange Fairgrounds, which are in Wrightstown, Pennsylvania. This two-day event is hosted in conjunction with the Huntingdon Valley Kennel Club.

Field Trial

The fields and woods of the English Setter Club facility in Medford are a popular site for AKC-sanctioned field trials. On the second weekend in *April*, the Vizsla Club of America holds their two-day trial.

New Jersey Beanfield Earthdog Club

Terriers have traditionally been dogs that "go to ground" after their prey. Earthdog trials are a series of events that test the dog's instincts for quarry and his determination to get his prey. No animals are harmed during an earthdog trial. The New Jersey Beanfield Earthdog Club holds regular trials at Village Green Farm in Crosswicks in late *May* and early *November*. For details, go to http://members.aol.com/greybrndle/njbeindex.html.

One of the world's most famous terriers is Toto from The Wizard of Oz. *Toto was a Cairn terrier whose real name was "Terry." And, even though Toto was referred to as a "he" in MGM's classic film, Toto was really a "she."*

Bordentown Events

In early *May* the Downtown Bordentown Association sponsors an annual Iris Festival and Art Show in the downtown area and in early *October* the town hosts the Cranberry Festival, complete with an arts and crafts show, music, vintage car show, and a Miss Cranberry Pageant. Well-mannered dogs are always welcome, although they are not eligible for the beauty pageant!

Burlington County Farm Fair

Held in late *July* at the Lumberton County Fairgrounds, this agricultural event is guaranteed to tempt the farm kid in anyone. From pig racing to horse shows to the standard 4-H events, this fair is fun for the whole family. Dogs can shine at their own events sponsored by local 4-H clubs with pet shows, Seeing Eye dog demonstrations, and more. For dates and details, go to www.burlcofarmfair.com.

City of Burlington

Fur-sure, you and your dog can enjoy some of the woof-abulous events held by the city of Burlington. The focus of these events is the historic district and the Riverfront Promenade. For specifics, go to the events calendar at www.tourburlington.org.

Summer Concert Series. Held weekly in *July* and *August*, the outdoor concerts at the Promenade Bandstand feature a range of musicians from jazz to big band. Come tune in the ears and enjoy the evening with your pooch, although you might want to ascertain his taste in music first—no howling allowed!

Festival of Lights. This all-day event is held in late *August* and is fun for the whole family, including those with four feet. During the day, the focus is on the street in the form of entertainment, dining, and shopping. Once dusk falls, the concert begins in the park and the illuminated boat parade starts down the river. The people event culminates with a fireworks display, so be sure to take your dog home a bit early.

Wood Street Fair Crafts & Art Show. This open-air street fair in the historic district has juried craft vendors, an art show, food vendors, street entertainment, fire and rescue demonstrations, and authentic period soldier encampments. Bring out the hound and walk a few blocks and enjoy the sights, sounds, and smells of an old-fashioned street fair together on the first Saturday after Labor Day in *September*.

Medford Township Events

The little town of Medford has a nice variety of events that get tails wagging. It is a dog-friendly town and many of the events are held at Kirby's. This mill was the last operating commercial mill in the state of New Jersey and is at 175 Church Street. For event details, look on the Special Events page or through the town Calendar at www.medfordtownship.com.

Summer Movies. Bring your chairs and/or blankets and join in the family fun on Tuesday evenings from late *June through August*. The movies are geared for families so you will not have to cover your dog's eyes or ears! Show times begin at dusk in Cranberry Park, which is behind the Municipal Center at 17 North Main Street.

Country Day at the Mill. Visit Kirby's Mill in the middle of *July* for a fun-filled afternoon. See the mill and sawmill in operation, displays of farm equipment, blacksmithing and coopery, basket and broom making, open-hearth cooking, a Civil War encampment, and carriage rides with Clydesdale horses.

Art Show & Sale. On the first Sunday in *August*, historic Kirby's Mill is the site of this annual event sponsored by the Medford Historical Society, featuring the work of many of the area's finest artists. Artists are welcome to set up without advance notice and well-mannered dogs are welcome to browse.

Apple Festival. In early *October*, Kirby's Mill hosts an apple festival in conjunction with the Main Street Scarecrow Contest. This is an all-day event, usually the second Saturday of the month.

Halloween Parade. The Rotary sponsors a family Halloween Parade down Main Street. It is usually the last Saturday evening before Halloween in *October*.

Valenzano Winery Harvest & Music Festival

Local craft vendors and jazz performers combine to set the stage for this *September* festival. With entertainment and gourmet food to complement the wine, a feast is available for everyone. Well-mannered dogs are welcome. The Valenzano Winery is located in Shamong. For more information, go to www.valenzanowine.com.

Cranberry Festival

In the middle of *October*, you can bring your dog to Chatsworth for this festival, which is a celebration of New Jersey's cranberry harvest, the third largest in the United States, and offers a tribute to the Pine Barrens and its culture. Held in the downtown area, the main attraction is the diverse showing of artists and crafters, antique dealers, and cranberry bog tours. For more information, go to www.cranfest.org.

Autumn in Moorestown

Sponsored by the Moorestown Business Association (MBA), Autumn in Moorestown is held on the third Saturday in *October* and is an arts and craft show, along with antiques, classic cars, pumpkin painting, and scarecrows. It is held on Main Street, a quaint, tree-lined street at the heart of the town's historic business district. For more information, go to www.moorestown.com.

Agility Trial

The Petit Basset Griffon Vendeen (PBGV) Association hosts one of the longest-running AKC agility trials in the state. Held every year in late *October*, this event brings out the agility dogs—no matter what the weather. It is a two-day event and is held at Mill Creek Park on Beverly-Rancocas Road in Willingboro.

West Jersey Volunteers for Animals

This local shelter holds a wide variety of fundraising events throughout the year, including yard sales, Easter Bunny pictures, and bowling nights. For details on up-coming events, go to the shelter web page at http://members.petfinder.org/~NJ75/.

Whitesbog Events

The Preservation Society hosts a variety of events, including the annual Blueberry Festival in late *June* and a monthly dog walk. Whitesbog is a dog-friendly village and you are welcome to bring along your four-footed pal to many of the events. For details, go to www.whitesbog.org.

Woodedge Stables

This large, private stable in Moorestown hosts a variety of "horsey" events and shows throughout the year. A premier training facility, the club also sponsors several three-day shows at the Horse Park in New Jersey. The stable grounds are large, horse people are very friendly, and dogs are always welcome at their events. The stable is on Borton Landing Road, just a mile or so from exit 40 on I-295.

Overnights

Wading Pines Camping Resort

This campground is in Chatsworth at 85 Godfrey Bridge Road. The campground is right on the Wading River and they have canoe and kayak rentals available. For more information, call 888-726-1313 or go to www.wadingpines.com.

You know you are a dog person when your idea of the ultimate present has a cold nose and a furry body versus a warm engine and metal body.

Ocean County

Stretching along the Atlantic Coastal Plain in central New Jersey, Ocean County is the second largest in the state in terms of size and one of the last New Jersey counties formed, Union being last. Ocean County was created from lands divided from Monmouth County in 1850. For much of its early history, the county was a rural center of agriculture and fishing. It was not until the latter part of the 1800s and early 1900s that the resort industry of the New Jersey shore was developed. In recent years, the county's growth has continued as people retire away from the more industrial areas to the north. Despite the large growth in population, Ocean County maintains a vast amount of protected open space—both land and water. In between the rivers and inlets and along the coast are quaint shore towns, immense state forests, and lots of dog-friendly folks.

Dog Day Out

Finding a way to spend the day with your pooch is a simple matter in Ocean County. Quaint towns and beachfront resorts are plentiful. There is a howling good county park system, a few first-rate state parks for canine explorations and even bigger adventures, and two of the best dog parks in the state. You may actually have to work hard to choose where to go since your dog will want to do them all. For more information on any of the county parks, go to www.oceancountygov.com.

Barnegat Lighthouse State Park

The Barnegat Lighthouse on the northern tip of Long Beach Island in Ocean County guided vessels bound to and from New York along the New Jersey coastline. Today, picnic tables are located along Barnegat Inlet, where visitors can relax over a picnic lunch and observe the waterway. There are no trails but visitors who enjoy getting sand between their toes can poke about the area along the jetty. From Route 72 in Ship Bottom, go north on Long Beach Boulevard and then left onto Broadway. The park entrance is on the right.

Bay Head Walkabout

There is something special about Bay Head! It is a charming little town, with plenty of stores to explore, eateries to snack through, and blocks of Victorian houses to gaze at. They also have a healthy dog community and are very dog-friendly. In fact, if you can carry your pooch, many of the art and gift stores are happy to have your dog shop with you. Municipal parking lots are scattered here and there.

Beach Haven Walking Tours

Beach Haven boasts a historical district with Victorian seaside houses from Third to Pearl and from Seaside to Bay Avenue. This area also contains the Long Beach Island Historical Museum, the Surflight Theater, and Veterans Bicentennial Park. Notable historic sites are marked with a white plaque inscribed in blue all through the downtown Victorian district. If you and your pooch want a guide, tours leave the museum Tuesday and Friday mornings. Call 609-492-3885 for details.

- A bit further south, you can strut your pup's stuff through the shops and eateries at Bay Village and Schooner's Wharf. Located at Ninth and Bay Avenues, these stores and restaurants provide a little of everything. Do not forget to stop by Buddy's Pet Stop for a special treat for your pal.

Beaches and Boardwalks

There are only a few towns and resort areas in Ocean County that allow dogs on beaches or on the boardwalks. Rules change quickly so watch for signs.

Barnegat Light. Dogs are allowed on the beach from October to April.

Beach Haven. Dogs are allowed on the beach from September (after Labor Day) through mid-May.

Harvey Cedars. Dogs are allowed on the beach from September 15 through April 30.

Lavallette. Dogs are never allowed on the beach—ocean or bayside. They are allowed on the boardwalk from mid-September to mid-May.

Long Beach Township. Dogs can be on the beach from October 2 to April 30.

Ship Bottom. Dogs are allowed on the beach—both ocean and bay—from October 1 through April 30. They can be on the bayside boardwalk anytime.

Berkeley Island

This county park is situated on a scenic peninsula jutting out into the calm waters of Barnegat Bay. It provides one of the best views of the bay in Ocean

County. Dogs are not allowed on the beach, but are welcome in the park. From Route 9 in the little town of Lanoka Harbor, go east onto Harbor Inn Road, north on Neary Avenue, and east on Brennan Concourse.

Cattus Island

The unspoiled, natural beauty of Cattus Island is sure to appeal to dogs as well as humans. This 500-acre county park has 6 miles of marked trails for your hound to roam about or you can walk a few miles along the fire roads. Seventy percent of the park consists of salt marshes and the Red Trail has a long boardwalk crossing the wetlands. The sand roads are all multi-use trails but the hiking trails are for pedestrians (two-footed or four-) only. For steamy summer days, there are picnic areas with grills, for hot dogs of course. From Route 27 in Toms River, take Fischer Boulevard north approximately 3 miles to Cattus Island Boulevard.

Colliers Mills Wildlife Management Area

The dog-training and exercise area is off CR 539, just east of New Egypt. It is on the north side of Success Lake, which is in the middle of the south area. Due to the lake, this is a popular spot for field trainers to work their dogs. From I-195, go southwest on CR 537 and then due south on Hawkins Road. The park office is near Colliers Mills and the gravel road to the dog-training area goes east from the lake. Remember—hunting is allowed in all WMAs and seasons extend from September to March.

Double Trouble State Park

Originally a cranberry farm and packing plant, the former company town, called Double Trouble, consists of cranberry bogs and fourteen historic structures dating from the late nineteenth century through the early twentieth century. Preservation efforts are just getting underway and most of the buildings are closed. Never mind, though, since the park features 7,336 acres of Pine Barrens habitat with over 12 miles of wide sand trails crisscrossing the forests, running along the river, and looping around the dry cranberry bogs. Paws prance and bodies wiggle for hiking here! Furthermore, Cedar Creek is an excellent stream for canoeing and kayaking and, of course, dog swimming. There is a very nice swimming hole at the bridge, about a quarter mile walk from the parking lot. For dry feet, the Nature Trail is a 1.5-mile, self-guided loop along a wide sand path that tours the village, saw mill, Cedar Creek, and cranberry bogs. There are no picnic facilities here. From the Garden State Parkway South, take exit 80, turn left off the exit ramp, and go south on Double Trouble Road about 4 miles. The park entrance is well marked.

Eno's Pond County Park

Paw stretches are delightful at this 23-acre county park. Eno's Pond and the surrounding area, with picnic tables and nature trails, make a refreshing dog stop. Located in Lacey Township, the park is on Lacey Road, east of Route 9.

The Grove at Shrewsbury

This elegant collection of thirty stores and restaurants is surrounded by lovely gardens. Stop for a bit of window shopping and saunter about with your pooch. The shops are on Route 35 in Shrewsbury.

Island Beach State Park

Arroowah! After the first visit, your dog is sure to howl for beach trips. Probably my dogs' favorite state park, Island Beach is a narrow barrier island stretching for 10 miles between the restless Atlantic Ocean and the historic Barnegat Bay. Over 3,000 acres and 10 miles of coastal dunes have remained almost untouched since Henry Hudson first described New Jersey from his ship in 1609. The park is split into the Southern and Northern Natural Areas, with access to portions of the Northern Natural Area being restricted to people using foot power. In the Southern Natural Area, however, dogs are allowed on the beach all year! From mid-June to Labor Day, dogs are not supposed to be in the lifeguard-protected bathing areas so go a little further south and enjoy a picnic on the beach or a swim in the surf with your furry friend. These areas are also open to cars and equestrians. Take Route 37 east to Route 35 south to the park entrance.

Ocean County Park

Originally part of financier John D. Rockefeller's vacation estate, this magnificent facility in Lakewood is a 323-acre park with a swimming beach, open fields, walking paths, and picnic areas. With its stately forests and lovely lakes, Ocean County Park offers activities all year round. Although there is no formal trail system, there are plenty of open fields, low-traffic roads, and paths connecting the facilities on which to get some decent paws-ercise. If you just want a short stroll, there is a sand path around the lake. Your dog, however, is going to whine for the *dog park*, which is about 4 acres with ample parking for everyone. There is a separate small-dog-only area that is mostly wooded with picnic tables for quiet time. The main area is open to any dog and has a wonderful mix of open field and woods. It also has a walking trail through the woods, running water, and during the summer a baby pool is provided for water-loving pooches. It is a woof-wonderful park with a very large, active dog community. To use either Ocean County dog park, you must purchase an Ocean County permit and male dogs must be neutered to receive a pass. For all the rules and details on purchasing an annual permit, go to www.co.ocean.nj.us/parks. The park entrance is on Route 88 in Lakewood.

8. Coconut and her mom spend a warm spring morning at the beach.

❖ While you are in the area, check out Lake Shenandoah County Park. The park entrance is across Route 88. Tall oaks and pines surround the gorgeous 100-acre Lake Shenandoah, which is the focal point of this park. There are three piers, one at the boat rental. Dock-jumping dogs and water lovers will find plenty of dog swim spots along the shoreline. The lake is also surrounded by informal trails and there is a picnic area.

Popcorn Park Zoo

Although for health reasons your dog cannot visit Popcorn Park Zoo, it is an animal lover's paradise and worth finding. The zoo was established in 1977 for the sole purpose of providing a refuge for wildlife that were sick, elderly, abandoned, abused, injured, or that could no longer survive in their natural habitat. As time went on, the facility was expanded to include exotic and domestic animals. Over two hundred of these animals and birds now live in spacious surroundings in the heart of the scenic Pine Barrens. The zoo, which is federally licensed, comprises seven acres and is operated by the Associated Humane Societies, which is a full-service humane society operating four animal care centers in New Jersey. From the Garden State Parkway, take exit 74 and go west on Lacey Road for 6.7 miles. Watch for signs to the park, which is on Humane Way.

Robert J. Miller Airpark

Located in the Robert J. Miller Airpark, directly across from the main terminal, this Ocean County off-leash area is an attractive spot for some dog time. With both woods and fields and picnic tables, this is a lovely *dog park* with an active dog community. To use either Ocean County dog run, you must purchase an annual permit, which can be obtained from the Parks & Recreation Division (www.co.ocean.nj.us), and male dogs must be neutered to receive a park pass. To find the park, take exit 77 on the Garden State Parkway southbound and go left onto Double Trouble Road. Make a right at the traffic light onto CR 530 and go about 3 miles to the park, which is on the left.

Stafford Forge Wildlife Management Area

The dog-training and exercise area is just north of the Garden State Parkway, near Tuckerton. It is in the southernmost area of the park, which encompasses almost 16,000 acres. In addition to the dog-training area, there are numerous sand roads crisscrossing the park, all of which make woof-wonderful dog hikes. On winter weekends, my dogs adore taking a break from all the snow and ice for a brisk hike along these roads, which tend to lose the snow quickly. From the Garden State Parkway, go north on CR 539 and make an immediate right onto Forge Road. The dog-training area is on the left, about 2 miles. Remember—hunting is allowed in all WMAs and seasons extend from September to March.

U-Cut Christmas Tree Farms

Wandering through fields of pine and spruce trees is great fun for the dog half of the family too. So put on the hats and gloves, grab the pooch, and go get a tree. Many of the tree farms are dog-friendly. Please do not let your dog "tag" the Christmas trees! For directions and more information on tree farms, go to www.njchristmastrees.org.

Holly Hill Nursery. In Forked River at 2211 Lacey Road, 609-693-5215.
Lone Silo Farm. In New Egypt at 139 Brynmore Road, 609-758-9449.
Yuletide Christmas Tree Farm. In New Egypt at 138 Evergreen Road, 732-349-2705.

Wells Mills

Wells Mills has the distinction of being the largest park in the Ocean County park system, encompassing over 900 acres of pine and oak forest within the Pine Barrens. A true-blue hound paradise, the park has miles of hiking trails with varying degrees of difficulty. It also contains beautiful Wells Mills Lake, with its own trails meandering around it, perfect for a leisurely stroll. Canoe rentals are available at a nominal cost and dogs are allowed. From Waretown, go west on Route 72 a short distance to Route 532 East. Turn right and proceed 3.8 miles to the park entrance on the right.

Winding River Park

This Dover Township park is a tail wagger. For long, peaceful walks with your pooch, there is a 3-mile, paved path winding through the woods along Toms River. Crisscrossing the paved path, there is a dirt trail that meanders deeper into the woods for more adventuresome hounds. Both trails are lightly used and are great for multi-dog walkers and stroller pushers. (Two quick cautions: water access is limited due to the strength of the current in Toms River where it passes through the park, and the field in the center of the park has quite a few cacti.) There is plenty of parking and two entrances. From Route 166 in Toms River, take Whitesville Road west and follow the signs. The southern entrance is on Route 37, a half mile west of the Parkway.

Paw-tacular Shopping

Buddy's Pet Stop and Gift Shop

Located in Schooner's Wharf in Beach Haven, this store has all the basics and some fun stuff thrown in for spoiling your pal or your dog friends. 609-492-8900.

R&R Feed and Pet Supply

For dog food and all the basics, this store in Tuckerton is the place to go. You will find it at 588 Route 9, 609-296-0300.

While traveling about in Ocean County, you can also get pet supplies at:

PETCO. In Toms River at 1331 Hooper Avenue, 732-473-9818.

PET VALU. In Bricktown in Laurel Square on Route 88, 732-836-9550. In Lanoka Harbor at the Lacey Mall, 609-242-1710. In Toms River at the Bay Plaza Shopping Center on Fischer Boulevard, 732-831-0117.

BEST-IN-COUNTY EVENTS

LIGHTHOUSE CIRCUIT ALL BREED DOG SHOW

Held at Robert J. Miller Airpark on CR 530, this AKC conformation show and obedience trial is sponsored by the Sand and Sea Kennel Club. It is usually the first weekend in *April* and runs for two days. All judging is outdoors. Your dog can be in the park. For more information, go to www.geocities.com/sandandseakennelclub.

The first formal dog show, held in 1859 in Newcastle, England, presented an enormous array of dogs and was held as a charity event. It was not until 1873 that the British Kennel Club was established. The American Kennel Club was established in 1884.

LT. LENNY'S 5K AND WAG-YOUR-TAIL TRAIL RUN

This race is held in early *April* in Winding River Park in Dover Township. There is a 5-K race on the paved bicycle trail for runners alone and a 5-K race on the wooded trail for owners with dogs. The event is sponsored by the Dover Township Police Department.

FIELD TRIALS

There are multiple AKC-sanctioned field trials for all the retrieving breeds in the county. All the events are held at the Assunpink Wildlife Management Area in New Egypt or Winslow Farms Conservancy in Winslow. These sites are also used by the Swamp Dog Club and the Long Island Retriever Club for events. For more information on field trials in the area, go to www.working-retriever.com.

SHREWSBURY RIVER RETRIEVER CLUB TRIAL. In *April* the club hosts a three-day trial. They also hold trials at these same locations some years in August and September. For details, go to http://members.aol.com/shrewsburyriver.

SOUTH JERSEY RETRIEVER CLUB TRIAL. In *April* and *September*, this club hosts a very large field trial with almost two hundred dogs competing in the three-day event. You can watch Labrador, golden, and Chesapeake Bay retrievers work at multiple competition levels.

Point Pleasant Street Fair

Usually held the first weekend in *June*, the street fair runs from Bridge Avenue to Beaver Dam Road. The event includes a pet parade, crafters, food vendors, live entertainment, and a whole lot more. For more information, go to www.pointpleasantchamber.com/streetfair.asp.

Art Shows

Ocean County hosts a variety of art and craft shows throughout the year and almost all are dog-friendly. Please note that there are a few exceptions: the Lavallette Juried Arts & Craft Show in early August and the Lavallette Heritage Festival do not allow dogs.

Art in the Park. This one-day show is held in the middle of *June*. It is a well-established art show with fifty local artists, a few demonstrations, music, and food at nearby shops and restaurants. The art show is in Centennial Park, just off Bridge Avenue in Bay Head. Specific event information can be found at www.bayhead.org.

Arts Festival. With over sixty professional artists, this show is a major event for the little town of Harvey Cedars, located on Long Beach Island. It is held in the middle of *July* at Sunset Park, on West Salem Avenue. Event details can be found at www.harveycedars.org.

Blue Claw Craft Show. Held the same weekend as the Blue Claw Crab Race, which is truly a crab race, this show is at Sunset Park in the middle of *August*. Visit www.harveycedars.org for more information.

Founders Day Art Fair & Street Festival. Seaside Heights hosts this one-day festival in late *September*. For exact date, check www.artsandcraftshows.net.

Concerts on the Green

Every Wednesday evening throughout the summer months, Beach Haven sponsors a series of concerts at Veterans Bicentennial Park, near Engleside Avenue and Amber Street. Concerts are free so bring a chair and enjoy.

Concerts at the Gazebo

Lavallette sponsors a series of free concerts at the gazebo, located at Philadelphia Avenue and Bay Boulevard. Concerts begin around July Fourth and are held every Sunday evening through Labor Day weekend. Bring your dog's blanket and a chair for yourself.

Music in the Park

Every Wednesday evening in the summer, the small town of Harvey Cedars on Long Beach Island sponsors a free, outdoor concert in Sunset Park. For a concert schedule, go to www.harveycedars.org.

Sounds of Summer

Berkeley Township hosts Tuesday-night concerts in Veterans Park. Concerts are typically scheduled for every other week in July and August. For more information, go to www.soundsofsummer.org.

Jersey Shore Craft Guild Summer Shows

These craft and vendor shows are held in Beach Haven at Bicentennial Park. The first is in *July*, after the big July Fourth weekend, and the second is in late *August*. Look for specialty pet vendors, like Elmo's Closet, who carry the latest, fabulous fabric collars and leashes.

Ocean County Fair

Dogs, horses, pigs, cats, and small pets are all part of the Ocean County 4-H Fair, which is usually held in late *July* at the Ocean County Fairgrounds in Robert J. Miller County Park. Please note that pets are not allowed on the fairgrounds. However, there are canine demonstrations every afternoon, including search & rescue, police, Seeing Eye, and competition dogs. The fair also has several dog shows. All require prior registration so pick up the information and forms before you bring out your dog. Event details are available at www.oceancountyfair.com. The park is on CR 530 in Berkeley Township.

Dogs love ice cream too! Although regular ice cream and frozen treats are not bad for dogs (assuming there is no chocolate and it is served on a limited basis), try this recipe and treat your pooch to a cool treat on hot days.

Frosty Dog Delight

1 qt vanilla yogurt
1 medium banana (ripeness adds flavor)
2 T peanut butter (natural style is better for dogs)
2 T honey

Puree the banana in a food processor or blender. Add the peanut butter and honey and continue processing until smooth. Add yogurt and process just long enough to blend all ingredients together. Place eighteen small paper cups (bathroom size) in a baking or pie pan and fill to about two-thirds full. Freeze until solid. Serve for tail wags.

New Jersey Ice Cream Festival

The annual New Jersey State Ice Cream Festival is in Toms River in late *July*. The festival runs along Washington Street between Hooper and Main Streets. For a small fee, you and your furry pal can taste ice cream from eight or nine different vendors and vote for your favorite flavor. The street is also filled with live entertainment, kids' rides, and fun for the entire family—dog included. For more information, call 732-341-8738 or go to www.downtowntomsriver.com.

Irish Festival

In the middle of *August*, you can find the Ancient Order of Hibernians at their annual Irish Festival. This one-day event, featuring traditional music, vendors, crafts, dancing, entertainment, and a food court, is at Veterans Park in Berkeley Township.

Point Pleasant Beach Arts & Crafts

This one-day arts and crafts show is held in *September* near Arnold and Bay Avenues in Point Pleasant Beach.

Manahawkin Good Ol' Days Festival

Over Labor Day weekend in *September*, Stafford Township sponsors a festival in Heritage Park, along the lake. The day's activities include a craft show and sale at Manahawkin Lake Park, featuring over a hundred crafters, all-day entertainment, rides and games for kids, food concessions, and free parking. The evening is capped off with a free drive-in movie at the Manahawkin Plaza on East Bay Avenue. For more information, go to www.staffordnj.gov/recreation/special.php.

Chowderfest

At Bayfront Park in early *October*, you can bring your dog along to enjoy the giant season's-end sale at the annual Chowderfest in Beach Haven. In between shopping excursions, you can devour all the chowder you can eat at the Chowder Cook-off Classic, as local restaurants compete to be the "King of Clams." Event dates can be found at www.discoversouthernocean.com.

Harvest Time in Bay Head

Sponsored by local businesses, this one-day event is in early *October* in downtown Bay Head. A key feature of this event is the Annual Dog Walk, which is usually a short, afternoon walk through the downtown area. You can round out your special dog day at the craft show, with more than forty professional crafters in Centennial Park. Details can be found at www.bayhead.org.

Pine Barrens Jamboree

With "Piney" music ringing through the air and genuine "Piney" crafters and artisans gathered together for food, fun, and friends, you and your dog can come celebrate the traditions of the Pine Barrens every *October*. This one-day event is held at Wells Mills County Park in Waretown. For event details, go to www.co.ocean.nj.us/parks/jamboree.html.

First Friday

Hosted by Toms River, this evening event is held the first Friday of every month, of course. Typically starting around 5 p.m., there is a variety of entertainment and activities in the downtown business district. Free parking is available after 5 p.m. Activities will vary each month in coordination with the seasons and holidays. For details, go to www.downtowntomsriver.com.

- Throughout the year, Toms River has a full calendar of events, including a two-day wooden boat show, annual chili and salsa cook-off, canoe and kayak race, Cruisin' Downtown events, and a Halloween parade. Many of the events are in Huddy Park. The events calendar is at www.downtowntomsriver.com.

Ship Bottom Events

Frequently referred to as the "gateway" to Long Beach Island, Ship Bottom is a dog-friendly spot along the beach so grab a cooler full of ice water and try some of these events on your hound. On Thursday evenings in *July*, the town hosts a series of free concerts on the boardwalk at Tenth Street Waterfront Park. There are also free "drive-in" movies for families to enjoy outdoors. For specific dates and event details, go to the event calendar at www.shipbottom.org.

Overnights

Need to get away for the weekend? Camping at any of these dog-friendly campgrounds can give you plenty of time to seriously spoil your pooch.

Baker's Acres Campground. In Parkertown at 230 Willets Avenue, 609-296-2664, www.bakersacres.com.

Butterfly Camping Resort. In Jackson on Butterfly Road, 732-928-2107, www.butterflycamp.com.

Cedar Creek Campground. In Bayville at 1052 Route 9, 732-269-1413, www.cedarcreeknj.com.

Sea Pirate Campground. In West Creek on the bay side of Route 9, 609-296-7400, www.sea-pirate.com.

You know you are a dog person when you sit on the floor if the dog got the chair first.

Camden County

Many of the early settlers in West Jersey (modern-day South Jersey) were Quakers, members of the Society of Friends who were persecuted in England for their religious beliefs and way of life. It took almost two hundred years after these first settlements were established before Camden County was created from Gloucester County. By the end of the nineteenth century, however, Camden had emerged as an industrial and commercial leader in the state. Today, the county covers 222 square miles, has thirty-seven municipalities, and is an eclectic landscape of old industrial areas and quaint historic towns. Pets and their people can find plenty to do and enjoy in the parks and towns.

Dog Day Out

Whether you want to stroll along the Delaware River, watch the rowing races on Cooper River, or just window shop through historic Haddonfield, your dog is sure to enjoy a day out in Camden. Many of the towns are slowly reclaiming defunct industrial sites and turning them into recreation areas. All in all, you might be surprised by what this county has to offer. Go to www.co.camden.nj.us for more information.

Challenge Grove

Located between Maria B. Greenwald and Wallworth Parks, this 17-acre park has a large picnic area, playground, and paved paths connecting all the facilities. Although not large itself, this park makes a good starting point for dogs that need a truly long walk. Heading north, then east through Greenwald Park and on to Cooper River Park, you can walk your pup all the way to Route 130, for a solid 8-mile round trip. The parking lot is just off Route 41, a mile south of Route 70 in Cherry Hill.

Cooper River Park

Tucked into the neighborhoods of Collingswood and Cherry Hill, Cooper River Park has a loop of paved paths and green lawns for tail-wagging walks, jogs, or lazy hours spent watching the rowing teams on the lake. Following along the curves of Cooper River, the 3 miles of trails are mostly in the open, making this a good dog walk at all times of the year. (Please note that for traffic-shy or really rambunctious dogs, you should plan your walk for the south side of the park because the path on the north side runs very close to the road.) There are also four picnic areas and a large playground, which guarantees kids should you be socializing a puppy. For a long ramble, use this park and the connecting Maria Greenwald Park. And you definitely do not want to miss the *dog park*. Camden County's leash-free pooch park is also located here. It has two enclosed runs with dog bowl fountains for the summer months. The runs are rated for dogs under thirty pounds and over thirty pounds. Both are located at the east end of North Park Drive, which is a great parking area for dog walkers, although a bit isolated. Additional parking areas are scattered along North Park Drive and South Park Drive, on either side of Cuthbert Boulevard, about a block south of Route 70.

Haddon Lake Park

Located on both sides of Kings Highway in Haddon Heights, this 79-acre county park is a favorite with local dog walkers. Almost 2 miles of paved paths run along Haddon Lake and Kings Run, providing lots of exercise time for four-footed family beasts. With landscaped gardens and three picnic areas, it is also a tail-wagging good place for a short stroll or a picnic lunch in the summer heat. Navigators will be happy to know that the park is easy to find. From exit 28 on I-295, it is less than a mile north on Route 168 to the turn onto Kings Highway. Parking is along North Park Avenue in the park.

A yip from Milan Kundera, "Dogs are our link to paradise. They don't know evil or jealousy or discontent. To sit with a dog on a hillside on a glorious afternoon is to be back in Eden, where doing nothing was not boring—it was peace."

Historic Haddonfield

Established in the early 1700s by Quakers, Haddonfield quickly became the center of commerce for the large, successful farms of south Jersey. Farmers came to town for all the necessities, while farm produce and animals supplied the growing needs of nearby Philadelphia. Today, the town's historic core, at the intersection of Haddon Avenue and Kings Highway, is listed on the National Register of Historic Places, and the wide sidewalks make it a woof-wonderful place to poke around with your pooch. Historic homes and businesses mingle with cafés and specialty stores for delightful window shopping and you can spoil your pup with a treat at one of the bakeries or coffee shops. And your dog will not want to miss an opportunity to shop for himself at Velvet Paws. Municipal parking lots are conveniently located throughout town. For more information, go to www.haddonfieldnj.org.

9. Kayla did some window shopping at Velvet Paws before going inside.

Maria B. Greenwald Park

The paved loop through Cooper River Park connects to the 1.2-mile paved path through this park, which in turn connects at the east end to Challenge Grove Park. The healthy squirrel population amused my hounds as we "strolled" in undignified leaps and bounds along the trail. There is also a 1.8-mile nature trail with a dirt surface that crisscrosses the paved path. This 47-acre Camden County Park is one block south of Route 70 in Cherry Hill. Parking is only available along Park Boulevard.

New Brooklyn Park

Located in Winslow Township, this large 758-acre county park encompasses New Brooklyn Lake, which is fed by the Great Egg Harbor River. With playgrounds, picnic areas, a 1.2-mile paved path, and a network of unmarked trails, your dog can shake off the house dust and enjoy the woods, soak in the lake, or just loosen up muscles bouncing around. From exit 8 on the Atlantic City Expressway, go north 1.5 miles on Williamstown-New Freedom Road and then make a right onto New Brooklyn Road. Follow the park signs.

Newton Lake Park

With 73 acres stretched out on both sides of Newton Lake, this county park provides all its canine visitors with plenty of space to stretch their paws, chase a few ducks, or just collect ear scratches from other park visitors. The paved path runs almost 2 miles along Newton Lake, passing picnic tables, playgrounds, and quiet green lawns. The park is located in Collingswood. Parking is only available along Lakeshore Drive, just off Cuthbert Boulevard.

U-Cut Christmas Tree Farms

When the temperature chills and the leaves are gone, it is time to get out and cut your tree or find a special holiday decoration. Many of the tree farms are Fido-friendly. For directions and more information on tree farms, go to www.njchristmastrees.org.

Culbertson's Nursery. In Atco at 672 Burnt Mill Road, 856-767-3221.
Lucca's Christmas Tree Farm. In Berlin at 133 Penbryn Road, 856-767-0189.

Wiggins Waterfront Park

Bring your dog out and let her strut her stuff along the Promenade in Camden's Waterfront Park. This 51-acre county park connects Campbell Field to the battleship *New Jersey* and offers dog visitors a nice spot to prowl along the Delaware River, with benches and bits of grass for quiet-time hugs and tummy scratches from their favorite human. Parking is available at the end of Mickle Boulevard. Follow signs for the State Aquarium.

Paw-tacular Shopping

Bill's Wonderland of Pets

If you need to restock while in the area, this pet supply store carries all the basics from leashes to dog food and is conveniently located at 600 White Horse Pike in Somerdale, 856-435-0800.

Velvet Paws

With treats and toys for your dog and a huge selection of gift items for every one of your dog friends, this store should not be missed by dog lovers or their dogs, who are welcome to come browse for themselves. The store is located in Historic Haddonfield at 107 Kings Highway East, 856-428-8889.

While traveling about in Camden County, you can also get pet supplies at:

Petco. In Pennsauken at 7024 Kaighns Avenue, 856-662-9692.
Pet Smart. In West Berlin at 215 Route 73 North, 856-753-9130. In Cherry Hill at 2135 Route 38, 856-910-1400.
Pet Valu. In Cherry Hill at 1469 Brace Road, 856-216-8455. In Laurel Springs in the Marketplace at Chews Landing, 856-309-1430. In Sicklerville at Winslow Plaza on Berlin Cross Keys Road, 856-629-3940.

Tail-Wagging Training Facilities

Camden County College

Offered through the Continuing Education Department of Camden County College, the Animal-Assisted Therapy (AAT) course teaches people how to use animals to help nursing home and hospital residents, the elderly, physically disabled and emotionally disturbed children, and others with special needs. Classes meet on Saturdays and include two lectures on planning and organizing AAT programs and field trips to see AAT in operation. The course is offered each year in the fall. For more information contact Camden County College or go to www.animaltherapy.net.

Tests have shown that owning a pet can help people attain a better level of physical and mental health. Petting your dog can lower your heart rate and your blood pressure, and even promote healing. Research has also shown that dog owners who suffered a heart attack had a better survival rate one year later than people without pets. Whether these health benefits are the result of your bond with your dog or the extra exercise you get through walks and visits to the park is not clear, but does it really matter? We know our lives are richer because we share them with our dog. I wonder if anyone has studied the benefits of having multiple dogs?

Wonder Dogs

With some of the best trainers in south Jersey on staff, this facility offers classes for everyone, whether you have a rambunctious puppy or a competitive hound on your hands. Group classes are run all year in household obedience, competitive obedience, rally, agility, flyball, and conformation showing. Check the events calendar for seminars on canine freestyle, behavior issues, and competitive matches. Located at 424D Kelley Drive in West Berlin. Call 856-767-6464 or go to www.wonderdogs.com for additional information.

Best-in-County Events

Obedience Trial

The best of the obedience dogs in the tri-state area trek to Camden County College in Blackwood for the Lower Camden County Dog Training Club obedience trial, held annually on the last weekend in *March.* During the one-day event, almost two hundred dogs compete on three levels. Admission charged.

Mid-Jersey Labrador Retriever Club

Although this very active club is not actually located in Camden, they do hold several of their annual events in the county. The club holds a variety of events, including a large match (practice show) in *April* in Cooper River Park and they have an AKC hunt test, just one of about five in New Jersey, in *September* at Blue Springs Kennel in Winslow. If you are a "Lab" person, this organization is definitely worth checking out. For more club information or specifics on events, go to www.mjlrc.org.

Cooper River Races

Every spring from April through June, Cooper River hosts multiple rowing events and races, including the National Collegiate Championships in early June. For a lazy few hours on the riverbank, bring your dog out to watch one of the races or catch the teams on a practice day. For an event schedule, go to www.cooperrowing.org.

Paws & Feet Walkathon and 5K Race

Held in the middle of *May* in Cooper River Park, this Animal Welfare Association (AWA)–sponsored race draws runners with two feet and four. Medals are awarded to people and pups for the 5K race, 5K walkathon, and 1-mile fun walk. For more information on events held by the Animal Welfare Association, go to www.awanj.org or call 856-424-2288.

Collingswood May Fair

Held in *May* along Haddon Avenue in Collingswood, it is a one-day event. For more information, go to www.collingswood.com.

- On Saturdays from May through November, you can also check out the Jersey fresh produce at the Collingswood Farmer's Market, located at Collings and Irvin Avenues.

Jazz Concerts

Wiggins Waterfront Park hosts the Sunset Jazz Series. These outdoor concerts are on Tuesday evenings from late June to mid-August. Bring a blanket big enough for you and your dog and you can scratch your dog's tummy in time to the music. Details can be found on the Camden County Parks events webpage at www.ccparks.com.

Woofstock

The very popular Woofstock is held in the middle of *September* at Lion's Lake Park in Voorhees. The annual event draws thousands of animal lovers for a day of creature fun, including pet contests and demonstrations. It is sponsored by the Animal Orphanage, a nonprofit animal shelter operating in the south Jersey area. This facility does not receive county or state money and yet almost two thousand animals are adopted from the shelter each year. To get all the news and events, go to www.theanimalorphanage.org. For the brave or those just trying to impress their Newfoundland, try the Polar Challenge and see what your dog thinks of your swimming in Sturbridge Lake in *March*!

Merchantville Events

The Main Street Merchantville organization sponsor events throughout the year in the downtown area, which is along Centre Street. All the events are dog-friendly. Bring your dog out for Merchantville's Birthday Celebration and Downtown Street Fair in early *June*. While you are in town, save time to walk through the historic districts, along Chestnut Street and West Maple Avenue. You can also check out the Handcrafts Festival in *October*, when the town hosts handcraft vendors from the tri-state area. It is a day of extraordinary shopping, food, and entertainment in the historic downtown area of Merchantville. For more information, go to the town website at www.merchantvillenj.com.

Haddonfield Festivals

Not only a delightful place to visit, Haddonfield also hosts several events that your dog might enjoy. On the second weekend in *July*, the downtown area hosts the two-day Craft & Fine Art Festival, while in the middle of *October* they hold the Fall Festival. For specific dates, go to www.haddonfieldnj.org.

Arktoberfest

With a shelter, therapy program, mobile spay/neuter van, and an overall commitment to educating people about companion animal issues, the Animal Welfare Association (AWA) is truly a blessing to the county and funds are always needed. If you want to help and spend quality time with your pet, check out the AWA events, like Arktoberfest. This fun-filled event is for the whole family and includes demonstrations, canine specialists, adoption groups, pet costume parades, and more. It is held in early *October* at Lion's Lake Park. For more information on Animal Welfare Association events, go to www.awanj.org or call 856-424-2288.

FOCAS Dog Walk

Registered as FOCAS (Friends of Camden Animal Shelter), the Animal Adoption Center was formed in 1990 to try to do something about the animal problem in Camden County. Located in Lindenwold, the group hosts a variety of fundraising events, including an annual dog walk. It is a "dog day" event, usually held the first weekend in *October* in one of the Camden County parks. For details, go to www.animaladoption.com.

You know you are a dog person when you receive a birth announcement, complete with newborn photos, celebrating the arrival of a litter of puppies.

Gloucester County

Founded in 1686, and once including present-day Atlantic and Camden Counties, this is the only county created by the people, rather than the government. In 1686, at a meeting of its proprietors, freeholders, and other inhabitants, the county was organized and a "Constitution of Gloucester County" was established. Now over three hundred years old, the county possesses and preserves its wonderful history in countless historic sites, beautiful parks, and historic towns. Visitors, with their human tag-alongs, are sure to find the eclectic mix of farm, town, and open space a delight.

Dog Day Out

Touring Gloucester County with your dog means more than just parks and lakes. Canine visitor can enjoy the quaint towns, a state university, and acres of wildlife management areas. Unfortunately, dogs are not allowed in any of the county parks, including Greenwich Lake, James Atkinson Memorial, Red Bank Battlefield, and Scotland Run.

Alcyon Lake Park

Once the nation's number one Superfund site, this area is now a park on the west shore of Alcyon Lake. With ball fields and a playground, the 38-acre Pitman town park allows dogs and the walking paths are long enough for some paws-ercise. The park entrance is on Carr Avenue. From Pitman, go west on CR 624 and look for the park on the left.

Glassboro Wildlife Management Area

The dog-training and exercise area is south off Route 322, just east of Glassboro. There are also miles and miles of unmarked trails and sand roads through this WMA. If your dog needs to hound-around rather than stroll on paths, this is definitely the place for him. The dog-training access is on the dirt track, off Route 47, about a mile south of Glassboro. Remember—hunting is allowed in all WMAs and seasons extend from September to March.

From 1953 through 1959, the beagle was America's most popular dog. In fact, since the AKC's inception in 1884, there has never been a time that the beagle was not one of the most popular breeds in this country. Arguably the most famous beagle is Snoopy, who first appeared in Charles Schulz's comic on October 4, 1950. Snoopy never spoke, did not actually walk upright until July of 1959, and had seven siblings, who made random appearances in the comic strip.

MONROE TOWNSHIP BIKEWAY

Need some prolonged pooch-ercise? This multi-purpose, paved path from Williamstown west to Fries Mill Road should do the trick. The 3.5-mile rail-trail can be accessed at Blue Bell Road and at Tuckahoe Road; both are a quarter mile south of Route 322 in Williamstown.

PITMAN WALKABOUT

Pitman is a state historical site. Developed as a summer camp, Pitman Grove is centered around an auditorium, which was built in 1882 for Methodist worship services. Twelve avenues, representing the disciples of Christ, fan out from the auditorium, like spokes on a wheel. Eventually small cottages were built on these avenues and this was the origin of the town. In 1905, Pitman Grove became the Borough of Pitman and the business district migrated a block east to Broadway. Today, Pitman Grove and Pitman are excellent places to tour with your dog. Start your walkabout at Ballard Park, a small township park across from Borough Hall, in downtown Pitman. Pitman Grove is one block west as is Betty Park, which is at the intersection of West Holly and Cedar Avenues. It has playground equipment, picnic tables, and provides water dogs with access to the Alcyon Lake.

ROWAN UNIVERSITY

Nestled beside historic Glassboro, Rowan University's tree-lined campus is just north of town along Mullica Hill Road and Carpenter Street. With forty-three buildings and over nine thousand students, this medium-sized state university is a dog-lightful place to saunter about with your furry pal. College campuses also make great places to toddle about with puppies. Parking permits are required for all campus lots but it is a short walk back to the campus, if you park in town.

U-Cut Christmas Tree Farms

When the leaves are gone and the world is decorated in red and green, it is time to get out and cut your tree. Many of the tree farms are dog-friendly. For directions and more information on tree farms, go to www.njchristmastrees.org.

Belly Acres Christmas Tree Farm. In Franklinville at 665 Royal Avenue, 856-694-0350.

Exley's Christmas Tree Farm. In Sewell at 1535 Tanyard Road, 856-468-5949.

Paw-tacular Shopping

Animal House Pet Supply

Shelf after shelf of premium dog foods and treats can make shopping for your dog's next meal a trifle difficult or truly scrumptious. The knowledgeable staff will help you select the best choice for your hound while she picks out her new toy, bed, and designer collar and leash set. The store is at 1509 Black Horse Pike in Williamstown, 856-629-7869.

Daminger's Country Store

With staff on hand to recommend a premium dog food for your special pal, this store is worth a slight detour. They also carry gourmet treats, cool supplies, and all the basics. It is located at 641 Main Street in Barnsboro, 856-468-0822.

Halo House Animal Resort

Located in Franklinville, this full-service kennel and grooming facility is also a pet health spa. Rather than a new toy, why not treat your pup to a hydrotherapy session with a massage or acupuncture? The pet therapy program has various facets that, when combined, provide healthy conditioning or recovery for your dog. To learn more about the pet therapy program, go to www.halohouseanimalresort.com.

For centuries, people in Nepal have observed an annual "Day of the Dog." They feed all the stray dogs and mark each dog with a red sign on the forehead or decorate them with flower garlands.

Swedesboro Pet Food and Supplies

If you are in western Gloucester County and find yourself in need of supplies, be it dog food or treats for your buddy, this store at 396 Kings Highway in Swedesboro will have what you need. 856-467-8668.

While traveling about in Gloucester County, you can also get pet supplies at:

Petco. In Deptford at 1730 Clements Bridge Road, 856-384-9609.
Pet Smart. In Woodbury at 1800 Clements Bridge Road, 856-853-0042.
Pet Valu. In Mullica Hill at the Mullica Hill Plaza on Bridgeton Pike, 856-223-8709. In Sewell in Mill Pond Village on Egg Harbor Road, 856-582-6612.

Tail-Wagging Training Facilities

A1 Total Control Dog Training Academy

Weekly training sessions are offered by A1 to educate and train you on how to handle your dog. The large facility, with indoor and outdoor settings, is located at 657 Bridgeton Pike in Mantua. For class schedules and details, call 856-468-8040 or go to www.a1totalcontrol.com.

Best-in-County Events

Gloucester County 4-H Fair and New Jersey Peach Festival

Held in late *July* at the Gloucester County 4-H Fairgrounds on Route 77 in Mullica Hill, the Gloucester County 4-H Fair and New Jersey Peach Festival features all the basics of a traditional 4-H fair, with a special emphasis on peaches. They also have a dog show so even your furry pal can have fun at the fair. For more information, go to the calendar at http://gloucester.rce.rutgers.edu.

Paws in the Park

Every year in the middle of *October*, Save the Animals Foundation (STAF) invites people to bring their dogs to a walk in the park to raise funds for ongoing programs. This is the only day of the year that dogs are allowed in James Atkinson Memorial Park in Sewell. The dog walkathon is just one of the many dog events held during the day. For more information, go to www.stafnj.org.

Overnights

Timberlane Campground

This family-owned campground is on 20 acres with both open and wooded sites, located at 117 Timberland Road in Clarksboro. For details, go to www.timberlanecampground.com or call 856-423-6677.

You know you are a dog person when your dog has his own website with links back to his parent kennel homepage or rescue alumni page.

Atlantic County

The first settlement in Atlantic County was in Somers Point, established in the late 1600s by John Somers. Many of the early settlers were whale men who relocated from New England, and early industries included shipyards, mills, iron furnaces, and brickyards. It was not until 1837 that Atlantic County was carved from Gloucester County and, about the same time, Dr Jonathan Pitney led a venture to develop a bathing village and health resort on the barrier island at the southern end of the county. The deal was sealed with a charter to operate a railroad from the boomtown of Camden and by 1854 engineer Richard Osborne had designed Atlantic City. Today, the beaches and boardwalks along the coast draw thousands of visitors, many of them with four feet. Keep the parks, shopping, and special events in this county on the whisker radar when you are out and about with your dog.

Dog Day Out

With many of the county parks open to dogs and a network of state forests, this county gets high tails from dog visitors. As in neighboring Cape May County, two of the larger parks, Northfield and Birch Grove, are wildlife refuges and, as such, do not allow dogs. And many of the township parks and boat launch areas do not allow dogs. No whimpering, though, as there are plenty of dog-friendly towns and Brigantine has a dog-friendly beach that is woof-wonderful. For more information on any of the county parks, go to the leisure page at www.aclink.org.

Atlantic County Bikeway

This paved 7.6-mile path running from Egg Harbor Township to Hamilton Township is a good place to walk your dog. It is a rail-trail on the old Pennsylvania Reading Seashore line so it is flat and wide. There are three parking areas: the Shore Mall on Black Horse Pike, the Atlantic County Vocational Technical

School, and in the middle at English Creek Avenue. Maps are posted at the parking lots showing approximate distances.

BEACHES AND BOARDWALKS

There are only a few towns in Atlantic County that allow dogs on beaches or on the boardwalks. Rules can change quickly so watch for signs.

BRIGANTINE. Dogs are allowed on the North-End Beach (beach area north of 14th Street) all year. Dogs are allowed on all the beaches from October 1 to May 29 but are never allowed on the sea wall walkway.

NORTH WILDWOOD. Dogs are allowed on the beach before May 15 and after September 15.

EDWIN B. FORSYTHE NATIONAL WILDLIFE REFUGE

This tract of federal land is over 20,000 acres of wetlands and forest. Located east of Smithville and Oceanville, the refuge has three distinct sections: Barnegat, Brigantine, and Holgate. Although dogs are allowed in Barnegat and Brigantine, this is a wildlife refuge and it is very popular with ornithologists. During spring, if you want to take your dog through the park, try the 8-mile driving loop, which starts on Great Creek Road. During the non-nesting season, there are plenty of short walks and longer ambles that you and your hound can use to explore the marshes. Dogs are never allowed in the Holgate area. Maps are available at the visitor's center near Oceanville. For more information, go to www.fws.gov/northeast/forsythe.

ESTELL MANOR PARK

This county park gets four paws up from the puppy patrol for its trails, extensive picnic areas, ponds, and wide-open spaces. It borders the Great Egg Harbor River, encompasses about 1,700 acres, and is the county's most popular park, with 13 miles of trails that wind through all types of habitats to thrill your hound's nose. For the people half, trails are not too sandy and cross mostly flat terrain, but can be wet due to beavers and wetlands. The park entrance is 3.5 miles south of Mays Landing on Route 50.

GALLOWAY TRACT

This county-owned tract of land is located in Galloway Township and encompasses over 371 acres. Unmarked hiking trails crisscross the park for serious forest explorations with adventuresome dogs. Trails can be accessed off Highlands Avenue, Seaview Avenue, Jimmie Leeds Road, or Great Creek Road.

GASKILL PARK

Located on the Great Egg Harbor River in Mays Landing, Gaskill Park makes for a good paw stretch. It has wonderful landscaping with brick paths, gazebos, and a large lawn. The picnic tables are along the river but across CR 617, which has heavy weekend traffic.

Lake Lenape Park

With nearly 2,000 acres and encompassing the 344-acre lake, this park in Mays Landing offers all its visitors a wide variety of activities. Besides swimming in Lake Lenape, dogs can snuffle their way down 10 miles of marked trails or just hang around and mooch food from their humans in the picnic area. On the west side of the lake, the park entrance is on CR 559, and on the east side, the park entrance is on Harding Highway.

Linwood Bikeway

Need to work those pads? The 6-mile-long rail-trail running from Black Horse Pike in Pleasantville through Linwood to Bethel Road in Somers Point should give them a workout. Use a short leash since the surface is paved so you are sure to have company on wheels. This is a suburban trail, passing through residential, commercial, and park areas. Individual trail segments are owned and maintained by the municipalities along the trail's route: Pleasantville, Northfield, Linwood, and Somers Point. The trail is paved except for a short segment of dirt between Northfield and Pleasantville. You can access the rail-trail in the middle at Wabash and Oak Crest Avenues in the center of Linwood, just two blocks east of Route 9. Parking is available at the ball field on Tabor Avenue.

Maple Lake Wildlife Management Area

Just south of Mays Landing, this 460-acre park has a 35-acre lake and several miles of unmarked trails. If your dog needs to get out and get lost in the woods for an afternoon, this park should satisfy his wild side. Alternately, he can swim off his doggie stress in the lake. The main parking area is on Maple Avenue, a mile west of Route 50.

Riverbend Park

Bordering the eastern shore of the Great Egg Harbor River in Egg Harbor Township, this 775-acre park gets paws prancing. A network of unmarked trails crisscrosses the park, offering plenty of fun for hounds and their tag-along humans. Sound-sensitive pups should probably skip this park, however, since the county Firearms Training Facility is located here. The park entrance is on CR 559.

Smithville

There is no place in south Jersey that surpasses the charm and atmosphere of Historic Smithville. With winding brick paths, a lake, and quaint shops dating back to the American Revolution, you can strut your dog's stuff all through town, treat your pal to an ice cream or hot dog, or just enjoy one of the special events, from craft and car shows to performances by the Olde Smithville Fife and Drum Corp. Visit www.smithvillenj.com for more information.

Tuckahoe Wildlife Management Area

The dog-training and exercise area is a mile east of Route 50 near Woodbine. It is at the north end of the WMA boarding Gibson's Creek Road, which is gravel. Trails meander away from all three parking lots and Gibson's Landing is a great place to swim your dog in the river. Remember—hunting is allowed in all WMAs and seasons extend from September to March.

Benji, whose real name was Higgins, was a beige-colored little mixed breed that rose to stardom in 1974 when he starred in the box office hit Benji. *At the ripe old age of seventeen, the original Benji gave up the cinema and retired, leaving a female look-alike pup to carry on in the sequel films* For the Love of Benji *(1977) and* Oh, Heavenly Dog *(1980).*

U-Cut Christmas Tree Farms

When the air cools and the world is decorated in red and green, slip into a warm coat and load the dog for the traditional tree cutting. Many of the tree farms are Fido-friendly. For more information on tree farms, go to www.njchristmastrees.org.

Holly Ridge Tree Farm. In Hammonton at 116 South Chew Road, 609-561-8575.

Petrongolo Evergreen Plantation. In Hammonton at 7541 Weymouth Road, 609-567-0336.

Weymouth Furnace

Although small, you should definitely keep this park on the whisker radar. An 11-acre park along the Great Egg Harbor River, it was once the site of an 1800s iron furnace and paper mill. Today, it is a woof-wonderful spot to swim your dog in the river or enjoy a quiet picnic lunch under the trees. The park entrance is on CR 559, a block north of Route 322.

Paw-tacular Shopping

Butterhof's Farm and Home Supply

With products for every stage of your pet's development, this store has all the right doggie stuff for dog-shopping addicts. It is located at 5715 White Horse Pike in Egg Harbor Township, 609-965-1198.

English Creek Supply

This store carries a wide range of high-end dog foods, specialty treats, and a grand selection of toys for all your dog's needs and all your wants. Located at 3088 English Creek Avenue in Egg Harbor Township, 609-641-6168.

Jake's Dog House

This store should come with a warning label for all credit-card-carrying dog owners! An unmatched selection of luscious treats is complemented by a woof-wonderful variety of toys, cool canine accessories, and plenty of dog-people gift items. One of several stores in New Jersey, the Atlantic County location is in the Tropicana Casino in Atlantic City. For more information, go to www.jakesdoghouse.com.

Without question, the most recognized gambling paintings ever created are the renderings of dogs playing poker by Cassius Coolidge. In fact, surveys have shown these paintings to be among the most recognizable artwork of any type. Coolidge was already known for his paintings of dogs when he was hired in 1903 by publishers Brown & Bigelow to create calendars and other advertising products. Coolidge produced sixteen paintings of dogs, with the Dogs Playing Poker *sequence being the most famous.*

Paw Dazzle

A little paw, a little magic, and "woof," you have Paw Dazzle. Wander in and select a new toy or a bag of treats for your favorite friend. Located on the Village Green in Historic Smithville, 609-748-7110.

Pet Pros Pet Supply

Need supplies quick? This store has all the basics from premium dog food to brushes to beds and is conveniently located at 112 Woodland Avenue in Somers Point, 609-927-3232.

While traveling about in Atlantic County, you can also get pet supplies at:

Pet Smart. In Mays Landing at 420 Consumer Square, 609-677-1620.

Tail-Wagging Training Facilities

Humane Society of Atlantic County

Training classes are offered year-round at the HSAC facility. The class schedule includes puppy kindergarten, basic good manners, canine good citizenship, agility, and rally obedience. Private obedience lessons and individual behavior consultations are also available. The shelter is located in Atlantic City on Route 30. For class schedules, go to www.humanesocietyac.org or call 609-347-2487.

The yellow dog that starred in the 1957 Disney classic Old Yeller *was bought for three dollars from an animal shelter by his trainer, Frank Weatherwax. His real name was Spike and his biggest challenge was learning how to look vicious, having spent most of his time playing with the family children. Spike also starred in the 1959 Paramount film* Dog of Flanders *and his son played Rontu in* Island of the Blue Dolphins, *while his grandson appeared with Steve McQueen and Robert Preston in* Junior Bonner.

Best-in-County Events

Agility Trial

In the middle of *June*, the South Jersey Agility Club hosts an agility trial at Buena Vista Family Campground in Buena. The three-day event draws agility competitors to the area in packs! Your dog can be in the campground.

Walk for the Animals

A nonprofit organization established in 1965, the Humane Society of Atlantic County hosts benefit dinners, charity golf outings, and fashion shows. One of the more popular events is the "Walk for the Animals" in Egg Harbor City. In the middle of *June*, this 2-mile walk begins at the Lake Pavilion. Their mission is to increase the number of pets adopted into loving homes. To this end, the shelter has multiple fundraisers throughout the year, some for people only and some for the dogs to join in. For more information, go to www.humanesocietyac.org or call 609-347-2487.

Bellview Winery

The climate and soil in southern New Jersey are near perfect for grapevines, which flourished here in the 1800's, hence the name of the nearby city of "Vineland." The Bellview Winery is a dog-friendly spot that has several festivals your dog might enjoy. In *June*, you can do the Jazz & Funk Festival and in *August*, you can try the Seafood Festival. In *October*, the winery, which is in Landisville, has a Harvest Festival. For more information, call 856-697-7172 or go to www.bellviewwinery.com.

All-Breed Show and Obedience Trial

In the middle of *October* you can find all the south Jersey dogs at Buena Vista Family Campground for the annual AKC conformation show and obedience

10. Catching the judge's eye, this little fellow goes on to win his class.

trial. Held by the South Jersey Kennel Club in conjunction with the Gloucester County Kennel Club, this two-day event draws over a thousand conformation entries and nearly a hundred obedience dogs every year.

OVERNIGHTS

Dogs love being outdoors and camping is a howling good time for most canines. All of these campgrounds in Atlantic County are Fido-friendly.

ARROWHEAD CAMPGROUND. In Egg Harbor at 163 Leektown Road, 609-296-8599.

BUENA VISTA CAMPING PARK. In Buena on Route 40, 609-697-2004, www.bvcp.com.

INDIAN BRANCH PARK CAMPGROUND. In Hammonton at 2021 Skip Morgan Road, 609-561-4719, www.indianbranchparkcg.com.

You know you are a dog person when you have traced your dog's family tree further than your own and you can effortlessly remember three generations of canine ancestors.

Salem County

Salem County lies in the southwest corner of the state. Founded in 1681, it is the oldest county and, at 338 square miles, it is also the smallest. Nearly half of the county is actively farmed, giving it a relatively rural character, much like Sussex County far away in the north. Its natural features include six rivers, more than 34,000 acres of meadow and marshland, tidal and freshwater wetlands, forty lakes and ponds, bay beaches, dunes, expansive woodlands, numerous streams, and critical headwaters. It also boasts a population of less than 65,000—the lowest population and the lowest density per square mile in New Jersey. Canines are more than welcome here and there are few, if any, "No Dogs" signs.

Dog Day Out

Salem County's vast array of natural resources and open spaces makes for a pleasant day out with your dog. Being so small and with many of its residents living on farms, there are no county parks but dogs are always welcome and accepted here.

Elmer Lake Wildlife Management Area

If your dog needs to muck about in the woods or romp along the lake shore, take him to this 279-acre WMA near Elmer. There is no formal trail system but local dog walkers and fishermen have cut plenty of paths through the woods. Parking is available at Elmer Lake, near the boat ramp. Route 40 bisects the park, just outside Elmer. Remember—hunting is allowed in all WMAs and seasons extend from September to March.

Finns Point Lighthouse

Located in the Supawna Meadows National Wildlife Refuge, the Finns Point Lighthouse was erected in 1876. It was first built in Buffalo, New York, then dismantled and shipped by rail to Salem. Its final journey was by mule-drawn wagon. It is in Pennsville at Fort Mott and Lighthouse Roads.

Fort Mott State Park

The fortifications seen today at Fort Mott were erected in 1896 in anticipation of the Spanish-American War. Visitors, and their favorite canines, can wander through the old batteries following interpretive signs with detailed descriptions of the fort. Just beyond the fortifications is the Delaware River shoreline, with great spots for walking and picnicking. Your dog can tour Fort Mott but cannot ride on the ferry to Pea Pod Island. The 104-acre state park is a few miles southeast along Fort Mott Road from downtown Pennsville.

Parvin State Park

In Parvin State Park, situated on the edge of the Pine Barrens, spring bursts out in bright colors and rich fragrances with blossoming dogwood, laurel, holly, magnolia, wild azalea, and hundreds of flowering plants. In any season, Thundergust Lake, Parvin Lake, and Muddy Run are popular for fishing and boating, and with 15 miles of trails to sniffle and snuffle along, your dog is sure to put a four-paws-up stamp on this 1,309-acre state park. There are also picnic tables with grills should you both be feeling the need for "dogs on the grill" versus "dogs on the trail." Canoes can be rented at the concession stand at 95-acre Parvin Lake and dogs are sometimes allowed in the rental boats. From Route 55, take exit 35 and follow signs to the main park entrance.

Riverview Beach Park

Located in downtown Pennsville along the Delaware River, this park was once an amusement park. Today, it is a spot for town events and festivals. Situated along the river with a large duck pond and meandering paths, it makes a good place for some paws-ercise. The park borders Route 49.

Throughout history witches were often accused of having "familiars," often described as low-ranking demons that help witches carry out spells and bewitchments. In the Salem trials in 1692, John Bradsheet was indicted for "inciting a dog to afflict." The dog was tried and hanged as a witch. Many modern witches do not believe the familiars are demons or spirits in animal form but simply animals whose psychic attunement makes them ideal partners in magical workings.

Salem River Wildlife Management Area

Located on Route 45 and bordering Mannington Creek, this WMA has unmarked trails winding through it from the parking lot. This is not an official dog-training area, but your dog can enjoy the woods and creek area off leash for most of the year anyway. Remember—hunting is allowed in all WMAs and seasons extend from September to March.

Best-in-County Events

Sunday at Salem

Once a month from May to November, you can enjoy a fur-fabulous Sunday with your canine at this arts and crafts show. Held at the Salem County Fairgrounds in Woodstown, this dog-friendly show also has a farmers' market, baked goods, and picnic-style dining for you and your dog to enjoy. Being pet-friendly, donations of dog and cat food are collected at the gate for the Salem County Humane Society. For specific dates, go to www.sjpumpkinshow.com.

Lure Coursing

Truly a hound event, lure coursing is fur-fabulous fun. AKC-sanctioned lure-coursing trials are held by the Jersey Rag Racers Whippet Association in the middle of *August* at Fort Mott State Park in Pennsville. It is usually a two-day event and dogs run rain or shine. Your dog can be in the park. Visit the club website at www.jrrwa.org for details.

Overnights

Dogs love being outdoors and camping is a howling good time for most canines. All of these campgrounds in Atlantic County are Fido-friendly.

Four Seasons Family Campground. In Pilesgrove at 158 Woodstown-Daretown Road, 856-769-3635, www.fourseasonscamping.com.

Yogi Bear's Jellystone Park. At Tall Pines Resort in Elmer at 59 Beal Road, 856-451-7479, www.tallpines.com.

You know you are a dog person when you can identify a Norwich from a cairn, an affenpinscher from a Brussels griffon, and a Cavalier from a toy spaniel.

Cumberland County

Home of the *Plain Dealer*, arguably New Jersey's first newspaper, and several of the state's first permanent settlements, Cumberland County has a long history. It was created from Salem County in January of 1748 by the Colonial legislature and named by Governor Jonathan Belcher in honor of his patron, William Augustus, Duke of Cumberland. Founded on a firm agricultural base, the county has maintained a quiet pace and lifestyle often considered lost along the east coast. Visitors are often surprised by the rich historic heritage, expansive farms, and small-town atmosphere of this southern county.

Dog Day Out

With vast wetlands, undisturbed stretches of the Delaware Bay, roadside vegetable stands, and a rich glassblowing heritage, Cumberland County has a natural beauty coupled with a long history. A trip through the county's towns and vast wildlife management areas offers delightful doggie adventures through every season. With miles of river and Delaware Bay beaches, your dog day out can easily include water sports, while the quaint towns are lovely spots to amble around slowly with your favorite pal. Many of the hiking parks in Cumberland County are wildlife management areas so please keep in mind that hunting is allowed in all WMAs and seasons extend from September to March.

Bridgeton Walkabout

The site of the Cohansey Bridge in the mid-1700s led to the development of this town, eventually renamed Bridgeton. Its importance grew when it was chosen as the seat of government for the newly created county of Cumberland. Today, Bridgeton is New Jersey's largest historic district, with over 2,200 homes and buildings on the National Register of Historic Places. It has touched and been touched by nearly every period of American history and has a charming aura that you and your dog can feel while you explore the area. Every dog will enjoy a meander along the Riverfront, a walkway along the Cohansey River between Route 49 and Commerce Street, while high-drive pups can join you on the Walking Tour, which features a wealth of historic attractions, including Potter's Tavern and the Old Broad Street Church. Town and tour maps are available to the navigators at the Tourist Information Center at 50 East Board Street.

Bridgeton City Park

This 1,100-acre township park is just a mile north of the historic district. It contains the 88-acre Sunset Lake and its small companion, Mary Elmer Lake. Tails wag happily on the marked trails and picnic areas of this very popular park. Dogs are not allowed, however, on the lakeside beach, in Cohanzick Zoo, or at any events held in the park. Follow Mayor Aitken Drive north from downtown; the park entrance is on West Park Drive.

Dutch Neck Village

This quaint country village opened to shoppers in 1976, and is a very nice place to stroll with your pooch and perhaps share a treat from one of the cafés. Be sure to visit the Old Arboretum, featuring 3 acres of unique plants and walkways. Dutch Neck Village is only a mile from Bridgeton. Take Fayette Street south to Chubby Hollow Rd and make a right onto Trench Street.

Edward G. Bevan Wildlife Management Area

This was formerly known as Millville WMA. The dog-training and exercise area is at Shaws Mill Pond. From Millville, go south on Cedarville Road to Newport Road. The gravel parking lot is on Shaws Mill Road and is well marked. The lake access makes this a popular spot for field trainers to work their dogs.

Gum Tree Corner Wildlife Management Area

For dogs that need space and freedom, go west about 8 miles from Bridgeton to this WMA along the county border. With over 800 acres and Newport Meadows to play in, your dog's grins will last the whole week. Trails are not marked. Parking is available off Causeway Road. Take CR 626 west from Bridgeton to CR 647 to Gum Tree Corner Road.

Greenwich Walkabout

Forty miles from Philadelphia is the little town of Greenwich, once the principal settlement of Cumberland County and a major port on the Cohansey River. Lost in time as roads replaced rivers as the primary transportation system, Greenwich is today much the same as it was three hundred years ago. The wide street, which is still called Ye Greate Street, was laid out in 1684 and its course has never been changed. If you want to discover a piece of the past and just stroll with your pal, Greenwich is worth the drive south. From Route 49 just west of Bridgeton, take CR 661 south to CR 607.

Rin Tin Tin was the first American canine movie star. He was rescued as a puppy in war-torn Germany and brought home by Lee Duncan, an American pilot in World War I, who was also his trainer. Rin Tin Tin first appeared in Where The North Begins *in 1925 and went on to make twenty-five movies, learning to sign his own contracts with a paw print.*

Heislerville Wildlife Management Area

Located along the Maurice River and Delaware Bay, this 6,700-acre WMA has unmarked hiking trails for house hounds that crave adventure and two beach areas for any dog that loves sand and/or water. From the parking area on East Point Road, it is a short walk down to Thompson Beach. A bit to the east along Moores Beach Road is another parking area that allows you to walk down to Moores Beach.

East Point Lighthouse is at the tip of Heislerville WMA. Built along the Delaware River in 1849, it is the last remaining lighthouse on the Delaware Bay and is maintained by the Maurice River Historical Society.

Manumuskin River Preserve

More than 3,500 acres, the Manumuskin River Preserve is the largest Nature Conservancy preserve in New Jersey. It was established to protect the globally rare plant joint-vetch and fifteen of New Jersey's threatened and endangered species of birds, which breed in the Manumuskin River Basin. Dogs are allowed in the preserve on the 2 miles of trails marked and approved for horseback riding. The trailhead parking lot is in Port Elizabeth on Schooner Landing Road, which is just off Route 55 at exit 21.

Menantico Ponds State Wildlife Management Area

Just southeast of Millville, this 400-acreWMA encompasses Menantico Sand Pond. For pups with a wild soul, the informal trail system here will elicit howls of delight. Access to the lake is on a gravel road. From Route 55, exit 24, go 1.3 miles east on Route 49.

Millville Walkabout

Stroll with your pooch through a town steeped in the history of American glassmaking and enjoy together the rich architectural history, lovely shops, and woof-wonderful places to get a snack. With a summertime farmer's market, evening events, and weekend festivals scheduled throughout the year, the Glasstown Arts District makes a great day out with your dog. Do not forget to stop into Puppy Love Pantry II. Several municipal parking lots are scattered about. For a map, parking, and/or directions, go to www.glasstownartsdistrict.com.

U-Cut Christmas Tree Farms

When the temperature chills and the leaves are gone, it is time to get out and cut your tree. Many of the tree farms are dog-friendly. For directions and more information on tree farms, go to www.njchristmastrees.org.

Airport Tree Plantation. In Millville at 2340 Cedar Street, 856-825-5212.

Fisher's Tree Farm. In Bridgeton at 461 Fairton-Millville Road, 856-451-2626.

Greenleaves Christmas Tree Farm. In Newport at 52 Newport Road, 856-447-3814.

Union Lake Wildlife Management Area

Union Lake is the largest lake in southern New Jersey. The WMA is just north of Millville and incorporates the 898-acre lake. With almost 5,000 acres to play in, the wild side of any dog is sure to surface. Trails are not marked but parking is available at the public boat launch, just off CR 608.

Paw-tacular Shopping

KC Stables Tack & Supply

For the hard-to-find canine supplies, try this equine supply store. They carry crates, kennels, heated pads, heated water bowls, joint supplements, and a variety of grooming items. The store is at 18 Lawrence Road in Bridgeton, 856-455-5342.

JV Pets

Need supplies while in the area? JV Pets has all the basics necessary to keep you trotting along on your day out. The store is located in the Main Street Shopping Center on Main Street in Vineland, 856-690-5884.

Puppy Love Pantry II

This dog-lightful store in the Millville Glasstown Arts District is a must visit in south Jersey. Not only do they carry fresh baked treats and the latest cool canine stuff, the store hosts fur-fabulous events, like animal art shows, puppy paw painting, dog psychic readings, and even a dog wedding, at which the bride and groom arrived via Rolls Royce. Dogs are always welcome to shop for themselves and a percentage of every purchase goes to local rescue groups. The shop is located at 202 North High Street in Millville, 856-327-5554.

Best-in-County Events

Dutch Neck Village Events

This small shopping village hosts several family-oriented events throughout the year, most notably the Strawberry Festival in *June*, the Peach Festival in

August, and the Fall Festival in *October*. A full calendar of events is available at www.dutchneckvillage.com.

Cumberland County Fair

This 4-H fair is held in early *July* at the Cumberland County Fairgrounds on Carmel Road in Millville. It includes a pet show and lots of animal exhibits. For entry details and exact dates, contact the Cumberland County Fair Association at 856-825-3820.

Harvest Festival

This Deerfield Township event is held in early *October* in the village of Rosenhayn. The festival highlights the community's agricultural heritage with farm-related displays, crafts, parades, food vendors, concerts, and recognition of the Farmer of the Year. For event details, go to the recreation page at www.deerfieldtownship.org.

Halloween on High

Dress up your pup (and yourself) and go trick-or-treating for dog treats and biscuits in the Glasstown Arts Historic District. Held on Halloween, *October* 31, this event is just howling good fun for dog families. For directions and details on this event and others, go to www.glasstownartsdistrict.com.

Millville Farmers' Market

The market is open every Saturday morning and is located at Buck and Pine Streets in downtown Millville. Most weekends include special events, entertainment, crafts, artists painting, and more. Look for the dog comfort station with water, treats, and poop bags sponsored by Puppy Love Pantry II.

South Jersey Pumpkin Show

This two-day family festival includes artists, crafters, concerts, a home and garden show, and, of course, pumpkins. Whether or not your dog loves pumpkins, his tail will wag right off at this dog-friendly event held at the Cumberland County Fairgrounds in the middle of *October*. For specific dates, go to www.sjpumpkinshow.com.

You know you are a dog person when your number one priority in purchasing a new home is whether the yard will please your dog.

Cape May County

In the 1620s, the Dutch West India Company sent Cornelius Jacobsen Mey to the New World with three ships. During his voyage up the Delaware Bay, he named the cape to the north Cape Mey. This cape still bears his name, although English settlers altered the spelling to May. The first settlers were whalers, who came south from Massachusetts around 1685 and, in 1692, Cape May County was formally created from land held by West Jersey. Almost two hundred years later, with the arrival of the railroad, Cape May became a popular resort for the upper classes. Many of these wealthy visitors built their own "cottages," which are now historic inns. Today's resort towns feature historic buildings, whale-watching trips, festivals, and, of course, beaches. Outdoor lovers can also visit the wetlands or inland forests. With miles of quaint shops to explore and famous boardwalks to stroll, this county offers plenty of activities for hound and human. It is a year-round resort and dog visitors often find more to do between October and March, after the summer crowds and nesting birds have gone, than in the summer.

Dog Day Out

The Cape May peninsula is one of the most famous bird-watching locations in North America. And, since birds do not typically think of dogs as friends, our favorite creatures must wait their turn for the parks and beaches. Many of the parks and almost all of the beaches and boardwalks in Cape May have dog restrictions. This includes the national and state parks since they too are wildlife refuges in this area. You can, however, get your furry friend out and about.

Beaches and Boardwalks

There are a few towns in Cape May County that allow dogs on beaches and boardwalks. Rules change quickly so watch for signs.

AVALON. Dogs are allowed on the beach and boardwalk from October 1 to the end of February.

CAPE MAY. Dogs are allowed on the beach and boardwalk from November 1 through March 31. Dogs are not allowed in the Washington Mall area, although there are no signs.

NORTH WILDWOOD. Dogs are allowed on the beach from September 16 to May 14.

STONE HARBOR. Dogs are allowed on the beach and boardwalk from October 1 to the end of February.

WILDWOOD. Dogs are allowed on the beach from November 1 to April 30 but are never allowed on the boardwalk.

Not all the victims of the Titanic *were people. Records show that there were twelve dogs on board with their first-class passengers. Two dogs, both Pomeranians, survived. The pets belonged to Elizabeth Barrett Rothschild and Margaret Hays. Another passenger, Ann Isham, refused a seat in the lifeboat when her dog was refused passage.*

BELLEPLAIN STATE FOREST

The 20,000 forested acres of Belleplain include stands of young pine, former agricultural areas, lowland swamps, and marshes. Established in 1928, the park has miles of trails for dog explorers. It definitely gets four paws up from the puppy patrol for day hikes on the 10 miles of marked trails around Lake Nummy and the nature center. The East Creek Trail is a nice 6.5-mile walk around the lake while the Pickle Pond Trail is a much shorter 1-mile walk. There are picnic areas, and trail maps are available. The park entrance is off CR 550 in Woodbine.

- If your dog is not "doing" woods, try the Woodbine Bike Path. It runs along parallel to CR 550 for 3 miles, with plenty of access points, including Lincoln Park and CR 610, at the intersection of Dehirsch Avenue.

CAPE MAY STATE PARK

In an effort to protect the threatened piping plovers and least terns, the park prohibits dogs on beaches during the nesting season, which means you can enjoy the beaches with your dog from September 16 to April 14. Dogs are never allowed on the trails and there are very few picnic areas. The contiguous beach, managed by the Nature Conservancy, follows the same dog restrictions. From Cape May, take CR 606 west toward Cape May Point and follow signs.

COLD SPRING BIKE PATH

For a serious power pad, try the bike path in Lower Township. The 2.7-mile path runs from Sally Marshall Crossing to Sandman Boulevard. This rail-trail runs parallel to Route 9 on the former West Jersey and Seashore Railroad Company rail bed. With bridges and a well-maintained surface, this trail is a dog favorite for miles around. Parking is available near historic Cold Spring Village.

Corson's Inlet State Park

This park was established in 1969 to help protect and preserve one of the last undeveloped tracts of land along the state's oceanfront. Since its primary function is as a wildlife sanctuary, both the dune trails and beaches are off limits to dogs during the nesting seasons. You can share this beautiful undeveloped beachfront and sand dunes area with your dog from September 16 to March 31. The park entrance is on CR 619, just south of Ocean City.

Higbee Beach Wildlife Management Area

This 1,000-acre WMA has a 1.5-mile stretch of beach that is managed specifically to provide habitat for migratory wildlife. Nevertheless, dogs are allowed year-round. Dogs must be on leash and under control at all times. This Delaware Bay beach has smaller waves than the Atlantic Ocean beaches and gets definite happy woofs from beach-going dogs. The parking area is at the end of CR 641, in Cape May Point.

- Just south of Higbee Beach is Sunset Beach. This beach also allows dogs year-round. Parking is available at the end of CR 606.

Historic Cold Spring Village

Dogs are more than welcome at this open-air, living history museum that depicts everyday life as it was experienced in a small south Jersey farm village during the nineteenth century. Stroll the shaded lanes on 22 acres as you step back in time with your dog and visit with crafters, tradesmen, housewives, and farmers of years gone by. The village is located 3 miles north of Cape May on Route 9 in Cold Spring. Admission charged. For details and event schedules, call 609-898-2300 or go to www.hcsv.org.

- On Sunday evenings in *July* and *August*, visitors are offered free concerts at the village gazebo. Performances are held light rain or shine and begin at 5:00 p.m.

Paw-tacular Shopping

Paw Prints of Cape May

With dog-people presents and accessories for every dog—big, furry, goofy, or just plain elegant, the folks at Paw Prints have something with which to indulge your favorite friend (or you). The shop is in Cape May at 315 Ocean Street, 609-898-1660.

Paw Prints

If you are not in Cape May, visit the second Paw Prints location in Stone Harbor at 281 96th Street, 609-368-3700.

Smeltzer & Sons Feed Supply

Need dog food or basic supplies while traveling about the cape area? Smeltzer's should have what you need to keep your day trotting along nicely. The store is located at 1139 South Route 9 in North Cape May, 609-465-4500.

Wagging Tail Pet Market

Should your favorite pal need supplies while in the Cape May area, this store has a bit of this and that to keep him healthy and happy. The shop is at 337 Route 9 in Cape May, 609-886-5999.

Whiskers

A whimsical and wonderful variety of whiskered goodies awaits your furry friend in this store located in the charming Victorian seaside resort of Cape May. It carries a wide array of fashions, accessories, jewelry, pottery, stationery, statues, toys, and treats for people and pets. Whiskers is at 605 Hughes Street, 609-898-1232.

Tail-Wagging Training Facilities

Jersey Devil Doggie Training

There are two programs offered for basic obedience training. The first is a two-week boarding and training program and the second is a six-week program that merges training and socialization. For more information, call 609-465-8844.

Devil Dog Training

Classes are held at the Humane Society for Ocean City. Group classes in basic obedience and beginner agility run for six weeks. Private instruction and in-home problem solving are also offered. For more information on classes, call 609-399-1028.

Best-in-County Events

Tri-State Basset Rescue

Wowing the crowd at the Board Waddle and at the Doo Dah Pawrade, the members of this club descend upon Ocean City in the middle of *April* for their annual fundraising weekend. With basset hound events scheduled all weekend, including the Basset Olympics on Friday, this annual gathering of the basset community is not to be missed. Events are only open to basset hounds but basset wanna-be's are welcome to watch. For details, go to www.tristatebassets.org.

Locked in a ratings war with Ed Sullivan, comedian Steve Allen hired a young and upcoming singer, Elvis Presley, to perform on his TV show in July of 1956. Elvis, dressed in white tie and tails, sang "Hound Dog" to a basset hound named Sherlock, who wore a black top hat.

Barks on the Boards

The Humane Society of Ocean City, a private, nonprofit, no-kill animal shelter, sponsors the annual Barks on the Boards. This very popular dog-walkathon is held on Saturday of Memorial Day weekend in *May* on the Ocean City boardwalk. It is open to all dogs and their people (someone has to be on the other end of the leash anyway) and is the only day dogs can be on the boardwalk. The Humane Society was established in 1964 to rescue and rehabilitate the stray and abandoned pets in Ocean City and the surrounding communities. They hold several other large fundraising events, including a pet fashion show in late March. For details and registration forms, go to www.petfinder.com/shelters/hsoc.html or call 609-399-2018.

West Cape May Events

The West Cape May events and festivals, including the Strawberry Festival in early *June*, are barking-good for dogs too. The festivals are very popular and members of the local dog community recommend visiting early (before 11 a.m.) unless your pooch is small enough to be carried through the crowd. Dogs are also welcome to come out for the *July* concert series and many of the shops in West Cape May welcome dogs. All events are held at Wilbraham Park. Visit the event calendar at www.westcapemay.us for more information.

Obedience Trial

This small AKC obedience trial is held every year in late *October* at the Middle Township High School in Cape May Court House. Sponsored by the Cape May County Dog Obedience Club, it draws the best of the local obedience and rally dogs to the competition. Due to space limitations, dogs not entered cannot be in the building.

All-Breed Show and Obedience Trial

Every year the Boardwalk Kennel Club sponsors an AKC conformation show in late *November*. The two-day show is held at the Wildwoods Convention Center in Wildwood and typically draws a thousand entries per day. It is a wonderful opportunity to inquire about a new breed, check in with your own favorite, or just watch the best of south Jersey's dogs strut their stuff. Dogs not entered are not allowed inside the building.

Overnights

Cape May is famous for its historic inns and quaint motels. Unfortunately, they seldom accept dog guests. The exceptions, which are delightfully dog-friendly, are listed below. It is always wise to check with the staff before booking.

Billmae Cottage. In Cape May at two locations: 1015 Washington Street and 103 Lafayette Street, 609-898-8558, www.billmae.com.

The Seagull. In Brigantine Beach, just north of Atlantic City, 800-550-5553, www.the-sea-gull.com.

Marquis de Lafayette Hotel. In Cape May at 501 Beach Avenue, 800-935-9667, www.marquiscapemay.com.

Highland House. In West Cape May at 131 North Broadway, 609-898-1198, www.highlandhousecapemay.com.

Camping

Another way to spend time with your house-hound is to take him on a camping trip. There are several dog-friendly campgrounds in the Cape May area. Policies change so remember to call ahead before planning your trip.

Big Timber Lake Camping Resort. In Cape May Court House at 116 Swainton-Goshen Road, 609-465-4456, www.bigtimberlake.com.

Beachcomber Camping. In Cape May at 42 Seashore Road, 609-886-6035, www.beachcombercamp.com.

Ocean View Resort Campground. In Ocean View at 2555 Route 9, 609-624-1675, www.ovresort.com.

Seashore Campsites. In Cape May on Seashore Road, 609-884-4010, www.seashorecampsites.com.

Whippoorwill Campground. In Marmora at 810 South Shore Road, 609-390-3458, www.campwhippoorwill.com.

You know you are a dog person when it makes perfect sense that "dog" spelled backward is "god."

New York City

For a different kind of day out with your pooch, you can take her into New York City. There are plenty of dog-friendly spots and some woof-abulous events for dogs. If you have a country dog that has no interest in city lights, there are several dog-lover events that belong on the whisker radar. You can tell your country pooch all about them when you get home.

Central Park

Central Park, a swath of green through Manhattan, makes an excellent doggie day trip. With 843 acres to explore, you and your dog are sure to enjoy multiple trips to this famous New York City park. Treat your pooch to a walk around the Lake, stroll through the Ramble, or you can go directly to "Dog Hill" in Central Park West, just north of 79th Street. This is a popular local dog community hangout. And your dog will not want to miss the statue of Balto, located at East Drive and 67th Street. This famous bronze statue is on the path leading north from Central Park Zoo. There are no parking areas in the park so use the public garages nearby.

Westminster Kennel Club Dog Show

The first Westminster dog show was held in 1877. No other continuously held sporting event in the United States is older except the Kentucky Derby, which predates Westminster by only two years. It originated as a show for sporting dogs, primarily setters and pointers, and was initiated by a group of hunters who met regularly at the Westminster Hotel in Manhattan. They decided to create a kennel club specifically for the purpose of holding a dog show, which they did in May of 1877. The show took place at Gilmore's Gardens and drew over 1,200 dogs. It proved so popular that its originally scheduled three days became four. It remained a three- or four-day show until 1941, when it changed to its current, two-day format. Now held every *February* at Madison Square Garden, Westminster is the premier AKC dog show in America and has become an international event. Tickets are available to all events but you should buy early and be prepared for a crushing crowd. For details, go to www.westminsterkennelclub.org.

Staten Island Companion Dog Training Club

Located on Staten Island, this active dog-training club offers classes taught by a variety of top-notch trainers, covering the competitive dog world from obedience to agility. They also hold household obedience classes and host an obedience trial and two agility trials every year. For more information on classes or events, go to www.sicdtc.net or call 718-761-8048.

Agility Trials. Held on Staten Island, these popular two-day events are in early *May* at Wolf's Pond Park and again at the end of *June* at Midland Beach Sports Field. They also hold a NADAC agility trial in late *August* at Wolf's Pond Park. Your dog is allowed to come watch the events at Wolf's Pond Park.

Obedience Trial. The club's obedience trial is held in New Jersey at East Freehold Park in Freehold (see Monmouth County). It is part of the Memorial Day shows in *May*.

Wolf's Pond Park on Staten Island is a paw-tastic spot to visit with your dog, even without an agility event. Dogs are allowed on a section of the beach during the off-season and there are miles of paved paths for great dog walks. The park entrance is easy to find off Hylan Boulevard.

Broadway Barks

Originally conceived as a program to promote the adoption of shelter animals, Broadway Barks has evolved into an event that focuses attention on the plight of homeless animals and provides much-needed exposure for the numerous shelters and rescue groups working throughout the city. Broadway Barks is held in the middle of *July* and you are welcome to bring your dog. For more information, go to www.broadwaybarks.com.

Service Dog Day

Every *September* the United States service dogs gather at the *Intrepid* Sea, Air & Space Museum for a celebration of all the types of service these dogs perform. Included in this special event are cancer sniffing, explosive detection, drug detection, therapy, assistance, and search and rescue. The U.S. War Dog Association is on hand to bring attention to dogs serving in the armed forces. Recognition is also given to an assortment of K-9 heroes and their special humans. Although your dog needs to relax at home for this one, dog lovers will not find a more thrilling celebration of the dog-human bond. The museum is at Pier 86 in New York City. For event details, go to www.bearsearchandrescue.org.

Halloween Dog Parade

Held every year in Tompkins Square Park, this Halloween Dog Parade is a howling good time with wonderful dogs in all kinds of crazy and unique costumes. The *October* afternoon includes games and fun dog stuff. Events begin around noon and are sponsored by First Run, a nonprofit organization that maintains the Tompkins Dog Run. Visit www.dogster.org for more information.

Event Calendar

January

Event	County
Obedience Trial, Princeton Dog Training Club	Middlesex
Obedience Trial, K-9 Obedience Club	Essex
Fire & Ice Festival, Mill Race Village	Burlington

February

Event	County
Garden State Specialty	Hudson
Super Pet Expo	Middlesex
Westminster Kennel Club Show	New York City
Winter Festival	Hunterdon

March

Event	County
Agility Trial, Afghan Hound Association	Monmouth
All-Breed Show and Obedience Trial	
New Brunswick Kennel Club	Middlesex
Hi-Hat Dinner Dance	Hudson
Obedience Trials	
First Dog Obedience Training Club	Bergen
Lower Camden County Dog Training Club	Camden

April

Event	County
Agility Trails	
Agility Association of Central New Jersey (JAG)	Monmouth
Delaware County Kennel Club	Burlington
Burlington County Kennel Club	Burlington
Kruisin' Kanines Agility Club	Mercer
All-Breed Show and Obedience Trial, Lighthouse Circuit	Ocean
BARKS Garage Sale	Sussex
Board Waddle, Tri-State Basset Rescue	Cape May

Event	County
Burlington County Earth Fair, Burlington Co. Animal Alliance	Burlington
Canine Cotillion, St. Hubert's	Morris
Doggie Easter Egg Hunt, Burlington Co. Animal Alliance	Burlington
4-H State Dog Show	Middlesex
Field Trials	
English Setter Club	Burlington
Shrewsbury River Retriever Club	Ocean
South Jersey Retriever Club	Ocean
Hunt Test, Eastern German Shorthaired Pointer Club	Monmouth
Intergroom Trade Show	Somerset
Lt. Lenny's 5K and Wag-Your-Tail Run	Ocean
Lure Coursing	
Greater Valley Forge Rhodesian Ridgeback Club	Hunterdon
Irish Wolfhound Association	Somerset
Match Shows	
Mid-Jersey Labrador Retriever Club	Camden
Peddler's Village	Hunterdon
Millburn Street Fair	Essex
Obedience & Rally Trial, Lower Bucks Dog Training Club	Mercer
Poodle Club Obedience Specialty	Morris

May

Event	County
Agility Trials	
Princeton Dog Training Club	Mercer
Staten Island Companion Dog Training Club	New York City
All-Breed Shows and Obedience Trials	
Burlington County Kennel Club	Burlington
Pocono Mountain Kennel Club	Warren
Trenton Kennel Club	Mercer
Staten Island, Plainfield, and Monmouth Kennel Clubs	Monmouth
Art in the Park, Upper Montclair	Essex
Bark Fest, St. Hubert's	Morris
Barks on the Boards	Cape May
Bethlehem Fine Arts & Craft Show	Warren
Collingswood May Fair	Camden
Crafts in the Park, Westwood	Bergen
Cranford Street Fair	Union
Earthdog Trial, New Jersey Beanfield Earthdog Club	Burlington
Fantasy Tea & Art Faire, Mill Race Village	Burlington
Fine Arts and Crafts Show, Verona	Essex
FOSRAS Dog Show, Somerset Regional Animal Shelter	Somerset

Herding Trial, Burlington County Kennel Club	Burlington
Highland Park Street Fair	Middlesex
Iris Festival, Bordentown	Burlington
Lord Stirling Family Fun Day	Somerset
Mutts at the Manor	Passaic
Paws & Feet Walkathon & 5K Race	Camden
Pet Fair	Union
SAVE Pet Jet Set	Mercer
Strut Your Mutt	Bergen
Walk-for-Animals	Union

June

Agility Trials	
Agility Association of Central New Jersey (JAG)	Monmouth
Bayshore Companion Dog Club	Monmouth
South Jersey Agility Club	Atlantic
Staten Island Companion Dog Training Club	New York City
All-Breed Shows and Obedience Trials	
Burlington County Kennel Club	Mercer
Huntingdon Valley Kennel Club	Mercer
Greater Philadelphia Dog Fanciers	Mercer
Applewood Winery Dog Day	Sussex
Art in the Park	Ocean
Art in the Park Show and Concert	Bergen
Arts & Craft Show	Union
Asbury Park Pet Parade	Monmouth
Birthday Celebration and Downtown Street Fair, Merchantville	Camden
Bonnie Brae Games	Somerset
Doggone Purrfect Golf Classic	Morris
Dream Stables Charity Dog Walk	Monmouth
Fine Arts and Crafts Show, Montclair	Essex
Fine Art & Contemporary Craft Show, Peddler's Village	Hunterdon
Jazz & Funk Festival, Bellview Winery	Atlantic
NADAC Agility Trial, Agility Assoc. of Central New Jersey	Monmouth
North Plainfield Street Fair	Somerset
PAHS Golf Classic	Union
Point Pleasant Street Fair	Ocean
Purina Incredible Dog Challenge	Hudson
Red Bank Jazz & Blues Festival	Monmouth
SAVE Walk-a-thon	Mercer
Somerville Street Fair	Somerset
Spring Arts & Craft Show, Chester	Morris

Strawberry Festival, West Cape May	Cape May
Strawberry Festival, Dutch Neck Village	Cumberland
Walk for the Animals	Atlantic

JULY

Agility Trial, Poodle Club of Lehigh Valley	Warren
Art Festival	Ocean
Bastille Day	Hunterdon
Broadway Barks	New York City
Burlington County Farm Fair	Burlington
Civil War Reenactment, Hamilton Township	Mercer
Country Day at the Mill, Medford	Burlington
Craft & Fine Art Festival, Haddonfield	Camden
Cumberland County Fair	Cumberland
Gloucester County 4-H Fair	Gloucester
Great Rubber Duck Race	Hunterdon
Jersey Animal Coalition Pet Show	Essex
Jersey Shore Craft Guild Summer Shows	Ocean
Monmouth County Fair	Monmouth
New Jersey Ice Cream Festival	Ocean
Obedience Trial, Town & Country Dog Training Club	Union
Ocean County Fair	Ocean
Passaic County Fair	Passaic
Sheep-Herding Trial	Warren

AUGUST

All-Breed Show and Obedience Trial Hunterdon Co. Kennel Club	Hunterdon
Antiques in the Park, Westwood	Bergen
Art Show and Sale, Medford	Burlington
Because Your Dog Is Worth It Too Day	Middlesex
Blue Claw Craft Show	Ocean
Clearwater Festival	Monmouth
Dog Day at the Museum of Agriculture	Middlesex
Festival of Lights, City of Burlington	Burlington
Hunterdon County 4-H Fair	Hunterdon
Irish Festival	Ocean
Jersey Shore Craft Guild Summer Shows	Ocean
Knowlton Riverfest	Warren
Lure Coursing, Jersey Rag Racers Whippet Assoc.	Salem
Middlesex County Fair	Middlesex
Peach Festival, Duck Neck Village	Cumberland
Peach Festival, Chester	Morris

Seafood Festival, Bellview Winery	Atlantic
Somerset County Fair	Somerset
Warren County Farmer's Fair and Balloon Festival	Warren

SEPTEMBER

Abbey Glen Memorial Day	Sussex
Agility Trials	
Delaware Valley German Shepherd Club	Hunterdon
Garden State Australian Shepherd Club	Sussex
Princeton Dog Training Club	Middlesex
All-Breed Shows and Obedience Trials	
Schooley's Mountain, Morris, and Sussex Hills Kennel Clubs	Morris
Newton County Kennel Club	Sussex
Pocono Mountain Kennel Club	Warren
Somerset Hills Kennel Club	Somerset
Art Across the River	Warren
Art in the Park, Highland Park	Middlesex
Art at the Oval, Livingston	Essex
Art on the Green	Middlesex
BARKS Garage Sale	Sussex
BASS Dog Show	Passaic
Brielle Day	Monmouth
Bloomfield Harvest Festival	Essex
Bloomsbury Fine Arts & Craft Festival	Hunterdon
Dog Day in the Park	Bergen
Dog Walkathon, Jersey Animal Coalition	Essex
Fall Arts & Craft Festival, Chester	Morris
Fall Craft Artists Festival	Bergen
Festival of the Sea	Monmouth
Festifall	Union
Field Trial, South Jersey Retriever Club	Ocean
FOCAS Dog Show	Bergen
Founders Day Art Fair & Street Festival	Ocean
Gladstone Driving Event	Somerset
Herding Trial, Burlington County Kennel Club	Burlington
Hunt Test, Mid-Jersey Labrador Retriever Club	Camden
Little Falls Street Fair & Craft Show	Passaic
Manahawkin Good Ol' Days Festival	Ocean
Mutts Marathon, Mount Pleasant Animal Shelter	Morris
New Jersey Sheep Dog Trials	Morris
Pasta Night, St. Hubert's	Morris
Paw Pals Dog Walkathon	Middlesex

Point Pleasant Beach Arts & Crafts	Ocean
Ride for the Animals	Mercer
Ridgewood Fall Craft Festival	Bergen
Riverside Festival of the Arts	Warren
Septemberfest, Hamilton Township	Mercer
Service Dog Day	New York City
Sheep and Fiber Festival	Hunterdon
Springfield Street Fair	Union
Tails on the Trails	Mercer
Valenzano Jazz & Blues Harvest Festival	Burlington
Walk for Homeless Paws	Passaic
Walk for Animals	Warren
Wood Street Fair Crafts & Art Show, City of Burlington	Burlington
Woofstock	Camden

October

Agility Trials	
Bayshore Companion Dog Club	Monmouth
Burlington County Kennel Club	Burlington
Petit Basset Griffon Vendeen Association	Burlington
All-Breed Shows and Obedience Trials	
Hatboro Kennel Club	Mercer
Ramapo Kennel Club	Sussex
South Jersey Kennel Club	Atlantic
Apple Festival, Medford	Burlington
Apple Festival, Chester	Morris
Arktoberfest	Camden
Art Fair	Essex
Arts & Craft Show	Union
Autumn in Moorestown	Burlington
Casino Night, People for Animals	Union
Chowderfest	Ocean
Closter Street Fair	Bergen
Cranberry Festival, Bordentown	Burlington
Cranberry Festival, Chatsworth	Burlington
Cranford Street Fair	Union
Dog Walk-a-thon	Union
Fair Lawn Street Fair & Craft Show	Bergen
Fall Country Harvest, Kuser Farm	Mercer
Fall Festival, Haddonfield	Camden
Fall Festival, Dutch Neck Village	Cumberland
Fanny Wood Day	Union
Fine Arts and Crafts Show, Montclair	Essex

FOCAS Dog Walk	Camden
Halloween Dog Parade	New York City
Halloween on High	Cumberland
Halloween Parade, Maplewood	Essex
Halloween Parade, Medford	Burlington
Handcrafts Festival, Merchantville	Camden
Harvest Festival, Bellview Winery	Atlantic
Harvest Festival	Cumberland
Harvest Festival, Highland Park	Middlesex
Harvest Time in Bay Head	Ocean
Hawthorne Street Fair	Passaic
Herding Trial, German Shepherd Dog Club	Sussex
Hounds & Harriers Run	Morris
Howl-o-ween Day, Burlington Co. Animal Alliance	Burlington
Howl-o-ween Hike, St. Hubert's	Morris
Hunt Test, Eastern German Shorthaired Pointer Club	Monmouth
Liberty Humane Society Dog Walk	Hudson
Metuchen County Fair	Middlesex
Metro Basset Bash & Howl-O-Ween Party	Bergen
Obedience Match, Peddler's Village	Hunterdon
Obedience Trial, Cape May County Dog Obedience Club	Cape May
Paws in the Park	Gloucester
Pine Barrens Jamboree	Ocean
Pooches and Polo Day	Hunterdon
Red Bank Pet Walk and Fair	Monmouth
SAVE Halloween Parade	Mercer
Skyhoundz Frisbee Competition	Monmouth
Somerville Fall Festival	Somerset
South Jersey Pumpkin Show	Cumberland
Thompson Park Day	Monmouth
Tri-State Pet Expo	Middlesex
Witches Ball, Mill Race Village	Burlington
WMASS Walk-A-Dog-Athon	Passaic

NOVEMBER

Agility Trials	
Fast Pawz	Monmouth
Garden State Norwegian Elkhound Club	Somerset
All-Breed Show and Obedience Trial, Boardwalk Kennel Club	Cape May
Earthdog Trial, New Jersey Beanfield Earthdog Club	Burlington
Tracking Trial, Lenape Tracking Club	Hunterdon

December

All-Breed Show and Obedience Trial Lehigh Valley Kennel Club	Warren
Pet Expo and Craft Show	Somerset
Lure Coursing, Irish Wolfhound Association	Somerset
Winter Wonderland, Kuser Farm	Mercer

About the Author

Diane Goodspeed is a mother of two and has always been fascinated by dogs. She currently competes in obedience and agility and is also an agility instructor for Top Dog Obedience in Flanders, New Jersey. The author of *Family-Friendly Biking in New Jersey and Eastern Pennsylvania*, she lives in Hackettstown, New Jersey.